A BOOK OF HOURS

AND OTHER CATHOLIC DEVOTIONS

A BOOK OF HOURS

AND OTHER CATHOLIC DEVOTIONS

THE CANTERBURY PRESS NORWICH

First published in 1998 by The Canterbury Press Norwich
(a publishing imprint of Hymns Ancient & Modern Limited
a registered charity)
St Mary's Works, St Mary's Plain
Norwich, Norfolk, NR3 3BH

First published in paperback 1999

ISBN 1–85311–242–9

Printed and bound in Great Britain by
Biddles Ltd, Guildford and King's Lynn

FOR MY PARENTS

NANCY AND BRENDAN FINNEGAN

WHO TAUGHT ME TO PRAY

CONTENTS

THE PSALTER

DEVOTIONS FOR THE SACRAMENTS

PUBLIC DEVOTIONS

OTHER DEVOTIONS

FOREWORD

The Revd and Rt Hon. Graham Leonard KCVO

Now the Catholic faith is this, that we worship one God in Trinity and Trinity in Unity.

S O SAYS that great Profession of Faith which is commonly called the Athanasian Creed. More a hymn than a creed, it was probably written about AD 450 and for centuries was recited regularly in the old Breviary. It is very good that it is included in *A Book of Hours* (p.215) both for its own sake and because it reminds us of the priority of worship in the Christian life. To some, those words from it come as a surprise. Few Christians, even Catholics, if asked what the Faith is would say that it was worship. Yet such an answer would be right and proper.

Catholic worship is both corporate and personal. Incorporated into Christ by Baptism, we are enabled to share in the perfect worship which our Lord offers, and to do so with the whole host of heaven. In the Mass, we offer the Holy Sacrifice from which alone flows that participation in the life of our Lord and in the worship of the Church which is his Body. It gives us the two commands: 'Do this', that is: to celebrate the Mass and to pray. We obey by celebrating the Liturgy, and by our own personal prayer.

But the personal prayer of Catholics has always taken two forms, corporate and private, in both of which we seek to be grasped by the majesty, glory and love of God; redemptive acts, and so come to adore him. The corporate and the private need to be related. Neither alone will suffice. So we should in our private prayer draw upon the heritage of the prayers of the Church which have been offered through the ages. While our private prayer can and should be intensely personal, related to our particular circumstances, it needs to be challenged and, where need be, corrected by the mind of the whole Body, the Church as it has sought to live the mystery. When this does not happen, we can find ourselves locked into the thought of this present age, and in danger of succumbing to the temptation to adapt the Faith to our ends.

A Book of Hours is designed to enable us to avoid this danger by sharing in the inexhaustible riches of the worship of the the Church throughout the ages.

A Book of Hours has many admirable qualities. While providing a necessary structure for prayer, thereby delivering us from the whim of the moment, it is flexible and can be readily adapted to individual needs, as the section on how to use the book makes clear. For many, the use of the Douai Bible, especially the Psalms, skilfully amended by Fr Finnegan, will be welcome, conveying as it does the religious significance of Scripture more effectively than some modern translations. Part II provides us with a truly marvellous storehouse of devotions which enables us to draw upon those of the saints of all ages.

Fr Finnegan is to be congratulated and thanked for a book which will be a great inspiration for that true devotion which is both corporate and personal.

G.L.

INTRODUCTION

VERNACULAR devotions have long formed the backbone of the piety of English-speaking Catholics throughout the world. Largely, this reflects the religious developments which took place in England from the beginning of the sixteenth century, and which clearly affected all those countries where English was spoken, initially in North America, and thereafter throughout all the areas which came within England's colonial sphere of influence.

The late Middle Ages saw a great flowering of prayer books throughout Western Europe known as 'Primers' or 'Books of Hours', designed to nourish the prayer life of the laity outside the elaborate Latin liturgy. At first, these were, as indeed any books were, very expensive, and often highly decorated and illuminated. The very name 'Book of Hours' conjures up to our minds images of sumptuously gilded and illustrated books such as the justly famous *Très Riches Heures* of the Duc de Berry. Clearly books such as these were the prized possessions of the very wealthy. The invention of printing, however, greatly increased the circulation of Primers or Books of Hours, as well as resulting in a simplification of the format, putting these books of devotion within the reach of a far greater number of people than had been the case formerly.

When Caxton set up his printing presses in London, at Westminster Abbey in 1476, he set to work and produced a Primer which is thought to be the first liturgical book printed in this country. From then on, editions of the Primer far surpassed in number any other class of literature. Latin Primers came under a variety of names: *Horæ beatæ Mariæ Virginis secundum usum Sarum*, for instance, or simply *Enchiridion,* or *Horarium*, or *Cursus* and, in one rare but significant edition, *Hortulus Animæ*, or 'Little Garden of the Soul'. Vernacular prayer books were usually known by the simple name of Primer. Dr Johnson's Dictionary defines a primer as 'a small prayer-book in which children are taught to read' hence the modern application of the word Primer, used to refer to any book designed to instil the basics of a subject into the memory of a neophyte. Many readers may remember with pleasure (or otherwise) the pedantic charms of Kennedy's *Latin Primer,* or Sweet's *Anglo-Saxon Primer.*

All these Primers and Books of Hours contained some consistent basic material. Almost invariably they began with a kind of very short Divine Office known as the Little Office of our Lady, and followed this with the Office of the Dead, the Seven Penitential Psalms, and the Litany of the Saints. All these are provided in this volume, with the exception of the Little Office of our Lady, which you will find in a shortened form for use on Saturdays (customarily dedicated to the honour of our Lady) in the Psalter section, which here fulfils the same function as the Little Office did in earlier Books of Hours. After those standard items, what was contained in the ancient books, as here, was very much up to the piety, taste and resources of the compiler.

It is commonly believed that when Henry VIII declared himself Head of the Church of England, he left the former Catholic doctrinal and devotional system intact, merely omitting the reverence given to the Papal office. In the history of the primers, we can see that this is not quite as simple as some would have it. In 1538, the King's delegate for religious matters, Thomas Cromwell, commissioned the Bishop of Rochester, John Hilsey, to provide a revised primer for the use of the English. This was accomplished by removing most of the references to our Lady in the office at the beginning, and substituting other versicles, antiphons and readings from the breviary, the whole being solely in the vernacular, this being the first time that the offices and psalms were printed in English, though earlier *manuscript* versions survive, and are used in this present volume. A shorter, simpler, version of the primer was also produced around the same time expressly for children, actively designed to help them learn to read and at the same time learn their prayers. Fr Thurston (*The Primer,* Burns & Oates 1923) supposes this to be based on a pre-existing Catholic model, the *Primarium pro Pueris*, of which no copies seem to have survived.

With the short-lived restoration of the Catholic religion under Queen Mary, it was felt that the use of English had become so well-established in the devotional life of the laity, that it was as well to leave the psalms and offices in the vernacular. Thus, the primers produced in that reign built on much of the material from the previous, and did not entirely revert to the earlier practice.

The final restoration of Protestantism in 1558 brought persecution to Catholics, but no end to the well-established custom of vernacular devotions among those who clung to the old faith. Primers both in Latin and English continued to be produced on the continent, though in a more restrained form. This restraint may in part be due to the increasingly extravagant claims of indulgences for, and saintly pedigree of, various prayers and devotions that had crept into the sixteenth-century primers all over western Europe. Pope St Pius V firmly established limits on this sort of material in his Bull *Superni Omnipotentis Dei* of 1571. Thereafter, the primers assumed a more uniform shape and content, and became considerably more careful and dignified, as befitted the new post-Reformation age of neo-Classical restraint and poise which preceded that of the Baroque.

A very important innovation for English Catholics took place about 1583, with the publication on the continent of the first edition of the *Manual of Prayers*. This entirely broke with the tradition of the Primers, and in one form or another continued to be used both privately and in public non-liturgical vernacular devotional services until very recent days, being revised from time to time. In some places you will still find this book used, though in the last hundred or so years it has become almost exclusively tailored for the use of churches, being printed and bound in large format appropriate to this location, and not for tucking into pocket or handbag.

In 1740, Bishop Challoner produced the first edition of one of the most enduring classics of English Catholic devotion: *The Garden of the Soul*. This has remained firmly in the hands of the laity, and has formed the spirituality of generations of English and Irish Catholics. Rare is the Catholic jumble sale where you will not find a few well-thumbed and tattered copies of this book with pious pictures pushed in here and there: evidence of a holy life and, it is to be hoped, a holy death.

In Challoner's time, and until the 'Second Spring' of Catholicism in the second half of the nineteenth century, Catholics unable to obtain a priest for Mass on Sundays would nevertheless gather together to pray. This practice is described in Bishop Ullathorne's remarkable autobiography, published under various titles, such as *From Cabin-Boy to Archbishop* or *The Devil is a Jackass.* The staple religious diet of these gatherings was formed by vernacular devotions, often taken from the books mentioned above, led by one of the district's laymen. The Rosary would be prayed, and very often the Jesus Psalter, which you will also find on page 305 in this publication. Frequently, a sermon would be read from a book. These devotions, embraced out of necessity, nourished the spirituality of generations of English Catholics, and they are probably the cause of the tradition in England of invariably praying the Rosary in the vernacular, whereas on the Continent until recent days it was far more common for even layfolk to pray it in Latin.

ॐ

The Modern Age

THE liturgical movement pioneered by Dom Prosper Guéranger (1805-1875) and the monks of Solesmes in the mid-nineteenth century led to the growth of a new kind of devotion, centred on the liturgy of the Church. The laity were encouraged now not to pursue their own devotions at Mass: reading their *Garden of the Soul* or saying the Sorrowful Mysteries of the Rosary as they had been accustomed. Instead, they were encouraged to buy Missals with parallel Latin and vernacular texts: to follow the liturgy of the Church as much as possible, and frame their devotions around it. In itself, this was nothing new: even before the Reformation there had been books, such as *The Lay-Folks' Mass Book,* designed to foster understanding of the action at the altar; but this all-absorbing interest in the liturgy as something that the *whole* Church does, and which is not just the province of the clergy, was an innovation, and it had a profound effect on the devotional life of ordinary Catholics.

These new layfolk Missals were of various shapes and sizes, but always had the main text of the Mass for at least Sundays and Holydays in parallel columns of Latin and a vernacular translation. Often these Missals contained, besides, other services presented in bilingual form: usually Sunday Vespers and Compline.

Almost invariably they also took on the role of the old Primer or *Garden of the Soul*, by including in the back a substantial treasury of prayers and devotions for devotional use *outside* Mass. A most remarkable fusion of all the devotional approaches was published in 1862: the *Crown of Jesus*. Here one finds the entire Ordinary of the Mass, together with propers for all Sundays and greater feasts. But there is much more besides: a huge treasury of devotions, ways of assisting at Mass for children, explanations of the faith and practices of the Church, and a large selection of hymns. It was, indeed, in the *Crown of Jesus* that many of the hymns known to Catholics today first made their appearance. Similarly one ought to draw attention to that most enduring and popular publication, *A Simple Prayer Book,* first published by the Catholic Truth Society in 1886, and still in print today.

With the growth of the liturgical movement in the latter half of the nineteenth and the first half of the twentieth centuries, an intense reforming climate was engendered, with the term *'Garden of the Soul* Catholic' being used as a term of disapprobation, meaning one who 'got on with his or her devotions' at Mass while the more enlightened Catholic followed the text in his or her Missal and *participated.* In their own way, while appearing more backward-looking, the *Crown of Jesus* and its many imitators sought to facilitate this new movement, encouraging Catholics to enter into the drama of the Mass.

Nobody today can deny that it is useful or desirable that people should be more directly involved in the Mass, but the change did have an unfortunate knock-on effect of allowing a genuine and ancient form of vernacular prayer to decay. For many, following the Mass became a substitute for personal prayer, a trend that has continued to this day. The Little Office of our Lady, which had once been a staple of lay devotion, all but died out. Part of the reason is that it had already become the province, largely, of communities of religious sisters who arose to re-evangelize the people following the turmoil of the French Revolution. Many communities of these hard workers used the Little Office of our Lady as a shorter substitute for the long Divine Office, the solemnities of which were seen as being impracticable to combine with hard pastoral work. The Little Office of our Lady, though shorter than the then Divine Office, is, besides, still rather longer than most lay people might choose. It also never varies from day to day, and many feel that, important though a fervent devotion to our Lady is, there are other important things that, rightly, ought to be the focus of prayer, at least some of the time.

It was the upheavals of the 1960s that made the greatest impact on the vernacular prayer of Catholics, however. For the first time, the public, liturgical prayer of the Church was in the vernacular. It became possible to focus *all* one's spiritual life on the liturgy. Many devout laity are now accustomed to celebrating the Divine Office itself in its new form of the *Liturgy of the Hours*. People no longer need bilingual Missals to follow the Mass, but listen and respond and actively participate.

Coupled with this new form of liturgical life is a widespread interest in *spirituality*, as a thing in itself. Just as before the liturgical movement nobody thought of liturgy as something to talk about, but rather something just to get on with, to just do, so now people do a great deal of talking about prayer, but I am not convinced that people in general *do* it as formerly. It has become the province of 'experts', rather than something proper to every Christian. In the religious bookshops one can see row upon row of books on different ways to pray, different techniques, different philosophies. I am convinced that the important thing is not *how* one prays, but *that* one prays. Prayer is not the acquisition of a technique. Prayer is above all an exercise of the will: one intends to pray; one *is* praying already. The justly famous Dom John Chapman of Downside Abbey had a tag: 'pray as you can, and not as you can't'. It seems an obvious comment to make, and yet how many devout people feel that they aren't really praying until they have reached some form of transforming union or ecstasy?

I am convinced that in prayer simplicity is the thing, together with honesty. This book is put together by someone perfectly willing to admit that he hasn't got the instant key to rapture in prayer. I, too, get distracted and sometimes bored when I sit or kneel in church. But I am also utterly convinced of the transforming power of prayer, and of the vitally important role that it plays in the daily life of a Christian.

Some Thoughts on Vocal Prayer

God is a spirit, and those who adore him must adore him in spirit and truth. *(John 4:24)*

THE spirit, the scholastics tell us, has three powers: will, memory, and understanding, or intelligence—the ability to organize and analyse information which is in the memory. It is with these faculties that we relate to God, because it is the soul which bears the closest resemblance to God. If this is true, it is clear that questions of *enjoyment* of prayer, as such, are largely irrelevant. Enjoyment may help prayer along, and encourage one to do it more often, but must not be confused with the thing itself. We pray simply because God is God, and to relate to God is the highest function, glory and ultimate destiny of the human being. We pray to adore, praise, thank him, to apologize for our short-comings and to ask him to fulfil our needs and those of our neighbour. In these acts the Christian truly becomes the Priest, and since prayer is not be confused with the practice of a technique, it is irrelevant what form this prayer takes. As far as bodily activity goes, at this time, the less there is, the better. But best of all is to try to involve the three faculties of the soul: the memory, understanding and will.

One of the best ways of doing this is the use of vocal prayer, meaning prayer following a text whether read or memorized, making it our own, and using it to focus our devotion. This should involve all our mental faculties and a few of our physical ones, too. I am a great enthusiast for the Christian who 'merely' wants to 'say his or her prayers'. Vocal prayer is a far surer path to God than any direct attempt to be a second St John of the Cross, because vocal prayer involves the crucial virtue of humility. And if you want more authority than mine for the transforming power of vocal prayer, look at what St Teresa of Avila has to say on the subject: you'll find it in the 'Our Father' section of this book, on page 303. Contemplative prayer is the work of God, and nothing we can do can bring it on, other than living a holy life, 'saying one's prayers', and being faithful. Leave progress in the hands of the Holy Spirit: the best of all teachers.

ℭ

How to Use this Book

S IMPLY: use this book as you want to. Deliberately, I have
avoided using any sort of 'official' prayer of the Church. The
purpose of this book is only to give you a resource to help you to
speak to your Creator, to help you find words to express your
prayer; words being, after all, the key to human meaning.

The first section is a Psalter, loosely based on the form of the
Divine Office. You will see that I have laid out prayers and psalms
for a potential day of seven 'hours', or prayer sessions, on the
principle of the psalmist's 'seven times daily will I praise you, O
Lord', and following the custom of the Church. I do not imagine
that many people have the leisure to interrupt their day seven
times. Some may: the sick and housebound, for instance, or those
who work at home in their own time, and they may wish to celebrate the entire Psalter. Others may wish simply to keep the
hours nearest to whenever they have time to pray, uniting themselves in spirit with those keeping the liturgical hours at that time.
In this way, the round of the day itself is sanctified. Some, wishing to establish a routine each day, may find the unchanging hours
each week a little arid. They should not feel constrained to the
form I have provided, but, for example, use the psalm from one
of the offices which do not form part of their routine instead of
the appointed one. Or they could interchange offices, praying
Vigils one week, and Lauds the next, or circulate the three midday offices of Terce, Sext, and None through three weeks.

In other words, as this is not an official prayer book of the
Church, feel free to modify it as you see fit. The intercessions
given, for instance, would be much better replaced with prayers
that have a particular relevance for you, the one who is praying:
use this opportunity, for instance, to intercede for members of
your family regularly, or for matters which occupy your concern.
Or simply omit them, if you dislike them!

The sign ✠ signifies a sign of the Cross, made customarily at
the beginning of each office, and at the beginning of the Gospel
Canticles: the Benedictus at Lauds, the Magnificat at Vespers
and the Nunc Dimittis at Compline. It is customary to recite these
standing.

On the feasts of great saints or your particular favourites, you may prefer to substitute the office provided on page 153 for the office of the day. Likewise, you may wish to celebrate the Office of the Dead on page 134 for someone you know who has died, or on All Souls' Day (2 November), or whenever it seems appropriate.

Spiritual reading is often considered the food of the spiritual life, and essential to any Christian who wishes to make progress in prayer. Hence, I have provided in the hour of Vigils an opportunity, modelled on the Office of Readings in the official *Liturgy of the Hours* for benefitting from this practice. Concerning what one might read, pride of place must, of course, go to the Scriptures. It is quite easy to obtain schemata, and even whole printed Bibles laid out in such a way as to cover the entire Bible during the course of a year. Alternatively, one might consider simply reading a book at a time. I would not myself counsel reading the Bible directly from Genesis to Revelation: most people who try this seem to get bogged down in Leviticus and Deuteronomy! I recommend starting with a Gospel, then an Old Testament book, then a letter from the New Testament, and so forth. Or you may care to follow the schema that I have suggested on page 446.

The second, spiritual, reading is not so easy to define. You may ask: what should I read? St Philip Neri, when asked this question, observed that one should, for preference, read authors whose names begin with S: he meant Saints, of course. Simply, I recommend that you read a page or two of any spiritual book that helps you in your devotion. For preference, read the classics. I have provided a list of suggestions on page 447 that ought to be fairly easily obtained from a religious bookshop, or possibly from a second-hand bookshop.

When reading, if something strikes you, don't think you have to struggle on to the end, as if you were reading at Mass. Pause and consider. Also, if you have time, close your eyes for five minutes after each reading and reflect on what you have read before saying the response.

The other sections of this book speak for themselves. I have attempted to assemble a collection of prayers which are not necessarily written by Catholics, but which Catholics may find useful. The collection as a whole is intended to reflect six hundred fruitful years of vernacular prayers in English. You will find many new prayers, and many old ones, especially some of the classics which I want to preserve for another generation's use. Likewise, I have translated some prayers from the Latin which formerly were accessible only to clerics. Use all these prayers simply as you find helpful, either on your own or in groups.

∾

Translations and Language

I MUST add a word about the translations used in this book. I gave some consideration to using a familiar translation of the Scriptures, especially of the Psalms, but then felt that there was advantage to be gained from using a less familiar one. Besides, the sum of money demanded as a royalty for use of a more familiar Psalter was considerably more than I was able to pay! So, since I was aiming for a classical flavour, I have gently updated the Douai-Challoner translation; aiming to retain a savour of the original which has formed the spirituality so many generations of English-speaking Catholics, while at the same time rendering it accessible to a modern reader, by removing some of the rather more bizarre renderings and comparing with more modern versions. Note, please, that the Psalms are numbered according to the traditional Catholic custom of following the system used in the Greek Septuagint. Thus, here, *The Lord is My Shepherd* appears as the twenty-*second* Psalm, and not the twenty-*third*, which non-Catholics may find a little confusing. Anybody wishing to compare with other translations will find that the Masoretic numbering more commonly favoured in the English-speaking world puts the psalm desired only one, or at most two, places away from its position in the Septuagint arrangement.

Clearly these days some thought has to be given to the use of inclusive language. After consultation with the publishers, and with those who are more experienced than I in these matters, the decision was made not to tamper with existing texts, which would in some cases amount to cultural vandalism, but in newly composed texts sensitively to use inclusive language when referring to humanity, while adhering to the traditional pronouns for the Deity.

The illustrations in this book come mostly from a Sarum Missal of 1555 and a Sarum Book of Hours of 1534, while the newer, more baroque, ones come from a Roman Missal of the seventeenth century which had been adapted for use in England whose Catholics were at that time under persecution.

Finally, I would like to thank the many people who have made this publication possible. To the Fathers and Brothers of the Oratories in Oxford and London, to Walter Hooper who so persistently encouraged me to produce this book, to Mhairi Ellis, Brian Brindley and especially the Revd William Perry who each laboured generously to prevent many a howler from reaching your eyes. If any remain, this must be my own fault. Also to Christine Smith for her encouragement, and to Fr Graham Leonard who not only wrote the foreword, but also gave me much good advice, all of which I have taken. I would like to thank those who helped me in the collection of material: Sister Brigid O'Brien, sadly recently deceased, Fr Jerome Bertram, Fr Dominic Jacob, Fr Nicholas Kearney, Peter Ward, Richard and Lepel Kornicki and family, Iestyn Evans, and of course, my own family from whom I first learnt whatever I know of the grace of prayer.

Seán A. Finnegan
Christmas Eve 1997

CALENDAR

Y OU *may care to use this calendar in deciding which of-*
fice to say. Days of particular importance are marked in
bold type. On those days it is especially recommended that you
use the office indicated. Saints that have particular relevance
to you—patrons, for instance, of your country or diocese, or
town—could be honoured with a special office. Other Saints
could be commemorated simply by using the collect in their
honour from your daily Missal, or the collect from the ends of
the Offices for the Greater Feasts of Saints at the end of the
normal daily office. If any of the Saints pique your curiosity,
there are several good dictionaries of Saints available which
you may care to consult. You may also care to write in the
margin of the calendar the anniversaries of your deceased
friends and family, a reminder to you to offer the Office for the
Dead on those occasions.

Legenda

pr	priest
bp	bishop
m	martyr
v	virgin
dc	doctor of the Church
p	pope
ap	apostle
comps	companions in martyrdom

JANUARY

∾

1. **Mary, Mother of God** *Saturday Office*
2. Ss Basil & Gregory *bps dcs*
3.
4. St Elizabeth Ann Seton (USA)
5. Blessed John Neumann *bp* (USA)
6. **The Epiphany of the Lord** *Sunday Office*
7. St Raymond of Peñafort
8.
9.
10.
11.
12.
13. St Hilary of Poitiers *bp dc*
        also St Kentigern *bp* (Scotland)
14.
15.
16.
17. St Antony of Egypt *abbot*
18.
19.
20. Ss Fabian & Sebastian *ms*
21. St Agnes *v m*
22 St Vincent *deacon m*
23.
24. St Francis de Sales *bp dc*
25. **Conversion of St Paul** *Office of Saints*
26. Ss Timothy and Titus *bps*
27. St Angela Merici *v*
28. St Thomas Aquinas *pr dc*
29.
30.
31. St John Bosco *pr*

FEBRUARY

∾

1. St Brigid *v* (Ireland)
2. **The Presentation** *Sunday Office*
3. St Blaise *bp m also* St Ansgar *bp*
4.
5. St Agatha *v m*
6. Ss Paul Miki & comps *ms*
7.
8. St Jerome Emiliani
9.
10. St Scholastica *v*
11. Our Lady of Lourdes   *Saturday Office if desired*
12.
13.
14. Ss Cyril *pr* & Methodius *bp*
15.
16.
17. Seven holy Servite founders
18.
19.
20.
21. St Peter Damian *bp dc*
22. **The Chair of St Peter** *ap   Office of Saints*
23. St Polycarp *bp m*
24.
25.
26.
27.
28.
(29.)

MARCH

∾

1. St David *in Wales, Office of Saints*
2.
3.
4. St Casimir
5.
6.
7. Ss Perpetua & Felicity *vs ms*
8. St John of God
9. St Frances of Rome
10. St John Ogilvie *pr m* (Scotland)
11.
12.
13.
14.
15.
16.
17. St Patrick *in Ireland, Office of Saints*
18. St Cyril of Jerusalem *bp dc*
19. **St Joseph** *Office of Saints*
20.
21.
22.
23. St Turibius of Mongrovejo
24.
25. **The Annunciation** *Office of Sundays*
26.
27.
28.
29.
30.
31.

APRIL

∾

1.
2. St Francis of Paola *hermit*
3.
4. St Isidore *bp dc*
5. St Vincent Ferrer *pr*
6.
7. St John Baptist de la Salle *pr*
8.
9.
10.
11. St Stanislaus *bp m*
12.
13. St Martin I *p m*
14.
15.
16.
17.
18.
19.
20.
21. St Anselm *bp dc*
22.
23. St George *m   in England, Office of Saints*
24. St Fidelis of Sigmaringen *pr m*
25. **St Mark** *Office of Saints*
26.
27.
28. St Peter Chanel, *pr m*
29. St Catherine of Siena *v dc*
30. St Pius V *p*

MAY

∾

1. St Joseph the Worker
2. St Athanasius *bp dc*
3. **Ss Philip and James** *aps   Office of Saints*
4.
5.
6.
7.
8.
9.
10.
11.
12. Ss Nereus & Achilleus *ms   also*   St Pancras *m*
13.
14. **St Matthias** *ap   Office of Saints*
15. St Isidore
16.
17.
18. St John I *p m*
19.
20. St Bernadine of Siena *pr*
21.
22.
23.
24. Our Lady Help of Christians
        in Australia, Saturday Office
25. St Bede the Venerable *pr dc*
        also St Gregory VII *p*
26. St Philip Neri *pr*
27. St Augustine of Canterbury
        in England, Office of Saints
28.
29.
30.
31. **The Visitation of the Blessed Virgin Mary**
        Saturday Office

JUNE

∾

1. St Justin *m*
2. Ss Marcellinus & Peter *ms*
3. Ss Charles Lwanga & comps, *ms of Uganda*
4.
5. St Boniface *bp m*
6. St Norbert *bp*
7.
8.
9. St Ephræm *deacon, dc also* St Columba *abbot*
10.
11. St Barnabas *ap*
12.
13. St Anthony of Padua *pr dc*
14.
15.
16.
17.
18.
19. St Romuald *abbot*
20. St Alban *m*
     in England, Office of Saints
21. St Aloysius Gonzaga
22. Ss John Fisher *bp m* & Thomas More *m*
     in England, Office of Saints
     also St Paulinus of Nola *bp*
23.
24. **Birth of St John the Baptist** *Office of Saints*
25.
26.
27. St Cyril of Alexandria *bp dc*
28. St Irenæus *bp m*
29. **Ss Peter & Paul** *aps Office of Saints*
30. First Martyrs of Rome

JULY

∾

1.
2.
3. **St Thomas** *ap   Office of Saints*
4. St Elizabeth of Portugal
5. St Anthony Mary Zaccaria *pr*
6. St Maria Goretti *v m*
7.
8.
9.
10. St Oliver Plunkett *bp m* (Ireland)
11. St Benedict *abbot*
12.
13. St Henry
14. St Camillus of Lellis *pr*
15. St Bonaventure *bp dc*
16. Our Lady of Mount Carmel
        Saturday Office if desired
17.
18.
19.
20.
21. St Laurence of Brindisi *pr dc*
22. St Mary Magdalene
23. St Bridget
24.
25. **St James** *ap   Office of Saints*
26. Ss Joachim & Anne *parents of our Lady*
27.
28.
29. St Martha
30. St Peter Chrysologus *bp dc*
31. St Ignatius Loyola *pr*

AUGUST

∽

1. St Alphonsus Liguori *bp dc*
2. St Eusebius of Vercelli *bp*
       also St Peter Eymard *pr*
3.
4. St John Vianney, *(Curé d' Ars) pr*
5. Dedication of the Basilica of St Mary Major
       Saturday Office if desired.
6. **The Transfiguration** *Sunday Office*
7. St Sixtus *p m* & Comps *ms*
       also St Cajetan *pr*
8. St Dominic *pr*
9.
10. St Lawrence *deacon m*
11. St Clare *v*
12.
13. Ss Pontian *p m* & Hippolytus *pr m*
14. St Maximilian Kolbe *pr m*
15. **The Assumption of Our Lady**
       Saturday Office
16. St Stephen of Hungary
17.
18.
19. St John Eudes *pr*
20. St Bernard *abbot dc*
21. St Pius X *p*
22. Our Lady, Queen and Mother
       Saturday Office if desired
23. St Rose of Lima *v*
24. **St Bartholomew** *ap Office of Saints*
25. St Louis *King of France*
       also St Joseph of Calasanz *pr*
26. Blessed Dominic Barberi (England)
27. St Monica
28. St Augustine *bp dc*
29. **Death of St John Baptist** *Office of Saints*
30.
31.

SEPTEMBER

∾

1.
2.
3. St Gregory the Great *p dc*
   in England, Office of Saints
4.
5.
6.
7.
8. **Birthday of Our Lady** *Saturday Office*
9. St Peter Claver *pr*
10.
11.
12.
13. St John Chrysostom *bp dc*
14. **The Triumph of the Cross** *Sunday Office*
15. Our Lady of Sorrows *Saturday Office if desired*
16. Ss Cornelius & Cyprian *ms*
17. St Robert Bellarmine *bp dc*
18.
19. St Januarius *bp m*
20. Ss Andrew Kim Taegon, Paul Chong Hasang
         & Comps *ms of Korea*
21. **St Matthew** *ap Office of Saints*
22.
23.
24. Our Lady of Ransom *in England, Saturday Office*
25.
26. Ss Cosmas & Damian *ms*
27. St Vincent de Paul *pr*
28. St Wenceslaus *king*
         also St Laurence Ruiz & Comps
29. **The Holy Archangels**
         Office of Saints or of Sunday
30. St Jerome

OCTOBER

∾

1. St Thérèse of the Child Jesus *(of Lisieux)* v dc
2. The Guardian Angels
3.
4. St Francis of Assisi *deacon*
5.
6. St Bruno *pr*
7. Our Lady of the Rosary *Saturday Office if desired*
8.
9. St Denis & Comps *ms*
　　also St John Leonardi *pr*
10. St Paulinus
11.
12.
13. St Edward the Confessor
　　in England, Office of Saints
14. St Callistus *p m*
15. St Teresa of Jesus *(of Avila)* v dc
16. St Margaret Mary Alacoque *v also* St Hedwig
17. St Ignatius of Antioch *bp m*
18. **St Luke** *Office of Saints*
19. Ss John Brébeuf, Isaac Jogues & comps
　　ms of Canada
20.
21.
22.
23. St John Capistrano *pr*
24. St Anthony Mary Claret *bp*
25. 40 Martyrs of England & Wales
　　England & Wales, Office of Saints
26.
27.
28. **Ss Simon & Jude** *aps Office of Saints*
29.
30.
31.

NOVEMBER

∾

1. **All Saints** *Office of Saints*
2. **All Souls** *Office of the Dead*
3. St Martin of Porres
4. St Charles Borromeo *bp*
5.
6. All Saints of Ireland (Ireland)
7.
8.
9. Dedication of the Lateran Basilica *Sunday Office*
10. St Leo the Great *p dc*
11. St Martin of Tours *bp*
12. St Josaphat *bp m*
13. St Frances Xavier Cabrini (USA)
14.
15. St Albert the Great *bp dc*
16. St Margaret of Scotland *in Scotland, Office of Saints*
          also St Gertrude *v*
17. St Elizabeth of Hungary
18. Dedication of the Basilicas of Ss Peter and Paul *aps*
19.
20.
21. The Presentation of Our Lady *Saturday Office*
22. St Cecilia *v m*
23. St Clement I *p m*
     St Columbanus *abbot*
24. St Andrew Dung-Lac & comps *ms of Vietnam*
25.
26.
27.
28.
29.
30. **St Andrew** *ap Office of Saints*

DECEMBER

∾

1.
2.
3. St Francis Xavier *pr*
4. St John Damascene *pr dc*
5.
6. St Nicholas *bp*
7. St Ambrose *bp dc*
8. **The Immaculate Conception of Our Lady**
        Saturday Office
9.
10.
11. St Damasus I *p*
12. St Jane Frances de Chantal
        also Our Lady of Guadalupe
            in USA, Saturday Office
13. St Lucy *v m*
14. St John of the Cross *pr dc*
15.
16.
17.
18.
19.
20.
21. St Peter Canisius *pr dc*
22.
23.
24.
25. **Christmas Day** *Sunday Office*
26. St Stephen *first martyr*
27. **St John** *ap Office of Saints*
28. The Holy Innocents *ms*
29. St Thomas Becket *bp m*
30.
31. St Sylvester *p*

MOVABLE FEASTS

∾

Sunday after January 6: **The Baptism of the Lord**
First Sunday after Pentecost: **Trinity Sunday**
Thursday after Trinity Sunday: **Corpus Christi** *Sunday Office*
Friday after 2nd Sunday after Pentecost: **The Sacred Heart of Jesus** *Sunday Office*
The next day:**The Immaculate Heart of Mary** *Saturday Office.*
The last Sunday of the liturgical year: **Christ the King**

THE PSALTER

*Seven times a day
will I praise you, O Lord*
Psalm 118

SUNDAY

And feasts of the Lord

Vigils

The night office

℣. O Lord, ✠ open my lips.
℟. **And my mouth shall declare your praise.**

Antiphon: I shall see your glory when I awake, O Lord.

Psalm 62a

O GOD, my God, for you I watch at break of day;
    for you my soul is thirsting.
    My flesh longs for you!
as in a desert land without way or water.
Thus in the sanctuary have I come before you
    to see your power and your glory.

For your loving-kindness is better than many lives:
    my lips will declare your praise.
Thus I will bless you all my life long,
    and in your name I will lift up my hands.
Let my soul be filled as with marrow and fat,
    and my mouth shall praise you with joyful lips.

I have remembered you upon my bed.
    On you I meditated in the morning
for you have been my helper;
    and I will rejoice under the cover of your wings.
My soul clings close to you;
    your right arm holds me tight.

Glory be to the Father, and to the Son,
    and to the Holy Spirit.
As it was in the beginning, is now and ever shall be,
    world without end. Amen.

Antiphon: I shall see your glory when I awake, O Lord.

℣. O Lord, open the scriptures to me.
℟. **May my heart burn within me as you teach me.**

First reading

One chapter from the scriptures, ideally the Sunday Gospel.

Response to the reading

℣. May my footsteps be firm, O Lord,
℟. **In obeying your word.**
℣. May I be pleasing to you, O Lord,
℟. **In obeying your word.**

Second reading

Spiritual reading at choice.

Te Deum

WE PRAISE you, O God!
We acknowledge you as Lord.
Everlasting Father: the whole world worships you.
The angels and the heavenly powers,
The Cherubim and Seraphim,
With endless voices cry:
Holy! Holy! Holy!
The Lord, the God of might!
The heavens and the earth are filled
with the splendour of your glorious reign!
The glorious Apostolic choir,
And the prophets numberless do cry
The white robed martyrs' army sings,
And the holy Church throughout the world
Acclaims you as the Holy One:
The Father, limitlessly great;
His worshipful and only Son
And Holy Spirit, Paraclete.

O Christ! You are the glorious King!
You are the Father's only Son
Who, that you might rescue sinful man,
Did not despise the Virgin's womb.
Death's sting you boldly overthrew
And opened heaven's mighty gates
For your believers to pass inside.

Now you are throned at God's right hand
And share the glory of the Father.
We wait for you to come as Judge.

So guide your servants here below,
For whom you shed your precious blood,
And give them glory with your saints.

Save your people, Lord, we pray,
And bless your own inheritance.
For ever rule us, raise us up.

For every day we bless your name,
We praise you to eternity,
For ever and for ever more.

O grant us, Lord, this very day
to pass without a stain of sin
Have mercy on us, Lord, we pray.

Your mercy, Lord, we here implore
For see, Lord, we have hoped in you.

In you, O Lord, I put my trust—
Never, then, abandon me!

Let us pray.

O GOD, our teacher, by your mighty Word made flesh, keep us, we pray, always attentive to your teaching and true in proclaiming your Word, Jesus Christ our Lord. Amen.

℣. Let us bless the Lord.
℟. **Thanks be to God.**

Lauds

At daybreak

℣. O God, ✠ come to my assistance.
℟. O Lord, be swift to my aid.
℣. Glory be to the Father, and to the Son, and to the Holy Spirit.
**℟. As it was in the beginning, is now and ever shall be,
world without end. Amen.**

ETERNAL maker of all things
Who rule the night-time and the day,
Grant us the changing season's round
Our fickle mortal minds to cheer.

Now daytime's herald sends to rest
That watcher through the deepest night,
Whose beams, to night-time travellers' eyes
Do cleave the dark from dark with light.

And thus awakened, scattering dark,
Light's bearer rises over all;
And leaving all their evil ways,
The wicked flee the deadly paths.

The mariner finds courage fresh,
The angry seas leave off their fret,
And at this hour flowed Peter's tears,
Blest water flowing from the Rock!

Look on us sinners, Jesu, Lord,
Reprove us with one kindly glance;
For in thy sight our sins do melt,
And tears anoint the wounds of guilt.

And be a light unto our sense
And drive dull sleep far from our minds,
That, praising thee at break of day,
We may perform our duties well.

All praise, O Christ, all praise to thee,
And to the Father glory be,
And likewise to the Holy Ghost
Both now and for eternity. Amen.

Aeterne Rerum Conditor

Ant. O let all the works of the Lord bless the Lord; praise and exalt him for ever.

Canticle of the Three Children: Daniel 3:37-68, 36

B LESS the Lord, you angels of the Lord,
   All you heavens, bless the Lord,
Bless the Lord, you waters over the heavens,
   All you stars of the heavens, bless the Lord!

Bless the Lord, you showers and dew,
   All spirits of God, bless the Lord.
Bless the Lord, fire and heat,
   Cold and heat, bless the Lord.
Bless the Lord, you dews and frosts,
   Ice and cold, bless the Lord.
Bless the Lord, ice and snow,
   Night and day, bless the Lord.
Bless the Lord, light and darkness,
   Lightning and clouds, bless the Lord.

Bless the Lord, O earth: praise and exalt him for ever.

Bless the Lord, mountains and hills,
   All things that grow on earth, bless the Lord.
Bless the Lord, O you springs,
   Seas and rivers, bless the Lord.
Bless the Lord, you whales and fishes,
   Beasts and cattle, bless the Lord.

Bless the Lord, you children of men.
Bless the Lord, O Israel: praise and exalt him for ever.

Bless the Lord, O you his priests,
   Servants of the Lord, bless the Lord.
Bless the Lord, just spirits and souls,
   Holy hearts and humble, bless the Lord.

Bless the Lord, Ananias, Azarias and Misael:
   praise and exalt him for ever.

Let us bless the Father, Son and the Holy Spirit:
   praise and exalt him for ever.
You are blessed, O Lord, in the vault of Heaven,
   to be praised and exalted for ever.

(*Glory be* is not said)

Ant. O let all the works of the Lord bless the Lord; praise and
exalt him for ever.

Short reading *Revelation 7:10,12*

S ALVATION to our God who sits upon the throne, and to the
Lamb! Benediction and glory and wisdom and thanksgiv-
ing, honour and power and strength to our God for ever and ever.
Amen.

The Benedictus

*The Gospel canticle is the heart of the Hour. Jesus Christ is the prom-
ised Day that will dawn on us from on high, and so the Church greets
every morning with this canticle from the first chapter of St Luke's Gospel (1:68-79): Zechariah's great hymn of praise upon the birth of his
son, John the Baptist.*

B LESSED ✠ be the Lord, the God of Israel,
who has visited and redeemed his people,
and has lifted up a horn of salvation for us
in the family of his servant David.
For this he swore through the mouths of holy men:
those who were prophets, from the beginning:
There would be salvation from our foes,
and from the hand of all those who hate us;
to comfort our fathers,
and to honour his holy covenant,
which oath once he swore to Abraham, our father,
that he would grant us,
that freed from the hand of our enemies,
and without fear, we may serve him,
in holiness and justice in his very presence all our days.
And you, my son, will be named Prophet of the Most High;
for you will go before the presence of the Lord
to prepare his way,
to teach knowledge of salvation to his people
that their sins may be forgiven,
through the merciful heart of our God,
when the Daystar shall visit us from on high

to enlighten those who sit in darkness
and in the shadow of death,
and guide our feet to the way of peace.

Glory be…

Intercessions   *Either these, or others at choice or need.*

Lord, bless our parish. *(pause for prayer)* ℟. **Hear us, we pray.**
Lord, bless our clergy and fill them with wisdom. *(pause)* ℟.
Lord, bless our young people and fill them with faith. *(pause)* ℟.
Lord, bless our sick and infirm. *(pause)* ℟.
Lord, bless those we find difficult and give us patience with them.
(pause) ℟.
Lord, bless our parish catechists, ministers, and all who gener-
ously give their time and energy to your Church. *(pause)* ℟.
Lord, bless all our people. *(pause)* ℟.

> Lord, have mercy.
> Christ, have mercy.
> Lord, have mercy.

> Our Father…

Let us pray.

L ORD, God Almighty, since you have brought us safely to
the start of this day, defend us as this day proceeds by your
mighty power, so that we do not fall into any sin, but that all our
words, our thoughts and actions may be so governed, as to be
ever righteous in your sight. Through our Lord Jesus Christ your
Son, who lives and reigns with you in the unity of the Holy Spirit,
one God for ever and ever. Amen.

> ℣. Let us bless the Lord.
> ℟. **Thanks be to God.**

ॐ   ॐ   ॐ

Terce

The third hour: mid-morning

℣. O God, ✠ come to my assistance.
℟. O Lord, be swift to my aid.
℣. Glory be to the Father, and to the Son, and to the Holy Spirit.
**℟. As it was in the beginning, is now and ever shall be,
world without end. Amen.**

COME, Holy Ghost, with God the Son
And God the Father, ever one;
Shed forth thy grace within our breast
And dwell with us a ready guest.

By every power, by heart and tongue,
By act and deed, thy praise be sung;
Inflame with perfect love each sense
That others' souls may kindle thence.

O Father, that we ask be done,
Through Jesus Christ, thine only Son;
Who, with the Holy Ghost and thee
Doth live and reign eternally. Amen.

Nunc nobis, Sancte Spiritus

Ant. Lord, give us your blessing for ever.

Psalm 132

BEHOLD how good and how pleasant it is
for brethren to dwell together in unity!

Like precious ointment upon the head
that ran down upon the beard,
ran down upon Aaron's beard,
down to the skirt of his robe.

Like the dew of Hermon which descends
   on the mount of Zion.
For there the Lord has commanded his blessing,
   and life for ever more.

Glory be...

Ant. Lord, give us your blessing for ever.

Short reading *1 John 4:16*

WE HAVE known and have believed the love which God has towards us. God is love, and he that abides in love abides in God, and God in him.

Let us pray.

O GOD, the protector of those who hope in you, without whom nothing is true, nothing holy, increase your mercy towards us so that with you as our leader and guide, we may so go through the things of temporary value as not to miss the things of eternal worth. Through Christ our Lord. Amen.

℣. Let us bless the Lord.
℟. Thanks be to God.

Sext

The sixth hour: at noon

℣. O God, ✠ come to my assistance.
℟. O Lord, be swift to my aid.
℣. Glory be to the Father, and to the Son, and to the Holy Spirit.
**℟. As it was in the beginning, is now and ever shall be,
world without end. Amen.**

O GOD of truth, O Lord of might,
Who orderest time and change aright,
And send'st the early morning ray,
And light'st the glow of perfect day:

Extinguish thou each sinful fire,
And banish every ill desire;
And while thou keep'st the body whole,
Shed forth thy peace upon the soul.

O Father, that we ask be done,
Through Jesus Christ, thine only Son;
Who, with the Holy Ghost and thee,
Doth live and reign eternally. Amen.

Rector potens, verax Deus

Ant. Lord, how I love your law.

Psalm 118 Aleph

B LESSED are the undefiled in the way,
who walk in the law of the Lord.
Blessed are they that keep his testimonies,
that seek him with their whole hearts.
For those who commit iniquities
have not walked in his ways.
You have commanded your commandments
to be kept most diligently.
O that my ways may be directed
to keep your statutes.

Then I shall not be confounded,
as I examine all your commandments.
I will praise you with uprightness of heart
when I have learnt your just decrees.
I will keep your statutes:
O, do not utterly forsake me!

Glory be...

Ant. Lord, how I love your law.

Short reading

Galatians 6:8-10

HE THAT sows according to the flesh will from the flesh reap corruption; but he who sows according to the Spirit will reap from the Spirit everlasting life. So let us not fail in doing good, for in due time we shall reap, if we do not fail. Therefore, whilst we have time, let us do good to all, but especially to those who are of the household of the faith.

Let us pray.

O GOD, you that have prepared good things for those who love you, pour your love into our hearts that we may love you in all and above all, and that we may come to what you have promised: that which surpasses all our desires. Through Christ our Lord. Amen.

℣. Let us bless the Lord.
℟. **Thanks be to God.**

ও   ও   ও

None

The ninth hour: afternoon

℣. O God, ✠ come to my assistance.
℟. O Lord, be swift to my aid.
℣. Glory be to the Father, and to the Son, and to the Holy Spirit.
**℟. As it was in the beginning, is now and ever shall be,
world without end. Amen.**

O GOD, Creation's secret force,
Thyself unmoved, all motion's source,
Who from the morn till evening ray
Through all its changes guid'st the day:

Grant us, when this short life is past,
The glorious evening that shall last;
That, by a holy death attained,
Eternal glory may be gained.

O Father, that we ask be done,
Through Jesus Christ, thine only Son;
Who, with the Holy Ghost and thee,
Doth live and reign eternally. Amen.

Rerum Deus tenax vigor

Ant. O Lord, I seek you with all my heart.

Psalm 118 Beth

H OW shall the young correct his way?
By obeying your words.
With my whole heart I have sought after you;
    let me not stray from your commandments.
Your words I have hidden in my heart,
    that I may not sin against you.
Blessed are you, O Lord:
    teach me your commandments.
With my lips I have pronounced
    all the judgements you have made.

I delight in the way of your testimonies
    as if in all riches.
I will meditate on your commandments;
    and I will consider your ways.
I will delight in your commandments;
    Never will I forget your words.

Glory be…

Ant. O Lord, I seek you with all my heart.

Short reading
Romans 8:22-24

WE KNOW that everything created groans and travails in pain until now; and not only the creation, but also ourselves, who have the first fruits of the Spirit, even we groan within ourselves as we wait for our adoption as sons of God, the redemption of our bodies. For we are saved in this hope.

Let us pray.

GRANT, Lord, that the world may be governed according to your order, and the Church may rejoice in tranquil devotion. Through Christ our Lord. Amen.

℣. Let us bless the Lord.
℟. Thanks be to God.

Vespers

Evening

℣. O God, ✠ come to my assistance.
℟. O Lord, be swift to my aid.
℣. Glory be to the Father, and to the Son, and to the Holy Spirit.
**℟. As it was in the beginning, is now and ever shall be,
world without end. Amen.**

O WONDROUS maker of the light,
  Who brought forth light to bless the day,
And with new light did glorify
Creation's first ecstatic dawn;

Who, morning unto evening joined,
Decreed that day should be its name,
Now that this day declines to eve
Hear all our heartfelt prayers and psalms:

That all our minds be free from fault,
Free from the weight of reckless sin,
That sin which, self-entangling, drowns,
Forgetting your eternal love.

We knock at heaven's secret place
That we may win the prize of life;
Now let us flee all evil thoughts
And cast away unholiness.

Grant this, most holy Father blest,
And Jesus with the Father one,
And Holy Spirit, Paraclete
While everlasting ages run. Amen.

Lucis Creator optime

Ant. The Lord will send forth his sceptre of power, and his
dominion will be for ever.

Psalm 109

THE Lord said to my Lord:
  'Sit at my right hand:
  your foes I will make your footstool.'

The Lord will send forth your sceptre of power from Zion:
rule in the midst of all your enemies!

Dominion is yours in the day of your strength
in the splendour of the saints;
from the womb before the daystar I begot you.

The Lord has sworn and he will not retract:
'You are a priest for ever,
according to the order of Melchizedek.'

The Lord standing at your right hand
has broken kings in the day of his wrath.

He shall judge among nations, heap high the bodies;
he shall break heads in many lands.

He shall drink of the brook by the way
and therefore shall he lift up his head.

Glory be...

Ant. The Lord will send forth his sceptre of power, and his
dominion will be for ever.

Short reading   *1 Peter 1:3-5*

B LESSED be the God and Father of our Lord Jesus Christ,
who according to his great mercy has regenerated us to a
living hope by the resurrection of Jesus Christ from the dead, and
to an inheritance which is incorruptible and undefiled, and which
cannot fade, reserved in Heaven for you, who by the power of
God are kept by faith for salvation which is ready to be revealed
in the last time.

The Magnificat

*The Gospel canticle is the heart of the Hour. This is the great hymn of
Mary, uttered, according to the first chapter of St Luke's Gospel (1:46-
55), just after Elizabeth, Mary's cousin and mother of John the Baptist,
greeted our Lady.*

M Y ✠ SOUL magnifies the Lord,
my spirit rejoices in God who is my Saviour,
who has looked upon the humility of his handmaiden.

Behold, all generations from now
    will acknowledge me blessed,
For the mighty one has done great things for me:
    Holy is his name!
His mercy is from one generation to the next on those who fear him.
    Mighty is his arm!
He has scattered the proud in the imagination of their hearts,
    and has put down the powerful from their thrones,
    exalting those of humble degree.
The hungry he has filled with good things,
    but the rich he has dismissed with nothing.
Remembering his mercy, he has helped his servant Israel,
    as he promised to our fathers,
    to Abraham and to his posterity for ever more.

Glory be…

Intercessions   *Either these, or others at choice or need.*

Lord, bless and give wisdom to N. our Pope. *(pause for prayer)*
    ℟. Hear us, O Lord.
Lord, bless and give wisdom to N. our Bishop. *(pause)* **℟.**
Lord, bless and give wisdom to our country's leaders. *(pause)* **℟.**
Lord, bless and give wisdom to our local government. *(pause)* **℟.**
Lord, grant rest to the dead. *(pause)* **℟.**

> Lord, have mercy.
> Christ, have mercy.
> Lord, have mercy.

> Our Father…

Let us pray.

LORD, as we have celebrated today the mystery of your Son's resurrection from the dead, grant that this celebration may bear fruit in our lives, that we too may one day rise with him to eternal life. Through the same Jesus Christ, your Son, who lives and reigns with you and the Holy Spirit, one God, world without end. Amen.

> ℣. Let us bless the Lord.
> **℟. Thanks be to God.**

ೞ   ೞ   ೞ

Compline

At the end of the day

℣. O God, ✠ come to my assistance.
℟. O Lord, be swift to my aid.
℣. Glory be to the Father, and to the Son, and to the Holy Spirit.
℟. As it was in the beginning, is now and ever shall be, world without end. Amen.

It is fitting here to make an examination of conscience, followed by an act of penance such as the Confiteor as at Mass, or an act of contrition (see p. 199).

(see p. 199).

B EFORE the ending of the day,
Creator of the world, we pray
That with thy wonted favour thou
Wouldst be our guard and keeper now.

From all ill dreams defend our eyes,
From nightly fears and fantasies;
Tread under foot our ghostly foe,
That no pollution we may know.

O Father, that we ask be done,
Through Jesus Christ, thine only Son;
Who, with the Holy Ghost and thee,
Doth live and reign eternally. Amen.

Te lucis ante terminum

Ant. Bless the Lord throughout the night.

Psalm 133

B EHOLD, bless the Lord,
all you servants of the Lord,
who stand in the house of the Lord,
in the courts of the house of our God by night.

Lift up your hands to the holy places,
and bless the Lord.

May the Lord bless you out of Sion,
he that made both Heaven and earth.

Glory be…

Ant. Bless the Lord throughout the night.

Short reading   *Revelation 22:4-5*

T HEY shall see God's face, and his name shall be on their
     foreheads. And night shall be no more; they shall not need
the light of the lamp nor the light of the sun, because the Lord
God shall enlighten them, and they shall reign for ever and ever.

The Nunc Dimittis

This Gospel canticle uses the words of Simeon, giving thanks to God
when he first set eyes on the Messiah.   *Luke 2:29-32*

Ant. Save us, O Lord, while we wake, and watch over us as we
sleep, that we may pass the night with Christ and rest in peace.

L ORD, ✠ now let your servant depart in peace,
            according to your promise;
         for my eyes have seen your salvation
      which you have prepared in the presence of all peoples,
   a light for revelation to the Gentiles,
      and for glory to your people Israel.

Glory be…

Ant. Save us, O Lord, while we wake, and watch over us as we
sleep, that we may pass the night with Christ and rest in peace.

Let us pray.

V ISIT this house, O Lord, we pray, and drive far from it the
     deadly power of the enemy. May your holy angels dwell
here instead, that we may be preserved in peace, with your blessing on us always. Through Christ our Lord. Amen.

The day is traditionally closed with an antiphon in honour of our Lady,
varied according to the liturgical season (see pp.341ff.). At any season
of the year, the following, Sub Tuum Præsidium, *may be said instead:*

W E FLY to thy patronage, holy Mother of God.
      Despise not our petitions in our necessities
   But deliver us from every evil,
   O glorious and blessed Virgin!

MONDAY

Vigils

℣. O Lord, ✠ open my lips.
℟. And my mouth shall declare your praise.

Antiphon: The Lord remembers the cry of the poor.

Psalm 9:10-19

THE LORD is a refuge for the poor,
    a timely helper in tribulation.
    Let those who know your name trust you:
for, Lord, you will never forsake those who seek you.

Sing to the Lord who dwells in Sion,
    Declare his mighty ways among the Gentiles;
for he who seeks recompense for blood has remembered them,
    he has not forgotten the cry of the poor.

Have mercy on me, O Lord, see my humiliation,
    you who lift me up from the gates of death;
that I may declare all your praises
    at the gates of the Daughter of Sion,
    and rejoice in your salvation.

The Gentiles have stuck fast in the trap which they made,
    their foot caught in the very snare they hid.
The Lord shall be known when he executes judgement.
    The sinner is snared in the works of his own hands.

Let the wicked go down into Hell,
    all the nations that forget God.
For the needy shall never be forgotten,
    nor the patience of the poor perish for ever.

Glory be...

Antiphon: The Lord remembers the cry of the poor.

℣. O Lord, inflame my heart,
℟. And I will teach your way to the poor.

First reading

One chapter from the scriptures.

Response to the reading

℣. Let me know your will, O Lord,
℟. And do it with all my heart.
℣. May I proclaim your word with my lips,
℟. And do it with all my heart.

Second reading

Spiritual reading.

Response to the reading

℣. I shall proclaim your decrees to the mighty,
℟. For your word is my delight.
℣. All night, O Lord, I have remembered your name,
℟. For your word is my delight.

Let us pray.

ALMIGHTY God, by whose just decrees we are governed, grant that all people may recognize your Word, and come to live by it. Through Christ our Lord. Amen.

℣. Let us bless the Lord.
℟. Thanks be to God.

❧   ❧   ❧

Lauds

℣. O God, ✠ come to my assistance.
℟. O Lord, be swift to my aid.
℣. Glory be to the Father, and to the Son, and to the Holy Spirit.
**℟. As it was in the beginning, is now and ever shall be,
world without end. Amen.**

S PLENDOUR of the Father's glory,
Radiance from eternal light,
Light of lights and fount of radiance,
Day that art the light of days,

Truest Sun that flows upon us,
Shining beam, eternal light:
Now command the Holy Spirit
Our dull senses to illume.

Let us also ask the Father:
He who sends most powerful grace,
He of everlasting glory:
Cast away all dangerous sin.

Now inspire us to do battle,
Blunt the teeth of tempter's power,
Be the downfall of our brashness,
Be the giver of thy grace.

Guide and rule our wayward spirits,
Make our bodies pure and true,
Stir our faith into a fire lest
Poisoned error us molest.

And may Christ our finest food be,
Give true faith to quench our thirst.
Joyfully we drink that sober
Spirit which inebriates.

May this joyful day so flourish,
Pure as dawn then may we be,
So that faith may shine like noonday
And no setting ever know.

As the dawn brings on the daylight,
So may dawn bring now to us
In the Father, all the Sonhood,
All the Father in the Word. Amen.

Splendor Paternæ gloriæ

Ant. Bless the righteous, O Lord.

Psalm 5

GIVE ear to my words, O Lord,
    understand my cry.
Hearken to the voice of my prayer,
    O my King and my God.

It is you to whom I pray, O Lord.
    In the morning you will hear my voice;
in the morning I will stand before you,
    and I will wait and watch.

You are no God who wills iniquity;
    neither can the sinner dwell near you.
The unjust shall not abide before your face.
    You hate all who work iniquity:
    you destroy all who speak lies.
The deceitful and bloody man
    the Lord abhors.

But as for me, through the multitude of your mercies
    I will come into your house.
I will worship in your holy temple,
    filled with reverence.

Conduct me, Lord, in your justice,
    because of my enemies;
    direct my way in your sight.
For there is no truth in their mouth,
    their heart is all vanity,
    their throat an open sepulchre,
    their tongues all deceit.

Judge them, O God.
    Let them fall from their devices.
Cast them out for their multitude of wickednesses;
    for they have provoked you, O Lord.

But let all those who hope in you be glad:
>> for you shall dwell within them,
>> and those who love your name shall glory in you.

For you will bless the just, O Lord:
>> You have crowned us,
>> as with a shield of your good will.

Glory be...

>> *Ant.* Bless the righteous, O Lord.

Short reading
Romans 13:11-13

NOW is the hour for us to rise from sleep. For now our salvation is nearer to us than when we first believed. The night is passed, the day is at hand. Let us therefore cast off the works of darkness and put on the armour of light; let us walk honestly as in the day.

The Benedictus

Luke 1:68-79

BLESSED ✠ be the Lord, the God of Israel,
>> who has visited and redeemed his people,
>> and has lifted up a horn of salvation for us
in the family of his servant David.
For this he swore through the mouths of holy men:
>> those who were prophets, from the beginning:
There would be salvation from our foes,
>> and from the hand of all those who hate us;
to comfort our fathers,
>> and to honour his holy covenant,
which oath once he swore to Abraham, our father,
>> that he would grant us,
that freed from the hand of our enemies,
>> and without fear, we may serve him,
>> in holiness and justice in his very presence all our days.
And you, my son, will be named Prophet of the Most High;
>> for you will go before the presence of the Lord
>> to prepare his way,

to teach knowledge of salvation to his people
that their sins may be forgiven,
through the merciful heart of our God,
when the Daystar shall visit us from on high
to enlighten those who sit in darkness
and in the shadow of death,
and guide our feet to the way of peace.

Glory be…

Intercessions   *Either these, or others at choice or need.*

Lord, strengthen those who give food to the hungry. *(pause for prayer)* ℟. **Hear us, Father.**
Lord, strengthen those who give drink to the thirsty. *(pause)* ℟.
Lord, strengthen those who give clothing to the naked. *(pause)* ℟.
Lord, strengthen those who give shelter to the homeless.
(pause) ℟.
Lord, strengthen those who care for the sick. *(pause)* ℟.
Lord, strengthen those who visit and help the imprisoned.
(pause) ℟.

Lord, have mercy.
Christ, have mercy.
Lord, have mercy.

Our Father…

Let us pray.

GOD of righteousness, grant us the sight to see what needs to be done, and the courage to do it. Through our Lord Jesus Christ, your Son, who lives and reigns with you in the unity of the Holy Spirit, one God for ever and ever. Amen.

℣. Let us bless the Lord.
℟. **Thanks be to God.**

ॐ   ॐ   ॐ

Terce

℣. O God, ✠ come to my assistance.
℟. **O Lord, be swift to my aid.**
℣. Glory be to the Father, and to the Son, and to the Holy Spirit.
℟. **As it was in the beginning, is now and ever shall be,**
world without end. Amen.

COME, Holy Ghost, with God the Son
And God the Father, ever one;
Shed forth thy grace within our breast
And dwell with us a ready guest.

By every power, by heart and tongue,
By act and deed, thy praise be sung;
Inflame with perfect love each sense
That others' souls may kindle thence.

O Father, that we ask be done,
Through Jesus Christ, thine only Son;
Who, with the Holy Ghost and thee,
Doth live and reign eternally. Amen.

Nunc nobis, Sancte Spiritus

Ant. Lord, your testimonies are my meditation.

Psalm 118 Gimel

DEAL generously with your servant:
enliven me and I shall keep your word.
Open my eyes that I may consider
the wondrous things of your law.
I am a sojourner on the earth;
hide not your commands from me.
My soul is ever longing for
and coveting your decrees.
You have rebuked the proud; they are cursed
who turn away from your commands.
Remove from me reproach and contempt
for I have sought after your will.

For princes sat and spoke against me,
    but your servant was studying your statutes.
Your will is my meditation;
    your statutes are my counsel.

Glory be...

Ant. Lord, your testimonies are my meditation.

Short reading

Amos 5:14ff

S EEK good, and not evil, that you may live; and the Lord God of hosts will be with you. Hate evil, and love good, and establish just judgement in the gate; it may be that the Lord, the God of hosts, will have mercy on the remnant of Joseph.

Let us pray.

O GOD, delighting in virtue and despising evil, make us strong in the same virtue, and grant us the grace to be ever ready to run according to your commands. Through Christ our Lord. Amen.

℣. Let us bless the Lord.
℟. **Thanks be to God.**

Sext

℣. O God, ✠ come to my assistance.
℟. O Lord, be swift to my aid.
℣. Glory be to the Father, and to the Son, and to the Holy Spirit.
**℟. As it was in the beginning, is now and ever shall be,
world without end. Amen.**

O GOD of truth, O Lord of might,
Who orderest time and change aright,
And send'st the early morning ray,
And light'st the glow of perfect day:

Extinguish thou each sinful fire,
And banish every ill desire;
And while thou keep'st the body whole,
Shed forth thy peace upon the soul.

O Father, that we ask be done,
Through Jesus Christ, thine only Son;
Who, with the Holy Ghost and thee,
Doth live and reign eternally. Amen.

Rector potens, verax Deus

Ant. Lord, revive me according to your word.

Psalm 118 Daleth

MY SOUL cleaves to the dust;
by your word give me life.
I have declared my ways and you have heard me:
    teach me your commands.
Make me understand the way of your statutes,
    and I will consider your wondrous works.
My soul is heavy with sorrow;
    by your word strengthen me.
Remove me from the way of iniquity,
    and by reason of your law, have mercy on me.
I have chosen the way of truth;
    I put to myself your judgements.

I have bound myself to your testimonies;
 Lord, do not put me to shame.
I have run the way of your commands;
 you have given joy to my heart.

Glory be…

Ant. Lord, revive me according to your word.

Short reading

Isaiah 58:6-11

IS NOT this, rather, the fast that I have chosen? Loose the bonds of wickedness, undo the oppressive burdens, let the broken go free, and break asunder every yoke! Give your bread to the hungry, and bring the needy and homeless into your house. When you see someone naked, cover him, and do not despise your own flesh. Then shall your light break forth like the morning, and your healing shall speedily arise; your justice shall go before your face, and the glory of the Lord shall gather you up. Then you shall call, and the Lord will hear; you shall cry, and he will say, Here I am. If you take away the chain from the midst of you, the pointing of the finger, and speaking what does no good, if you pour out your soul for the hungry and satisfy the soul of the afflicted, then shall your light rise up in darkness and your darkness shall be as the noonday. And the Lord will give you rest continually, and will fill your soul with brightness, and rescue your bones, and you shall be like a watered garden, and like a fountain of water, whose waters shall not fail.

Let us pray.

LORD, pour your love into our hearts that we may love you above all things, and our neighbour as ourselves. Through Christ our Lord. Amen.

℣. Let us bless the Lord.
℟. Thanks be to God.

None

℣. O God, ✠ come to my assistance.
℟. **O Lord, be swift to my aid.**
℣. Glory be to the Father, and to the Son, and to the Holy Spirit.
℟. **As it was in the beginning, is now and ever shall be,**
   world without end. Amen.

O GOD, Creation's secret force,
   Thyself unmoved, all motion's source,
Who from the morn till evening ray
Through all its changes guid'st the day:

Grant us, when this short life is past,
The glorious evening that shall last;
That, by a holy death attained,
Eternal glory may be gained.

O Father, that we ask be done,
Through Jesus Christ, thine only Son;
Who, with the Holy Ghost and thee,
Doth live and reign eternally. Amen.

Rerum Deus tenax vigor

Ant. Lead me in the path of your commandments.

Psalm 118 He

S ET before me the way of your statutes, O Lord,
   and I will always seek after them.
Give me understanding, and I will search your law
   and I will keep it with my whole heart.
Lead me in the path of your commandments;
   for this I have desired.
Incline my heart to your testimonies,
   and not to covetousness.
Turn away my eyes from vanities:
   give me life in your way.
Fulfil the word you have spoken
   to the servant who stands in your fear.

Turn away from the reproach I dread,
for your judgements are delightful.
Behold, I have longed after your precepts:
give me life in your justice.

Glory be…

Ant. Lead me in the path of your commandments.

Short reading
1 Samuel 2:8

THE Lord raises up the needy from the dust; he lifts the poor from the dunghill, that they may sit with princes and hold a throne of glory.

Let us pray.

TAKE away, Lord, our heart of stone, and give us a heart of tenderness for you and our neighbours. Through Christ our Lord. Amen.

℣. Let us bless the Lord.
℟. Thanks be to God.

Vespers

℣. O God, ✠ come to my assistance.
℟. O Lord, be swift to my aid.
℣. Glory be to the Father, and to the Son, and to the Holy Spirit.
**℟. As it was in the beginning, is now and ever shall be,
   world without end. Amen.**

O BLEST Creator of the earthly sphere,
   Who 'stablished dry land firm upon its base,
In separating land from land you toiled,
And driving fretful waters to their place;

Who from that soil brought seeds of various kinds,
Bright flowers to beautify both hill and vale,
Abundant fruits that hang from many a bough,
Delightful food supplying without fail:

Cleanse with the freshness of your grace the wounds
Which mar the beauty of our sin-seared minds
And wash away with tears our evil deeds,
Grind down whatever sin unto us binds.

Now let our souls obey your just commands,
And let no evil thing to us draw nigh,
That filled with good, we may in you rejoice,
And come at last to eternal life on high.

Eternal Father, hear our earnest prayer,
And you, O equal, sole-begotten Son,
Who with the Holy Spirit reign supreme,
One only God, while endless ages run. Amen.

Telluris alme conditor

Ant. The Lord of hosts is with us: the God of Jacob is our stronghold.

Psalm 45

O UR GOD is for us a refuge and strength,
   a helper in troubles which have hit us hard:

Therefore we shall not fear
    though the earth should be troubled,
    and the mountains collapse into the heart of the sea;
Though its waters roar and are troubled,
    though mountains are shaken by its strength.

The Lord of hosts is with us:
    the God of Jacob is our stronghold.

The stream of a river makes joyful God's city,
    the tabernacle made holy by the Most High's dwelling.
God is in its midst, it shall not be moved;
    God will help it at the break of day.
Nations were troubled, kingdoms were humbled:
    he uttered his voice; the earth trembled.

The Lord of hosts is with us:
    the God of Jacob is our stronghold.

Come and behold the works of the Lord
    the wonderful things he has done upon earth
    making wars to cease to the ends of the world;
He shall destroy the bow, and break the weapons;
    the shields he shall burn in the fire.
'Be still and see that I am God,
    I will be exalted among the nations,
    I will be exalted on the earth!'

The Lord of hosts is with us:
    the God of Jacob is our stronghold.

Glory be…

Ant. The Lord of hosts is with us: the God of Jacob is our stronghold.

Short reading   *2 Corinthians 1:3-4*

B LESSED be the God and Father of our Lord Jesus Christ,
the Father of mercies and the God of all comfort, who comforts
us in all our tribulation, so that we also may be able to comfort those
who are in any distress, with the comfort with which we ourselves are
comforted by God.

The Magnificat

Luke 1:46-55

M Y ✠ SOUL magnifies the Lord,
    my spirit rejoices in God who is my Saviour,
    who has looked upon the humility of his handmaiden.
Behold, all generations from now
    will acknowledge me blessed,
For the mighty one has done great things for me:
    Holy is his name!
His mercy is from one generation to the next on those who fear him.
    Mighty is his arm!
He has scattered the proud in the imagination of their hearts,
    and has put down the powerful from their thrones,
    exalting those of humble degree.
The hungry he has filled with good things,
    but the rich he has dismissed with nothing.
Remembering his mercy, he has helped his servant Israel,
    as he promised to our fathers,
    to Abraham and to his posterity for ever more.

Glory be…

Intercessions   *Either these, or others at choice or need.*

For those unjustly deprived of freedom, *(pause for prayer)*
    ℟. **Hear us, O Lord.**
For those who lack the necessities of life, *(pause)* ℟.
For those who fight evil with good, *(pause)* ℟.
For an end to famine and war, *(pause)* ℟.
Grant rest to those who have given their lives for justice or truth.
    (pause) ℟.

Lord, have mercy.
Christ, have mercy.
Lord, have mercy.

Our Father…

Let us pray.

L ORD, grant us the gift to be always contemplating what is right, and make us well-disposed to putting it into action, that we who can do nothing without you may be worthy to live as you wish. Through our Lord Jesus Christ, your Son, who lives and reigns with you and the Holy Spirit, one God, world without end. Amen.

℣. Let us bless the Lord.
℟. Thanks be to God.

Compline

℣. O God, ✠ come to my assistance.
℟. O Lord, be swift to my aid.
℣. Glory be to the Father, and to the Son, and to the Holy Spirit.
℟. As it was in the beginning, is now and ever shall be, world without end. Amen.

Examination of conscience, and act of penance.

B EFORE the ending of the day,
Creator of the world, we pray
That with thy wonted favour thou
Wouldst be our guard and keeper now.

From all ill dreams defend our eyes,
From nightly fears and fantasies;
Tread under foot our ghostly foe,
That no pollution we may know.

O Father, that we ask be done,
Through Jesus Christ, thine only Son;
Who, with the Holy Ghost and thee,
Doth live and reign eternally. Amen.

Te lucis ante terminum

Ant. The Lord is with us in tribulation.

Psalm 90

H E THAT dwells in the help of the most High
shall abide in the protection of the Almighty.
He shall say to the Lord: You are my protector,
and my refuge: my God in whom I will trust!

For he has delivered me from the snare
of the hunter, and from the barbed word;
he will shelter you with his shoulders
and under the protection of his wings you will flee.

His truth shall compass you as with a shield:
    you will not be afraid of the terror in the night,
Nor the arrow that flies in the day,
        nor the scourge that stalks in the darkness
        nor the destroying noonday devil.

A thousand may fall by your side,
        and ten thousand at your right hand,
        never shall it come nigh to you.

Open your eyes and consider,
        and you will see the reward of the wicked.
You, O Lord, are my hope:
        and have made your refuge on high.

There shall no evil come upon you,
        nor shall the scourge come near your dwelling.
For he has given his angels charge over you,
        to keep you in all your ways.

In their hands they shall bear you up,
        lest you dash your foot against a stone.
You shall walk upon the asp and the basilisk
        and trample underfoot the lion and the dragon.

Because he hoped in me, I will deliver him;
        I will protect him for he has known my name.
He shall cry to me, and I will hear him:
        I am with him in tribulation and I will glorify him.

With length of days I will fill him;
        and I will show him my salvation.

Glory be...

Ant. The Lord is with us in tribulation.

Short reading   *1 Thessalonians 5:9-11*

FOR GOD has not destined us for wrath, but to purchase salvation by means of our Lord Jesus Christ, who died for us so that whether we watch or sleep we might live together with him. Because of this, encourage one another and edify one another, as you are doing already.

The Nunc Dimittis

Luke 2:29-32

Ant. Save us, O Lord, while we wake, and watch over us as we sleep, that we may pass the night with Christ and rest in peace.

L ORD, ✠ now let your servant depart in peace,
    according to your promise;
    for my eyes have seen your salvation
  which you have prepared in the presence of all peoples,
a light for revelation to the Gentiles,
    and for glory to your people Israel.

Glory be…

Ant. Save us, O Lord, while we wake, and watch over us as we sleep, that we may pass the night with Christ and rest in peace.

Let us pray.

V ISIT this house, O Lord, we pray, and drive far from it the deadly power of the enemy. May your holy angels dwell here instead, that we may be preserved in peace, with your blessing on us always. Through Christ our Lord. Amen.

Antiphon in honour of our Lady, pp.341ff.
or:

W E FLY to thy patronage, holy Mother of God.
    Despise not our petitions in our necessities
  But deliver us from every evil,
  O glorious and blessed Virgin!

∾   ∾   ∾

TUESDAY

Vigils

℣. O Lord, ✠ open my lips.
℟. **And my mouth shall declare your praise.**

Ant. Come, let us worship the Lord.

Psalm 94

COME, let us praise the Lord with joy;
    let us joyfully sing to God our Saviour.
    Let us come before his presence with thanksgiving,
and make a joyful noise to him with psalms.

For the Lord is a great God,
    and a great king above all gods.
For in his hand are all the depths of the earth;
    and the heights of the mountains are his.
For the sea is his, and it was he that made it
    and his hands formed the dry land.

Come, let us adore and fall down;
    let us kneel before the Lord who made us,
for he is the Lord our God,
      and we are the people of his pasture,
      and the sheep fed by his hand.

If only today you would hear his voice!
    Harden not your hearts
as at the provocation,
      as on that day of temptation in the desert
      when your fathers tempted me;
      when they proved me, and saw my works.

Forty years long I was offended with that generation
    and I said: 'These always err in their hearts,
    these men have not known my ways.'
So I swore in my wrath
    that they shall not enter into my rest.

Glory be…

Ant. Come, let us worship the Lord.

℣. Keep my eyes from what is false.
℟. **By your word give me life.**

First reading

One chapter from the scriptures.

Response to the reading

℣. This is my comfort in sorrow,
℟. **That your promise gives me life.**
℣. And I shall answer those who taunt me,
℟. **That your promise gives me life.**

Second reading

Spiritual reading.

Response to the reading

℣. Keep me from the way of error;
℟. **Teach me your law.**
℣. I have chosen the way of truth;
℟. **Teach me your law.**

Let us pray.

ALMIGHTY God, grant us greater faith, hope and charity and, that we might come to what you promise, make us to love what you command. Through Christ our Lord. Amen.

℣. Let us bless the Lord.
℟. **Thanks be to God.**

Lauds

℣. O God, ✠ come to my assistance.
℟. O Lord, be swift to my aid.
℣. Glory be to the Father, and to the Son, and to the Holy Spirit.
**℟. As it was in the beginning, is now and ever shall be,
world without end. Amen.**

THE fair-winged chorus of the dawn
Proclaims the coming of the light,
And Christ, the soul's awakener,
Bids us arise now into life.

Now cast away, he cries, your beds,
You drowsy captives of your sleep!
Be upright, sober, pure, alert,
And for my coming vigil keep.

To Jesus lift our voices loud,
Now clamour, praying without sleep;
For prayer directly from the heart
That heart from slumbering will keep.

So, Christ, dispel our lazy sleep,
And break the chains of slothful night,
And break the power of sins long past,
And fill us with the grace of light.

To God the Father glory be
And to his only Son, our Lord,
Who with the Holy Spirit, three
Yet one eternal is adored. Amen.

Ales diei nuntius

Ant. Sing to the Lord: praise his glorious name.

Psalm 146

PRAISE the Lord, for praising him is good;
It is joyful and comely to sing his praise!

The Lord builds up Jerusalem
  he will gather together the dispersal of Israel.
It is he who heals the broken-hearted,
  he binds up all their bruises.
He can tell the number of the stars,
  and calls each one by its name.

Great is our Lord, and great is his power;
  the acts of his wisdom are numberless.
The Lord lifts up the meek;
  and brings the wicked down to the dust.
Sing to the Lord with praise:
  sing to our God upon the harp!

It is he who covers the heavens with clouds;
  and prepares rain for the earth,
making grass to grow on the mountains
  and herbs for the service of men.

He gives the beasts their food
  and feeds the young ravens that call upon him.
His delight is not in the power of the horse,
  nor his pleasure in the strength of a man's legs.
But the Lord takes pleasure in those who fear him,
  and in those who hope in his mercy.

Glory be…

Ant. Sing to the Lord: praise his glorious name.

Short reading   *1 Thessalonians 5:4-5*

B UT YOU, brethren, are not in darkness, that day should
  overtake you like a thief. For you are all children of light
and children of the day; we are not of the night nor of darkness.

The Benedictus

Luke 1:68-79

BLESSED ✠ be the Lord, the God of Israel,
who has visited and redeemed his people,
and has lifted up a horn of salvation for us
in the family of his servant David.
For this he swore through the mouths of holy men:
those who were prophets, from the beginning:
There would be salvation from our foes,
and from the hand of all those who hate us;
to comfort our fathers,
and to honour his holy covenant,
which oath once he swore to Abraham, our father,
that he would grant us,
that freed from the hand of our enemies,
and without fear, we may serve him,
in holiness and justice in his very presence all our days.
And you, my son, will be named Prophet of the Most High;
for you will go before the presence of the Lord
to prepare his way,
to teach knowledge of salvation to his people
that their sins may be forgiven,
through the merciful heart of our God,
when the Daystar shall visit us from on high
to enlighten those who sit in darkness
and in the shadow of death,
and guide our feet to the way of peace.

Glory be…

Intercessions *Either these, or others at choice or need.*

Lord, bless all teachers and educators. *(pause for prayer)*
   ℟. **Lord have mercy.**
Lord, bless all those who care for the sick. *(pause)* ℟.
Lord, bless all those who labour to make you better known.
   (pause) ℟.
Lord, strengthen the vocation of nuns and sisters. *(pause)* ℟.

Lord, strengthen the vocation of brothers and priests. *(pause)* **R̶.**
Lord, strengthen the vocation of all married people. *(pause)* **R̶.**

Lord, have mercy.
Christ, have mercy.
Lord, have mercy.

Our Father...

Let us pray.

G OD of mercy and goodness, in whose gift it is that we should serve you worthily and well, grant that we may run towards the fulfilment of your promises, without offence, and with alacrity. Through our Lord Jesus Christ, your Son, who lives and reigns with you in the unity of the Holy Spirit, one God for ever and ever. Amen.

V̶. Let us bless the Lord.
R̶. Thanks be to God.

Terce

℣. O God, ✠ come to my assistance.
℞. O Lord, be swift to my aid.
℣. Glory be to the Father, and to the Son, and to the Holy Spirit.
**℞. As it was in the beginning, is now and ever shall be,
world without end. Amen.**

C OME, Holy Ghost, with God the Son
    And God the Father, ever one;
Shed forth thy grace within our breast
And dwell with us a ready guest.

By every power, by heart and tongue,
By act and deed, thy praise be sung;
Inflame with perfect love each sense
That others' souls may kindle thence.

O Father, that we ask be done,
Through Jesus Christ, thine only Son;
Who, with the Holy Ghost and thee,
Doth live and reign eternally. Amen.

Nunc nobis, Sancte Spiritus

Ant. I shall always keep your law for ever and ever.

Psalm 118 Vau

L ET your mercy come upon me, O Lord,
    your salvation according to your word.
So shall I answer those who reproach me,
    that I have trusted in your word.
Do not take the word of truth utterly out of my mouth
    for in your word I have greatly hoped.
So shall I always keep your law
    for ever and ever.
I shall walk in freedom,
    for I have sought your commandments.
I have spoken of your will before kings
    and I was not ashamed.

I delighted also in your commandments:
    which I have loved.
And I lifted up my hands to your decrees which I love
    and I contemplate your judgements.

Glory be...

Ant. I shall always keep your law for ever and ever.

Short reading   *Isaiah 55:8-11*

FOR my thoughts are not your thoughts, nor your ways my
ways, says the Lord. For as the heavens are exalted above
the earth, so are my ways exalted above your ways and my
thoughts above your thoughts. And as the rain and the snow come
down from Heaven, and return there no more but soak the earth,
and water it, and make it spring up, and give seed to the sower
and bread to the eater, so shall my word be, which goes forth
from my mouth; it shall not return to me empty, but it shall do
whatsoever I please, and shall prosper in the things for which I
sent it.

Let us pray.

O GOD of truth, send us the Holy Spirit to be our advocate
and guide, according to your promise. Through Christ our
Lord. Amen.

℣. Let us bless the Lord.
℟. **Thanks be to God.**

Sext

℣. O God, ✠ come to my assistance.
℞. **O Lord, be swift to my aid.**
℣. Glory be to the Father, and to the Son, and to the Holy Spirit.
℞. **As it was in the beginning, is now and ever shall be, world without end. Amen.**

O GOD of truth, O Lord of might,
 Who orderest time and change aright,
And send'st the early morning ray,
And light'st the glow of perfect day:

Extinguish thou each sinful fire,
And banish every ill desire;
And while thou keep'st the body whole,
Shed forth thy peace upon the soul.

O Father, that we ask be done,
Through Jesus Christ, thine only Son;
Who, with the Holy Ghost and thee,
Doth live and reign eternally. Amen.

Rector potens, verax Deus

Ant. This has been my reward, the keeping of your law.

Psalm 118 Zain

B E MINDFUL of your word to your servant;
 in which you gave me hope.
This has comforted me in humiliation,
    that your word has given me life.
Though the proud have greatly despised me,
    I have not left your law.
I remembered, O Lord, your judgements of old,
    and these are my comfort.
I am seized with indignation
    at the wicked who forsake your law.

Your commandments have become my song
    in the place of my wanderings.
In the night I remember your name, O Lord,
    and I have kept your law.
This is what has been my reward:
    because I have sought the keeping of your law.

Glory be...

Ant. This has been my reward, the keeping of your law.

Short reading   *1 Samuel 16:7b*

THE Lord sees not as man sees; for man sees those things which are merely apparent, but the Lord sees the heart.

Let us pray.

LORD, help us to rise above petty hypocrisy and self-seeking. May our outward appearance show a true heart within. Through Christ our Lord. Amen.

℣. Let us bless the Lord.
℟. Thanks be to God.

൲   ൲   ൲

None

℣. O God, ✠ come to my assistance.
℟. O Lord, be swift to my aid.
℣. Glory be to the Father, and to the Son, and to the Holy Spirit.
**℟. As it was in the beginning, is now and ever shall be,
world without end. Amen.**

O GOD, Creation's secret force,
Thyself unmoved, all motion's source,
Who from the morn till evening ray
Through all its changes guid'st the day:

Grant us, when this short life is past,
The glorious evening that shall last;
That, by a holy death attained,
Eternal glory may be gained.

O Father, that we ask be done,
Through Jesus Christ, thine only Son;
Who, with the Holy Ghost and thee,
Doth live and reign eternally. Amen.

Rerum Deus tenax vigor

Ant. Lord, your mercy fills the earth; teach me your statutes.

Psalm 118 Heth

MY PORTION is the Lord;
I have said: I will keep your law.
With all my heart I implore your kindness;
　　have mercy on me according to your word.
I have thought on my ways
　　and turned my feet to do your will.
I am ready and am not troubled
　　to obey your commandments.
The cords of the wicked encompassed me,
　　but I have not forgotten your law.

I rose at midnight to give you praise
    for your just judgements.
I am friend to all those who fear you,
    and who keep your commandments.
The earth, O Lord, is full of your mercy:
    teach me your statutes.

Glory be…

Ant. Lord, your mercy fills the earth; teach me your statutes.

Short reading
Galatians 5:22-25

B UT THE fruit of the Spirit is charity, joy, peace, patience, benignity, goodness, longanimity, mildness, faith, modesty, continency, chastity; against such there is no law. And those who are Christ's have crucified their flesh with its vices and desires. If we live in the Spirit, let us also walk in the Spirit.

Let us pray.

S END us, Lord, the gifts of your Holy Spirit in abundance, that we may reap the fruits in our lives and walk by the same Spirit. Through Christ our Lord. Amen.

℣. Let us bless the Lord.
℟. Thanks be to God.

Vespers

℣. O God, ✠ come to my assistance.
℟. **O Lord, be swift to my aid.**
℣. Glory be to the Father, and to the Son, and to the Holy Spirit.
℟. **As it was in the beginning, is now and ever shall be,
world without end. Amen.**

G LORY to thee, my God, this night,
For all the blessings of the light;
Keep me, O keep me, King of Kings,
Beneath thy own almighty wings.

Forgive me, Lord, for thy dear Son
The ill that I this day have done,
That with the world, myself, and thee,
I, ere I sleep, at peace may be.

Teach me to live, that I may dread
The grave as little as my bed;
Teach me to die, that so I may
Rise glorious at the awful day.

O may my soul on thee repose
And with sweet sleep mine eyelids close,
Sleep that may me more vigorous make
To serve my God when I awake.

Praise God, from whom all blessings flow,
Praise him, all creatures here below,
Praise him above, ye heavenly host,
Praise Father, Son and Holy Ghost. Amen.

Thomas Ken

Ant. May we be blessed by the Lord, who made Heaven and
earth.

Psalm 113

W HEN Israel came out of Egypt,
the house of Jacob from a barbarous people,
Judah was made his sanctuary,

Israel his dominion.
The sea looked and fled:
    even the Jordan turned back;
the mountains skipped like rams,
    and the hills like the lambs of the flock.

Why was it, O sea, that you fled,
    that you were turned back, O Jordan?
You mountains, that you skipped like rams,
    and you hills, like lambs of the flock?

At the presence of the Lord the earth quaked,
    at the presence of the God of Jacob,
who turned the rock into pools of water
    and the stony hill into fountains of waters.

Not to us, O Lord, not to us,
    but to your name give glory,
for your mercy and your truth's sake,
    lest the Gentiles say: 'Where is their God?'

But our God is in Heaven;
    he does all things as he wills.
The idols of the Gentiles are silver and gold,
    the work of the hands of men.

They have mouths yet cannot speak;
    they have eyes yet cannot see;
they have ears yet cannot hear;
    they have nostrils yet cannot smell.
They have hands yet cannot feel;
    they have feet yet cannot walk.
Nor can they cry out through their throats.

Let those who make them become like them,
    and all such who trust in them.

The house of Israel hopes in the Lord;
    he is their helper and their protector.
The house of Aaron hopes in the Lord;
    he is their helper and their protector.
Those who fear him hope in the Lord;

he is their helper and their protector.
The Lord remembers us,
    and has blessed us;
He has blessed the sons of Israel.
    He has blessed the sons of Aaron.
He has blessed all those who fear him,
    both the little and the great.

May the Lord add blessings upon you,
    upon you and upon your children.
May you be blessed by the Lord,
    he who has made Heaven and earth.

The Heaven of heavens is the Lord's
    but the earth he has given to the children of men.
The dead shall not praise you, O Lord,
    nor any of those who go down into Hell.
But we that live bless the Lord
    from this time, now and for ever.

Glory be...

Ant. May we be blessed by the Lord, who made Heaven and
earth.

Short reading

2 Thessalonians 2:12-17

B UT WE ought to give thanks to God always for you, brethren, beloved of God, because God has chosen you as first
fruits of salvation, through sanctification by the Spirit and faith
in the truth. To which he has called you by our gospel, so that
you may obtain the glory of our Lord Jesus Christ. Therefore,
brethren, stand fast and hold to the traditions which you have
learned either by word or by our letter. Now may our Lord Jesus
Christ himself, and God our Father, who has loved us and has
given us everlasting consolation and good hope in grace, comfort your hearts and confirm you in every good work and word.

The Magnificat

Luke 1:46-55

M Y ✠ SOUL magnifies the Lord,
    my spirit rejoices in God who is my Saviour,
who has looked upon the humility of his handmaiden.

Behold, all generations from now
　　will acknowledge me blessed,
For the mighty one has done great things for me:
　　Holy is his name!
His mercy is from one generation to the next on those who fear him.
　　Mighty is his arm!
He has scattered the proud in the imagination of their hearts,
　　and has put down the powerful from their thrones,
　　exalting those of humble degree.
The hungry he has filled with good things,
　　but the rich he has dismissed with nothing.
Remembering his mercy, he has helped his servant Israel,
　　as he promised to our fathers,
　　to Abraham and to his posterity for ever more.

Glory be…

Intercessions *Either these, or others at choice or need.*

Keep us firm in your faith, O Lord. *(pause for prayer)*
　　R̹. Grant our prayer, we beg.
Sanctify us: make us saints, O Lord. *(pause)* **R̹.**
Give us courage to do good and avoid evil. *(pause)* **R̹.**
Overcome our wayward dispositions. *(pause)* **R̹.**
Lord, grant rest to those of our friends who have died. *(pause)* **R̹.**

Lord, have mercy.
Christ, have mercy.
Lord, have mercy.

Our Father…

Let us pray.

O GOD, our refuge and strength, heed the devout prayers of your Church, and grant that what we beg in faith may truly come to pass. Through our Lord Jesus Christ, your Son, who lives and reigns with you and the Holy Spirit, one God, world without end. Amen.

V̹. Let us bless the Lord.
R̹. Thanks be to God.

☙　　☙　　☙

Compline

℣. O God, ✠ come to my assistance.
℟. O Lord, be swift to my aid.
℣. Glory be to the Father, and to the Son, and to the Holy Spirit.
℟. As it was in the beginning, is now and ever shall be,
world without end. Amen.

Examination of conscience, and act of penance.

B EFORE the ending of the day,
Creator of the world, we pray
That with thy wonted favour thou
Wouldst be our guard and keeper now.

From all ill dreams defend our eyes,
From nightly fears and fantasies;
Tread under foot our ghostly foe,
That no pollution we may know.

O Father, that we ask be done,
Through Jesus Christ, thine only Son;
Who, with the Holy Ghost and thee,
Doth live and reign eternally. Amen.

Te lucis ante terminum

Ant. Into your hands I commend my spirit, Lord.

Psalm 30:2-9

I N YOU, O Lord, I have hoped.
Let me never be confounded.
In your justice, deliver me:
    Bow your ear; make haste to rescue me.

Be to me a God, a protector,
    and a house of refuge to save me,
for you are my strength and my stronghold,
    and for your name's sake, lead me and nourish me.

Bring me out of this snare
   which they have hidden for me:
   for you are my protector, Lord.
Into your hands I commend my spirit:
   It is you who will redeem me, O Lord, God of truth.

You hate those who have empty regard for vanities,
   but I have hoped in the Lord:
I will be glad and rejoice in your mercy,
   for you have looked upon my humiliation,
and have saved my soul out of distress:
   you have not placed me in the hands of the enemy,
   but set my feet in a spacious place.

Glory be…

Ant. Into your hands I commend my spirit, Lord.

Short reading *Ephesians 4:26-27*

B E ANGRY (if you must) but do not sin; do not let the sun go
down upon your anger, and give no place to the devil.

The Nunc Dimittis

Luke 2:29-32

Ant. Save us, O Lord, while we wake, and watch over us as we
sleep, that we may pass the night with Christ and rest in peace.

L ORD, ✠ now let your servant depart in peace,
   according to your promise;
   for my eyes have seen your salvation
which you have prepared in the presence of all peoples,
a light for revelation to the Gentiles,
   and for glory to your people Israel.

Glory be…

Ant. Save us, O Lord, while we wake, and watch over us as we
sleep, that we may pass the night with Christ and rest in peace.

Let us pray.

V ISIT this house, O Lord, we pray, and drive far from it the
  deadly power of the enemy. May your holy angels dwell
here instead, that we may be preserved in peace, with your blessing on us always. Through Christ our Lord. Amen.

Antiphon in honour of our Lady, pp.341ff.
or:

W E FLY to thy patronage, holy Mother of God.
  Despise not our petitions in our necessities
But deliver us from every evil,
O glorious and blessed Virgin.

∾   ∾   ∾

WEDNESDAY

Vigils

℣. O Lord, ✠ open my lips.
℟. And my mouth shall declare your praise.

Antiphon: In your decrees I find instruction, Lord.

Psalm 18

THE HEAVENS show forth the glory of God
and the firmament declares the work of his hands.
Day unto day tells the tale
and night unto night shows forth knowledge.

There are no speeches, no languages,
where their voices are not understood.
Their sound goes forth through all the earth,
and their words to the very ends of the world.

Among them he has pitched his tent of the sun:
coming forth like a bridegroom from the bridal chamber,
rejoicing like a giant to run the way.
His going out is from the end of Heaven,
and its circuit to the other end of the same.
Nothing can be hidden from his heat.

The law of the Lord is immaculate,
converting the soul.
The rule of the Lord is faithful,
giving wisdom to little ones.

The commands of the Lord are right,
rejoicing hearts.
The rule of the Lord is lightsome,
enlightening the eyes.

The fear of the Lord is pure,
    enduring for ever and ever.
The judgements of the Lord are true
    and righteous altogether.

They are more to be desired than gold,
    and many precious stones,
sweeter also than honey,
    than honey from the honeycomb.

Furthermore, in them your servant finds teaching;
    in keeping them is great reward.
But who, then, can understand sins?
    From secret sins cleanse me.

From the sin of presumption keep your servant
    lest it rule me.
Then shall I be without spot,
    cleansed from gravest sin.

And may the words of my mouth,
    the meditations of my heart,
be pleasing in your sight, O Lord,
    my helper, my Redeemer!

Glory be…

Antiphon: In your decrees I find instruction, Lord.

℣. I trust in you, O Lord.
℟. It is you who are my God.

First reading

One chapter from the scriptures.

Response to the reading

℣. Your word is a lamp for my steps,
℟. Joy to the heart, light for the eyes.
℣. I shall walk in the way of your commands:
℟. Joy to the heart, light for the eyes.

Second reading

Spiritual reading.

Response to the reading

℣. The vaults of the heavens
℟. Cry out your praise, O Lord.
℣. The saints and the angelic hosts
℟. Cry out your praise, O Lord.

Let us pray.

ALMIGHTY and eternal God, look upon our feebleness with pity, and stretch out your mighty arm to protect us. Through Christ our Lord. Amen.

℣. Let us bless the Lord.
℟. Thanks be to God.

Lauds

℣. O God, ✠ come to my assistance.

℟. **O Lord, be swift to my aid.**

℣. Glory be to the Father, and to the Son, and to the Holy Spirit.

℟. **As it was in the beginning, is now and ever shall be, world without end. Amen.**

NOW THAT daylight fills the sky,
We lift our hearts to Christ on high,
That he, in all we do or say,
Would keep us free from harm today.

Would guard our hearts and tongues from strife;
From anger's din would hide our life;
From all ill sights would turn our eyes;
Would close our ears from vanities:

Would keep our inmost conscience pure;
Our souls from folly would secure;
Would bid us check the pride of sense
With due and holy abstinence.

So we, when this new day is gone,
And night in turn is drawing on,
With conscience by the world unstained
Shall praise his name for victory gained.

All laud to God the Father be;
All praise, eternal Son, to thee;
All glory, as is ever meet,
To God the holy Paraclete. Amen.

Iam lucis orto sidere

Ant. Praise the name of the Lord, for he alone is exalted.

Psalm 148

PRAISE the Lord from the heavens,
praise him in the high places.

Praise him, all his angels,
  praise him, all his hosts.
Praise him, O sun and moon,
  praise him all you stars and light.
Praise him, Heaven of heavens
  and you waters above the heavens.
Praise the name of the Lord.

For he spoke and they were made:
  he commanded and they were created.
He established them for ever,
  he made a decree which shall not pass away.

Praise the Lord from the earth,
  you dragons and all deeps,
fire, hail, snow, ice,
  stormy winds which fulfil his word;
Mountains and all hills,
  fruitful trees and all cedars,
Beasts, and all cattle,
  serpents and feathered fowls;
Kings of the earth and all people:
  princes and all judges of the earth;
Young men and maidens,
  the old with the younger:
Praise the name of the Lord
  for his name alone is exalted.
The praise of his name
  is exalted above Heaven and earth.

He exalts the horn of his people.
  He is the praise of all his saints,
of the children of Israel,
  of the people who draw near him.

Glory be...

Ant. Praise the name of the Lord, for he alone is exalted.

Short reading   *Wisdom 7:28-30*

G OD loves no one so much as the one who dwells with wisdom. For she is more beautiful than the sun, and above all
the order of the stars. Compared with the light she is found to be
surpassing, for light is succeeded by the night, but no evil can
overcome wisdom.

The Benedictus

Luke 1:68-79

B LESSED ✠ be the Lord, the God of Israel,
who has visited and redeemed his people,
and has lifted up a horn of salvation for us
in the family of his servant David.
For this he swore through the mouths of holy men:
those who were prophets, from the beginning:
There would be salvation from our foes,
and from the hand of all those who hate us;
to comfort our fathers,
and to honour his holy covenant,
which oath once he swore to Abraham, our father,
that he would grant us,
that freed from the hand of our enemies,
and without fear, we may serve him,
in holiness and justice in his very presence all our days.
And you, my son, will be named Prophet of the Most High;
for you will go before the presence of the Lord
to prepare his way,
to teach knowledge of salvation to his people
that their sins may be forgiven,
through the merciful heart of our God,
when the Daystar shall visit us from on high
to enlighten those who sit in darkness
and in the shadow of death,
and guide our feet to the way of peace.

Glory be...

Intercessions *Either these, or others at choice or need.*

Lord, protect all those who travel, and those who protect them.
    (pause for prayer) ℟. **Guard us and save us, Lord.**
Lord, protect those in our armed forces, and end all wars.
    (pause) ℟.
Lord, protect our police, and preserve their sense of justice.
    (pause) ℟.
Lord, protect our judges and lawyers, and grant them wisdom.
    (pause) ℟.
Lord, protect our own sense of justice and help us always to do
    what is right. *(pause)* ℟.

Lord, have mercy.
Christ, have mercy.
Lord, have mercy.

Our Father...

Let us pray.

G OD of mercy and goodness, in whose gift it is that we should
    serve you worthily and well, grant that we may run towards
the fulfilment of your promises, without offence, and with alacrity. Through our Lord Jesus Christ your Son, who lives and reigns
with you in the unity of the Holy Spirit, one God for ever and
ever. Amen.

℣. Let us bless the Lord.
℟. **Thanks be to God.**

ॐ   ॐ   ॐ

Terce

℣. O God, ✠ come to my assistance.
℟. O Lord, be swift to my aid.
℣. Glory be to the Father, and to the Son, and to the Holy Spirit.
**℟. As it was in the beginning, is now and ever shall be,
world without end. Amen.**

COME, Holy Ghost, with God the Son
And God the Father, ever one;
Shed forth thy grace within our breast
And dwell with us a ready guest.

By every power, by heart and tongue,
By act and deed, thy praise be sung;
Inflame with perfect love each sense
That others' souls may kindle thence.

O Father, that we ask be done,
Through Jesus Christ, thine only Son;
Who, with the Holy Ghost and thee,
Doth live and reign eternally. Amen.

Nunc nobis, Sancte Spiritus

Ant. The law from your mouth is good to me.

Psalm 118 Teth

LORD, you have dealt well with your servant,
according to your word.
Teach me goodness, discipline and knowledge:
I have believed your commandments.
Before I was humbled, I went wrong,
but now I keep your word.
You are good, and in your goodness
teach me your statutes.
The proud have conceived lies about me
but with all my heart will I keep your commands.
Their minds are curdled like milk,

but your law is my delight.
It was good for me to have been humbled,
    that I may learn your commandments.
The law from your mouth is good to me;
    dearer than thousands in silver or gold.

Glory be…

Ant. The law from your mouth is good to me.

Short reading
1 Corinthians 12:4-7

NOW THERE are diversities of graces, but the same Spirit; and there are diversities of ministries, but the same Lord; and there are diversities of operation, but it is the same God who works all in all. And the manifestation of the Spirit is given to everyone for profit.

Let us pray.

O GOD, who at the third hour poured your Holy Spirit upon our Lady and the Apostles: renew your gift of the same Spirit within us at this time, that we may perfectly serve you, and come to our eternal reward. Through Christ our Lord. Amen.

℣. Let us bless the Lord.
℟. **Thanks be to God.**

Sext

℣. O God, ✠ come to my assistance.
℟. O Lord, be swift to my aid.
℣. Glory be to the Father, and to the Son, and to the Holy Spirit.
**℟. As it was in the beginning, is now and ever shall be,
world without end. Amen.**

O GOD of truth, O Lord of might,
Who orderest time and change aright,
And send'st the early morning ray,
And light'st the glow of perfect day:

Extinguish thou each sinful fire,
And banish every ill desire;
And while thou keep'st the body whole,
Shed forth thy peace upon the soul.

O Father, that we ask be done,
Through Jesus Christ, thine only Son;
Who, with the Holy Ghost and thee,
Doth live and reign eternally. Amen.

Rector potens, verax Deus

Ant. Let my heart be undefiled in your commandments, O Lord.

Psalm 118 Jod

YOUR hands made me and formed me:
give me understanding to learn your commands.
Those who fear you will see me and be glad,
for I greatly hope in your word.
I know, O Lord, that your judgements are right
and that you were right to have humbled me.
O let your mercy be now for my comfort,
according to your promise unto your servant.

Let your tender mercies come to me and I shall live,
    for your law is my delight.
Let the proud be ashamed who have been unjust to me,
    but I will contemplate your precepts.
Let those who fear you turn to me,
    and those who know your decrees.
Let my heart be undefiled in your commandments
    that I may not be confounded.

Glory be...

Ant. Let my heart be undefiled in your commandments, O Lord.

Short reading   *1 Corinthians 12:12-13*

FOR as the body is one and has many members, and all the members of the body, though they are many, yet are one body, so also is Christ. For in one Spirit we were all baptized into one Body—Jews or Gentiles, slaves or free—and of one Spirit we have all been made to drink.

Let us pray.

SET aside, Lord, our envies and our selfish jealousies: help us to realize the true value of each person in building up the Church, the Body of Christ: that your Kingdom may come and your will be done. Through the same Christ our Lord. Amen.

℣. Let us bless the Lord.
℟. Thanks be to God.

👁 👁 👁

None

℣. O God, ✠ come to my assistance.
℟. O Lord, be swift to my aid.
℣. Glory be to the Father, and to the Son, and to the Holy Spirit.
**℟. As it was in the beginning, is now and ever shall be,
world without end. Amen.**

O GOD, Creation's secret force,
Thyself unmoved, all motion's source,
Who from the morn till evening ray
Through all its changes guid'st the day:

Grant us, when this short life is past,
The glorious evening that shall last;
That, by a holy death attained,
Eternal glory may be gained.

O Father, that we ask be done,
Through Jesus Christ, thine only Son;
Who, with the Holy Ghost and thee,
Doth live and reign eternally. Amen.

Rerum Deus tenax vigor

Ant. Lord, because of your love give me life.

Psalm 118 Caph

MY SOUL longs after your salvation:
and in your word I strongly hope.
My eyes strain to see your word fulfilled.
Saying: O when will you comfort me?
I have become like a bottle in the smoke;
I have not forgotten your statutes.
How many days must your servant endure?
When will you avenge me on my foes?

The wicked have dug pitfalls for me,
>   which are against your law.
All your commandments are true;
>   be my help when they persecute me unjustly.
They almost made an end of me on earth,
>   but I have not forsaken your commandments.
Give me life according to your mercy
>   and I will keep the commands of your mouth.

Glory be…

Ant. Lord, because of your love give me life

Short reading
2 Corinthians 12:24b, 25-26

GOD has so tempered the Body together, that there may be no schism in the Body, but that the members might be mutually caring, one for another. So if one member should suffer, all the members suffer with it; or if one member is glorified, all the members rejoice with it.

Let us pray.

ALMIGHTY God, as you have made the Church the mystical Body of your Son, give all its members care for each other, that the Church may be extended throughout the world. Through Christ our Lord. Amen.

℣. Let us bless the Lord.
℟. Thanks be to God.

෨   ෨   ෨

Vespers

℣. O God, ✠ come to my assistance.
℟. O Lord, be swift to my aid.
℣. Glory be to the Father, and to the Son, and to the Holy Spirit.
**℟. As it was in the beginning, is now and ever shall be,
world without end. Amen.**

O HEAVENLY maker of mankind,
   Alone who gave each thing its place,
By whose command the earth brought forth
Both reptiles and the feral race.

And ordered that those mighty beasts
Who live their lives at your behest
Be subject to your servants' word,
Who are of your creation best.

Then drive away those passions bold
Which trouble your poor servants here,
And sins ingrained by habit old
Of thought, or word, or deed, or fear.

Grant us reward of heavenly joy
O grant us gifts of heavenly grace!
And break the chains of strife, that peace
May lead us all to see your face.

Grant this, O loving Father God,
And Jesus Christ, your only Son,
Who with the Holy Spirit blest
Reign ever three and ever one. Amen.

Plasmator hominis, Deus

Ant. Your throne, O God, shall endure for ever.

Psalm 44

M Y HEART has uttered noble words.
   To the king I must speak of what I have done;
my tongue like the pen of a swift scribe.

You are beautiful above all the children of men;
    grace is poured upon your lips:
    therefore God has blessed you for ever.

O most mighty one, gird your sword upon your thigh,
    With your comeliness and beauty
    begin, prosper, and reign!
Because of truth, and kindness and justice,
    your own right hand shall keep you safe.

Your arrows are sharp: peoples will fall beneath you,
    even in the midst of the King's enemies.

Your throne, O God, is for ever and ever:
The sceptre of uprightness is the sceptre of your kingdom.

You have loved justice and have hated iniquity.
    Therefore God, your God, has anointed you
    with the oil of gladness above your fellows:
Your garments are perfumed with myrrh, aloes and cassia;
    from the ivory palace music shall delight you.

The daughters of kings are among your attendants.
    On your right stands the queen
    in garments of gold of Ophir.

Hearken, O daughter, and see: give ear to my words:
    forget your people and your father's house.
And the king will greatly desire your beauty.
    He is your lord; then adore him.

And the daughters of Tyre shall entreat with gifts,
    all the rich of the people shall beg your favour.
The glory of the daughter of the king is in golden borders,
    clothed round about with varieties.

She is conducted to the king with her virgin companions.
    They are brought with gladness and rejoicing;
    they enter within the temple of the king.

Instead of your fathers you shall have sons:
>you shall make them princes over all the earth.

They shall remember your name throughout all generations.
>Therefore shall people praise you for ever and for ever.

Glory be…

Ant. Your throne, O God, shall endure for ever.

Short reading   *1 Thessalonians 2:13*

THEREFORE we also thank God without ceasing, because when you received the word of God which you heard from us, you received it not as the word of men but (as it is indeed) the word of God, who is at work in you that have believed.

The Magnificat

Luke 1:46-55

MY ✠ SOUL magnifies the Lord,
>my spirit rejoices in God who is my Saviour,
>who has looked upon the humility of his handmaiden.
Behold, all generations from now
>will acknowledge me blessed,
For the mighty one has done great things for me:
>Holy is his name!
His mercy is from one generation to the next on those who fear him.
>Mighty is his arm!
He has scattered the proud in the imagination of their hearts,
>and has put down the powerful from their thrones,
>exalting those of humble degree.
The hungry he has filled with good things,
>but the rich he has dismissed with nothing.
Remembering his mercy, he has helped his servant Israel,
>as he promised to our fathers,
>to Abraham and to his posterity for ever more.

Glory be…

Intercessions   *Either these, or others at choice or need.*

Grant us faith in its fullness, O Lord. *(pause for prayer)*
  ℟. **Kyrie eleison.**
Grant us hope for our salvation. *(pause)* ℟.
Give us charity in abundance. *(pause)* ℟.
Make us perfect in your sight, O Lord. *(pause)* ℟.
Lord, grant rest to the dead in Purgatory. *(pause)* ℟.

Lord, have mercy.
Christ, have mercy.
Lord, have mercy.

Our Father …

Let us pray.

A LMIGHTY God, our heavenly Father, hear the prayers
of your children, and grant that what we ask in faith may be
according to your holy will. Through our Lord Jesus Christ, your
Son, who lives and reigns with you and the Holy Spirit, one God,
world without end. Amen.

℣. Let us bless the Lord.
℟. **Thanks be to God.**

℘   ℘   ℘

Compline

℣. O God, ✠ come to my assistance.
℟. O Lord, be swift to my aid.
℣. Glory be to the Father, and to the Son, and to the Holy Spirit.
**℟. As it was in the beginning, is now and ever shall be,
world without end. Amen.**

Examination of conscience, and act of penance.

B EFORE the ending of the day,
Creator of the world, we pray
That with thy wonted favour thou
Wouldst be our guard and keeper now.

From all ill dreams defend our eyes,
From nightly fears and fantasies;
Tread under foot our ghostly foe,
That no pollution we may know.

O Father, that we ask be done,
Through Jesus Christ, thine only Son;
Who, with the Holy Ghost and thee,
Doth live and reign eternally. Amen.

Te lucis ante terminum

Ant. I will bless the Lord who even at night directs my heart.

Psalm 15

P RESERVE me, God, I put my trust in you.
I say to the Lord: You are my God.
All I have is nothing without you.

He has placed in me a wonderful love
for the saints, great men, who are in the land.
Those who run after other gods shall have great trouble.
I will not offer their offerings of blood.
I will not mention their name with my lips.

The Lord is my portion and my cup;
it is you who will restore my inheritance to me.
My lines have fallen in pleasant places:
welcome is my heritage to me.

I will bless the Lord who gives me understanding,
even at night he advises my heart.
I set the Lord always in my sight:
because he is at my right hand, I shall not fall.

Therefore my heart is glad, my tongue rejoices;
even my flesh shall rest in hope.
For you will not leave my soul in Hell,
nor let your holy one know corruption.

You have made known to me the way of life,
you will fill me with joy when I see your face,
at your right hand are delights for ever more.

Glory be…

Ant. I will bless the Lord who even at night directs my heart.

Short reading   *1 Thessalonians 5:23-24*

M AY the God of peace himself sanctify you in all things:
that your whole spirit and soul and body may be preserved
blameless at the coming of our Lord Jesus Christ. He who has
called you is faithful, and he will do it.

The Nunc Dimittis

Luke 2:29-32

Ant. Save us, O Lord, while we wake, and watch over us as we
sleep, that we may pass the night with Christ and rest in peace.

L ORD, ✠ now let your servant depart in peace,
according to your promise;
for my eyes have seen your salvation
which you have prepared in the presence of all peoples,

a light for revelation to the Gentiles,
and for glory to your people Israel.

Glory be…

Ant. Save us, O Lord, while we wake, and watch over us as we sleep, that we may pass the night with Christ and rest in peace.

Let us pray.

V ISIT this house, O Lord, we pray, and drive far from it the deadly power of the enemy. May your holy angels dwell here instead, that we may be preserved in peace, with your blessing on us always. Through Christ our Lord. Amen.

Antiphon in honour of our Lady, pp.341ff.
or:

W E FLY to thy patronage, holy Mother of God.
Despise not our petitions in our necessities
But deliver us from every evil,
O glorious and blessed Virgini

ℭ   ℭ   ℭ

THURSDAY

Vigils

Baptism

℣. O Lord, ✠ open my lips.
℟. **And my mouth shall declare your praise.**

Antiphon: My soul is thirsting for God, the God of my life.

Psalm 41

L IKE the hart that pants after fountains of water,
    so my soul is yearning after you, O my God.
    My soul is thirsting for God, the living God;
when can I come and appear before the face of God?

My tears have become my bread day and night,
    as I hear it said to me daily: Where is your God?
These things I remembered, and poured out my soul:
    how I would go with the rejoicing multitude
    even into the house of God,
amid loud cries of joy and thanksgiving,
    the crowd keeping joyful festival.

Why so sad, my soul, why so troubled within me?
    Hope in God; I will still give him praise,
    my salvation and my God.

My soul is troubled within me, therefore I will think of you,
    from the land of Jordan and Hermon, from the Hill of Mizar.
Deep is calling on deep, in the roar of your cataracts:
    your heights and all your billows have passed over me.

In the daytime the Lord has granted his loving-kindness;
    and at night I sang of him: a prayer to the God of my life.
I sing to God: my Redeemer, why have you forgotten me?
    Why must I go mourning while my enemy afflicts me?

While my bones are broken, my enemies reproach me,
    saying to me day after day: Where is your God?
Why so sad, my soul, why so troubled within me?
    Hope in God; I will still give him praise,
    my salvation and my God.

Glory be...

Antiphon: My soul is thirsting for God, the God of my life.

℣. You shall ask, and you shall receive,
℟. **A spring of living water inside you.**

First reading

One chapter from the scriptures.

Response to the reading

℣. Go, then, and teach all nations:
℟. **Baptize them in the name of the Father, and of the Son, and of the Holy Spirit.**
℣. Let the little children come to me: do not stop them.
℟. **Baptize them in the name of the Father, and of the Son, and of the Holy Spirit.**

Second reading

Spiritual reading.

Response to the reading

℣. From his wounded side flowed blood and water.
℟. **Christ comes to us in water and in blood.**
℣. There are three witnesses, the Spirit, the water, and the blood; and these three agree.
℟. **Christ comes to us in water and in blood.**

Let us pray.

ALMIGHTY God, whose Son gave himself as the sacrifice for our salvation, and from whose wounded side flowed blood and water, the fountain of sacramental life in the Church, renew within us the grace of the sacraments, first received in our baptism. Through the same Christ our Lord. Amen.

℣. Let us bless the Lord.
℟. **Thanks be to God.**

❧   ❧   ❧

Lauds

The Eucharist

℣. O God, ✠ come to my assistance.
℟. **O Lord, be swift to my aid.**
℣. Glory be to the Father, and to the Son, and to the Holy Spirit.
℟. **As it was in the beginning, is now and ever shall be,
world without end. Amen.**

> LORD, enthroned in heavenly splendour,
>   First-begotten from the dead,
> Thou alone, our strong defender,
> Liftest up thy people's head.
>   Alleluya, Alleluya,
> Jesu, true and living Bread!
>
> Paschal Lamb, thine offering, finished
> Once for all when thou wast slain,
> In its fullness undiminished
> Shall for ever more remain.
>   Alleluya, Alleluya,
> Cleansing souls from every stain.
>
> Life-imparting, heavenly Manna,
> Stricken Rock with streaming side,
> Heaven and earth with loud hosanna
> Worship thee, the Lamb who died,
>   Alleluya, Alleluya,
> Risen, ascended, glorified!

G.H. Bourne

Ant. I will go in to the altar of God: the God of my joy.

Psalm 42

> DEFEND me, O God, and distinguish my cause
>   from that of an unholy nation.
> From unjust and deceitful men
>   deliver me, O God.

For you, O God, are my strength,
    why have you cast me off?
Why do I go sorrowful
    and afflicted by the foe?

Send forth your light and your truth;
    these have directed me,
and brought me unto your holy mountain
    and into your tabernacles.

And I will go in to the altar of God,
    the God of my gladness and joy.
Upon the harp I will give you thanks,
    O God, my God.

Why so sad, my soul,
    why so troubled within me?
Hope in God; I will still give him praise,
    my salvation and my God.

Glory be...

Ant. I will go in to the altar of God: the God of my joy.

Short reading   *1 Corinthians 11:23-24*

FOR I received from the Lord that which I also delivered to you, that the Lord Jesus the same night in which he was betrayed took bread, and giving thanks, broke it, and said, 'Take and eat: this is my Body which shall be delivered for you. Do this in commemoration of me.' In the same way also the chalice, after he had eaten, saying, 'This chalice is the new testament in my blood. Do this, as often as you drink it, for the commemoration of me.' For as often as you shall eat this bread and drink the chalice, you shall show the Lord's death until he come.

The Benedictus

Luke 1:68-79

B LESSED ✠ be the Lord, the God of Israel,
who has visited and redeemed his people,
and has lifted up a horn of salvation for us
in the family of his servant David.
For this he swore through the mouths of holy men:
those who were prophets, from the beginning:
There would be salvation from our foes,
and from the hand of all those who hate us;
to comfort our fathers,
and to honour his holy covenant,
which oath once he swore to Abraham, our father,
that he would grant us,
that freed from the hand of our enemies,
and without fear, we may serve him,
in holiness and justice in his very presence all our days.
And you, my son, will be named Prophet of the Most High;
for you will go before the presence of the Lord
to prepare his way,
to teach knowledge of salvation to his people
that their sins may be forgiven,
through the merciful heart of our God,
when the Daystar shall visit us from on high
to enlighten those who sit in darkness
and in the shadow of death,
and guide our feet to the way of peace.

Glory be…

Intercessions   *Either these, or others at choice or need.*

Lord Jesus, deepen our faith in your real presence in the Eucharist. *(pause)* ℟. **You, Lord, have the words of eternal life.**
Grant us the grace to receive Communion worthily. *(pause)* ℟.
Help all our priests to offer your sacrifice reverently and well.
(pause) ℟.
Strengthen with your grace those deprived of the Eucharist.
(pause) ℟.
Deepen the reverence and faith of those who bring communion
to the sick. *(pause)* ℟.

> Lord, have mercy,
> Christ, have mercy,
> Lord, have mercy.
>
> Our Father...

Let us pray.

G OD, who has given us in this wonderful Sacrament a memorial of your passion, grant, we beg, that we may so honour it in this life that the redemption which it signifies may be ours in the life to come. Through our Lord Jesus Christ your Son, who lives and reigns with you in the unity of the Holy Spirit, one God for ever and ever. Amen.

> ℣. Let us bless the Lord.
> ℟. **Thanks be to God.**

Terce

Confirmation

℣. O God, ✠ come to my assistance.
℟. **O Lord, be swift to my aid.**
℣. Glory be to the Father, and to the Son, and to the Holy Spirit.
℟. **As it was in the beginning, is now and ever shall be,
world without end. Amen.**

COME, Holy Ghost, with God the Son
And God the Father, ever one;
Shed forth thy grace within our breast
And dwell with us a ready guest.

By every power, by heart and tongue,
By act and deed, thy praise be sung;
Inflame with perfect love each sense
That others' souls may kindle thence.

O Father, that we ask be done,
Through Jesus Christ, thine only Son;
Who, with the Holy Ghost and thee,
Doth live and reign eternally. Amen.

Nunc nobis, Sancte Spiritus

Ant. O Lord, how wonderful is the work of your Spirit in us.

Psalm 118 Lamed

FOR ever, O Lord, your word
stands firm in Heaven.
Your truth lasts unto all generations,
as the earth which you created:
Which, by your ordinance, endures to this day;
for all things serve you.
Unless your law had been my meditation
I might have perished in my abjection.
Your precepts I will never forget,
for by them you have given me life.

I am yours: save me,
    for I have sought your statutes.
Though the wicked have waited to destroy me,
    still I meditate on your will.
I have seen that all perfection has its limits,
    but broad indeed is your command.

Glory be...

Ant. O Lord, how wonderful is the work of your Spirit in us.

Short reading   *1 Corinthians 12:13*

IN ONE Spirit we were all baptized into one Body—Jews or Gentiles, whether slaves or free; and of one Spirit all were made to drink.

Let us pray.

O GOD, the lover of truth, and source of every blessing, grant, through the Holy Spirit dwelling within us, that we may be confirmed in truth, and truly blessed. Through Christ our Lord. Amen.

℣. Let us bless the Lord.
℟. Thanks be to God.

ლ   ლ   ლ

Sext

Sacrament of Penance

℣. O God, ✠ come to my assistance.
℟. **O Lord, be swift to my aid.**
℣. Glory be to the Father, and to the Son, and to the Holy Spirit.
℟. **As it was in the beginning, is now and ever shall be, world without end. Amen.**

O GOD of truth, O Lord of might,
Who orderest time and change aright,
And send'st the early morning ray,
And light'st the glow of perfect day:

Extinguish thou each sinful fire,
And banish every ill desire;
And while thou keep'st the body whole,
Shed forth thy peace upon the soul.

O Father, that we ask be done,
Through Jesus Christ, thine only Son;
Who, with the Holy Ghost and thee,
Doth live and reign eternally. Amen.

Rector potens, verax Deus

Ant. Lord, restrain my feet from evil ways.

Psalm 118 Mem

O HOW have I loved your law!
It is ever in my mind.
Your command makes me wiser than my foes;
for it is mine for ever.
I have understood more than all my teachers
because your testimonies are my meditation.
I have understanding above the ancients
because I have sought your commandments.
I have restrained my feet from every evil way
that I may keep your word.
I have not turned away from your judgements,

because you have taught me your law.
How sweet are your words to my palate!
more than honey in my mouth.
By your commandments I gain understanding,
and so I hate every way of iniquity.

Glory be...

Ant. Lord, restrain my feet from evil ways.

Short reading
Ephesians 1:3-8

B LESSED be the God and Father of our Lord Jesus Christ, who has blessed us with spiritual blessings in the heavenly places in Christ, as he chose us in him before the foundation of the world, that we should be holy and unspotted before him in love. He predestined us to be his own adopted children through Jesus Christ, according to the purpose of his will, to the praise of the glory of his grace with which he graced us in his beloved Son. In him we have redemption through his blood, the remission of sins, according to the riches of his grace which he lavished upon us in all wisdom and prudence.

Let us pray.

A LMIGHTY Father, whose own dear Son died on the cross for our forgiveness, overcome our bashfulness, give us a true sense of shame for our sins, and help us to seek your pardon in the Sacrament of Penance. Through the same Christ our Lord. Amen.

℣. Let us bless the Lord.
℟. Thanks be to God.

None

Holy Orders

℣. O God, ✠ come to my assistance.
℟. O Lord, be swift to my aid.
℣. Glory be to the Father, and to the Son, and to the Holy Spirit.
**℟. As it was in the beginning, is now and ever shall be,
world without end. Amen.**

O GOD, Creation's secret force,
Thyself unmoved, all motion's source,
Who from the morn till evening ray
Through all its changes guid'st the day:

Grant us, when this short life is past,
The glorious evening that shall last;
That, by a holy death attained,
Eternal glory may be gained.

O Father, that we ask be done,
Through Jesus Christ, thine only Son;
Who, with the Holy Ghost and thee,
Doth live and reign eternally. Amen.

Rerum Deus tenax vigor

Ant. Your laws are the joy of my heart, O Lord.

Psalm 118 Nun

YOUR word is a lamp to my feet
and a light to my paths.
I have sworn and am determined
to keep the judgements of your justice.
Lord, I have been humbled exceedingly:
give me life according to your word.
Accept, O Lord, the free offering of my mouth
and teach me your judgements.
My soul is continually in my hands,
yet I have not forgotten your law.

Sinners have laid a snare for me:
>> but I have not erred from your precepts.
I have your laws as an eternal inheritance,
>> because they are the joy of my heart.
I have inclined my heart to do your will for ever
>> and this is my reward for ever more.

Glory be…

Ant. Your laws are the joy of my heart, O Lord.

Short reading   *Isaiah 61:1-2*

T HE SPIRIT of the Lord is upon me, because the Lord
has anointed me: he has sent me to preach to the meek; to
heal the contrite of heart, to preach release to the captives, and
deliverance to those who are imprisoned; to proclaim the acceptable year of the Lord, and the day of vengeance of our God; to
comfort all who mourn.

Let us pray.

P ROTECT with your grace, Lord, those whom you have called
to share your sacred ministry by the laying on of hands. May
they be gentle but ardent servants of the Gospel, seeking not to
be served but to serve, and to do your will in all things. Through
Christ our Lord. Amen.

℣. Let us bless the Lord.
℟. Thanks be to God.

Vespers

Holy Marriage

℣. O God, ✠ come to my assistance.
℟. O Lord, be swift to my aid.
℣. Glory be to the Father, and to the Son, and to the Holy Spirit.
**℟. As it was in the beginning, is now and ever shall be,
world without end. Amen.**

LOVE Divine, all loves excelling,
Joy of Heaven, to earth come down,
Fix in us thy humble dwelling,
All thy faithful mercies crown.

Jesu, thou art all compassion,
Pure unbounded love thou art;
Visit us with thy salvation,
Enter every trembling heart.

Come, almighty to deliver,
Let us all thy life receive;
Suddenly return and never,
Never more thy temples leave.

Thee we would be always blessing,
Serve thee as thy hosts above,
Pray, and praise thee without ceasing,
Glory in thy perfect love.

Finish then thy new creation,
Pure and spotless let us be;
Let us see thy great salvation,
Perfectly restored in thee.

Changed from glory into glory,
Till in Heaven we take our place,
Till we cast our crowns before thee
Lost in wonder, love and praise!

C. Wesley

Ant. You are beautiful, my love, comely as Jerusalem.

Psalm 127

O BLESSED are all that fear the Lord,
that walk in his ways!

You shall eat the fruit of the labour of your hands,
   You will be blessed: it shall be well with you;
Your wife like a fruitful vine
   that grows on the wall of your house;
your children like olive plants,
      round about your table.

Behold, thus shall the one be blessed
   that fears the Lord.
May the Lord bless you out of Sion:
   and may you see the good things of Jerusalem
   all the days of your life.
May you live to see your children's children.
   Peace upon Israel!

Glory be...

Ant. You are beautiful, my love, comely as Jerusalem.

Short reading   *Song of Songs 8:6-7*

M ANY waters cannot quench love, neither can the floods
drown it. If a man should give all the substance of his house
for love, it would be despised as nothing.

The Magnificat

Luke 1:46-55

M Y ✠ SOUL magnifies the Lord,
      my spirit rejoices in God who is my Saviour,
      who has looked upon the humility of his handmaiden.
Behold, all generations from now
   will acknowledge me blessed,
For the mighty one has done great things for me:
   Holy is his name!

His mercy is from one generation to the next on those who fear him.
   Mighty is his arm!
He has scattered the proud in the imagination of their hearts,
   and has put down the powerful from their thrones,
   exalting those of humble degree.
The hungry he has filled with good things,
   but the rich he has dismissed with nothing.
Remembering his mercy, he has helped his servant Israel,
   as he promised to our fathers,
   to Abraham and to his posterity for ever more.

Glory be…

Intercessions   *Either these, or others at choice or need.*

Let us pray for all those are married. *(pause for prayer)*
   ℟. May your love be upon us, O Lord.
For those who are preparing for marriage. *(pause)* **℟.**
For those whose marriage is a source of pain. *(pause)* **℟.**
For the gift of understanding between married people. *(pause)* **℟.**
Lord, give comfort to those who have been widowed. *(pause)* **℟.**

Lord, have mercy.
Christ, have mercy.
Lord, have mercy.

Our Father…

Let us pray.

L ORD, you who does not wish that human beings should be
alone, renew the grace of the Sacrament of Marriage within
those whom you have called to this state, and enable them to bear
the difficulties with fortitude, and the joys with gratitude. Through
our Lord Jesus Christ, your Son, who lives and reigns with you
and the Holy Spirit, one God, world without end. Amen.

℣. Let us bless the Lord.
℟. Thanks be to God.

❧   ❧   ❧

Compline

Anointing

℣. O God, ✠ come to my assistance.
℟. O Lord, be swift to my aid.
℣. Glory be to the Father, and to the Son, and to the Holy Spirit.
**℟. As it was in the beginning, is now and ever shall be,
world without end. Amen.**

Examination of conscience, and act of penance.

BEFORE the ending of the day,
Creator of the world, we pray
That with thy wonted favour thou
Wouldst be our guard and keeper now.

From all ill dreams defend our eyes,
From nightly fears and fantasies;
Tread under foot our ghostly foe,
That no pollution we may know.

O Father, that we ask be done,
Through Jesus Christ, thine only Son;
Who, with the Holy Ghost and thee,
Doth live and reign eternally. Amen.

Te lucis ante terminum

Ant. Your mercy, Lord, will follow me all the days of my life.

Psalm 22

THE LORD is my shepherd; so I shall need nothing.
He has set me in a place of pasture.
He has led me by the waters of tranquillity;
    he has restored my soul.
He has led me on the paths of justice,
    for his own name's sake.
For if I should walk in the midst of the shadow of death
    I will fear no evils, for you are there with me.
Your rod and your staff:
    these have comforted me.
You have prepared a table before me
    in the sight of those that afflict me.
You have anointed my head with oil;
    and my cup is overflowing.
And so your mercy will follow me

all the days of my life.
And I shall dwell in the house of the Lord
    unto length of days.

Glory be…

Ant. Your mercy, Lord, will follow me all the days of my life.

Short reading   *James 5:14-16*

IS ANYONE sick among you? Let him bring in the priests of the church, and let them pray over him, anointing him with oil in the name of the Lord; and the prayer of faith shall save the sick man, and the Lord will raise him up; and should he be in sins, they shall be forgiven.

The Nunc Dimittis
Luke 2:29-32

Ant. Save us, O Lord, while we wake, and watch over us as we sleep, that we may pass the night with Christ and rest in peace.

LORD, ✠ now let your servant depart in peace,
    according to your promise;
    for my eyes have seen your salvation
which you have prepared in the presence of all peoples,
a light for revelation to the Gentiles,
    and for glory to your people Israel.

Glory be…

Ant. Save us, O Lord, while we wake, and watch over us as we sleep, that we may pass the night with Christ and rest in peace.

Let us pray.

VISIT this house, O Lord, we pray, and drive far from it the deadly power of the enemy. May your holy angels dwell here instead, that we may be preserved in peace, with your blessing on us always. Through Christ our Lord. Amen.

Antiphon in honour of our Lady, pp.341ff.
or:

WE FLY to thy patronage, holy Mother of God.
    Despise not our petitions in our necessities
But deliver us from every evil,
O glorious and blessed Virgin!

FRIDAY

Vigils

℣. O Lord, ✠ open my lips.
℟. **And my mouth shall declare your praise.**

Antiphon: They tear holes in my hands and my feet.

Psalm 21

O GOD, my God, why have you forsaken me?
Why so far from my salvation;
Why so far from the cries of my affliction?

O my God, I cry by day, and you will not listen,
I cry by night and I find no comfort.

Yet you, O God, are holy,
dwelling in the praise of Israel.
In you our fathers hoped;
they hoped, and you delivered them.
They cried to you, and they were saved;
they trusted in you and were not confounded.

But I am a worm and no man,
the reproach of men, and the outcast of the people.
All who see me laugh me to scorn.
They turn their lips, they shake their heads.
'He hoped in the Lord, let him deliver him;
let him save him, seeing he delighted in him.'

For you are the one who drew me out of the womb,
my hope from my mother's breast.
I was cast upon you from the womb,
from my mother's womb you are my God.
Do not leave me; for tribulation is very near,
for there is no one else to help me.

Many young bulls have surrounded me,
fat bulls have besieged me.
They open wide their mouths against me,
as a lion, ravening and roaring.

I am poured out like water,
  and all my bones are scattered.
My heart is become like wax,
  melting in the midst of my body.
My strength is dried up like a potsherd,
  and my tongue cleaves to my jaws;
  you have brought me down into the dust of death.

For many dogs have encompassed me,
  the council of the malignant besieges me.
They have dug holes in my hands and my feet;
  I can count all my bones.

And they have looked and stared upon me;
  they parted my garments among them.
  And upon my vesture they cast lots.

But you, O Lord, do not keep away!
  My strength, look to my defence!
Deliver, O God, my soul from the sword,
  all I have from the grip of the dog.
Save me from the lion's mouth,
  my humble soul from the horns of the unicorns.

I will declare your name to my brethren
  and in the midst of the assembly will I praise you.
You who fear the Lord, praise him;
  all the children of Jacob, glorify him.
Let all the children of Israel fear him,
  for he has not slighted or despised
  the supplication of the poor man.
From him he has not hidden his face,
  but he heard him when he cried.

You are my praise in the great congregation.
  I will pay my vows in the sight of those who fear him.
The poor shall eat and shall be filled.
  They shall praise the Lord, that seek him.
  Their hearts shall live for ever and ever!

All the ends of the earth shall remember
  and shall be converted to the Lord.
All the families of the Gentiles shall adore in his sight.
  For the Kingdom is the Lord's;
  and he shall have dominion over the nations.

All those who sleep in the earth shall worship him alone,
    all who go down to the dust shall fall down before him.

And my soul shall live for him,
    and my descendants shall serve him.
A generation to come shall be declared to the Lord,
    and they shall show forth his justice
    to a people yet unborn:
These things the Lord has done.

Glory be…

Antiphon: They tear holes in my hands and my feet.

℣. Lord, remember me,
℟. When you come into your Kingdom.

First reading

One chapter from the scriptures.

Response to the reading

℣. We adore you, O Christ,
℟. Because by your holy cross you have redeemed the world.
℣. And we bless you,
℟. Because by your holy cross you have redeemed the world.

Second reading

Spiritual reading.

Response to the reading

℣. Christ was obedient even to accepting death on a cross,
℟. So God has raised him high.
℣. Let every knee bend at the name of Jesus,
℟. For God has raised him high.

Let us pray.

ALMIGHTY God, whose Son Jesus Christ ascended for us the altar of the cross, grant that we may respond with like generosity to the needs of our neighbours. Through Christ our Lord. Amen.

℣. Let us bless the Lord.
℟. Thanks be to God.

Lauds

℣. O God, ✠ come to my assistance.
℟. O Lord, be swift to my aid.
℣. Glory be to the Father, and to the Son, and to the Holy Spirit.
**℟. As it was in the beginning, is now and ever shall be,
world without end. Amen.**

GLORY be to Jesus,
Who, in bitter pains,
Poured for me the life-blood
From his sacred veins.

Grace and life eternal
In that Blood I find;
Blest be his compassion,
Infinitely kind.

Blest through endless ages
Be that precious stream,
Which from endless torment
Doth the world redeem.

Abel's blood for vengeance
Pleaded to the skies;
But the Blood of Jesus
For our pardon cries.

Oft as it is sprinkled
On our guilty hearts,
Satan in confusion
Terror-struck departs.

Oft as earth, exulting,
Wafts its praise on high,
Hell with terror trembles,
Heaven is filled with joy.

Lift ye then your voices;
Swell the mighty flood;
Louder still and louder
Praise the precious Blood.

Viva! Viva! Gesù

Ant. A contrite and humbled heart, O God, you will not spurn.

Psalm 50

HAVE MERCY on me, O God,
    according to your great mercy.
And according to the multitude of your tender mercies
    blot out my iniquity.

Wash me yet more from my iniquity
    and cleanse me from my sin.
For I know my iniquity;
    and my sin is always before me.
Against you only have I sinned;
    and done evil before you.

That you may be justified in your sentence
    and may overcome when you are judged:
Behold, I was conceived in iniquities,
    and in sin did my mother give me life.

For behold, you love truth in the heart;
    and in secret you have made wisdom known to me.
You shall sprinkle me with hyssop and I shall be cleansed;
    you shall wash me; I shall be made whiter than snow.

You shall make me hear joy and gladness,
    and the bones that have been humbled shall rejoice.
Turn away your face from my sins
    and blot out all my iniquities.

Create a clean heart in me, O God,
    and renew a right spirit within me.
Do not cast me away from your face,
    nor take away your holy spirit from me.

Give me the joy of your salvation;
    and strengthen me with a willing spirit.
I will teach the unjust your ways
    and the wicked shall be converted to you.

Deliver me from blood, O God, the God of my salvation,
    and my tongue shall extol your justice.
O Lord, you will open my lips
    and my mouth shall declare your praise.

For if you had desired sacrifice,
    I would indeed have given it,
    but in burnt offerings you would not delight.
A sacrifice to God is an afflicted spirit:
    a contrite and humbled heart O God,
    you will not spurn.

Deal favourably, O Lord in your goodness, with Sion:
    that the walls of Jerusalem may be built up.
Then you will accept the sacrifice of justice,
    oblations and whole burnt offerings:
then they will lay calves upon your altar.

Glory be...

Ant. A contrite and humbled heart, O God, you will not spurn.

Short reading   *1 Peter 2:20-24*

WHEN, in doing well, you suffer for it patiently, this is
praiseworthy before God. For to this you are called, because Christ also suffered for you, leaving you an example, that
you should follow his steps who committed no sin; neither was
guile found in his mouth. Who, when he was reviled, did not
revile in return; when he suffered, he did not threaten; but he
trusted to him who judges justly. Who himself bore our sins in
his body upon the tree, that we, being dead to sin, should live to
righteousness. By his wounds you have been healed.

The Benedictus

Luke 1:68-79

BLESSED ✠ be the Lord, the God of Israel,
    who has visited and redeemed his people,
    and has lifted up a horn of salvation for us
in the family of his servant David.

For this he swore through the mouths of holy men:
    those who were prophets, from the beginning:
There would be salvation from our foes,
    and from the hand of all those who hate us;
to comfort our fathers,
    and to honour his holy covenant,
which oath once he swore to Abraham, our father,
    that he would grant us,
that freed from the hand of our enemies,
    and without fear, we may serve him,
    in holiness and justice in his very presence all our days.
And you, my son, will be named Prophet of the Most High;
    for you will go before the presence of the Lord
    to prepare his way,
to teach knowledge of salvation to his people
    that their sins may be forgiven,
    through the merciful heart of our God,
when the Daystar shall visit us from on high
    to enlighten those who sit in darkness
    and in the shadow of death,
    and guide our feet to the way of peace.

Glory be…

Intercessions   *Either these, or others at choice or need.*

Lord, forgive our sins. *(pause for prayer)* ℟. **Hear us, Father.**
Lord, deepen our compassion for the sufferings of your Son.
    (pause) ℟.
Lord, strengthen our determination to see the face of your Son in
    all those who suffer. *(pause)* ℟.
Lord, help us to take up our crosses to follow your Son. *(pause)* ℟.
Lord, help us to 'make up in our sinful bodies what lacks to the
sufferings of Christ'. *(pause)* ℟.

Lord, have mercy.
Christ, have mercy.
Lord, have mercy.

Our Father…

Let us pray.

L OOK upon your family, Lord, for which our Lord Jesus Christ did not hesitate to give himself into the hands of murderers and undergo the torments of the cross. Through the same Jesus Christ your Son, who lives and reigns with you in the unity of the Holy Spirit, one God for ever and ever. Amen.

℣. Let us bless the Lord.
℟. **Thanks be to God.**

Terce

℣. O God, ✠ come to my assistance.
℟. O Lord, be swift to my aid.
℣. Glory be to the Father, and to the Son, and to the Holy Spirit.
**℟. As it was in the beginning, is now and ever shall be,
world without end. Amen.**

COME, Holy Ghost, with God the Son
And God the Father, ever one;
Shed forth thy grace within our breast
And dwell with us a ready guest.

By every power, by heart and tongue,
By act and deed, thy praise be sung;
Inflame with perfect love each sense
That others' souls may kindle thence.

O Father, that we ask be done,
Through Jesus Christ, thine only Son;
Who, with the Holy Ghost and thee,
Doth live and reign eternally. Amen.

Nunc nobis, Sancte Spiritus

Ant. Lord, uphold me according to your word, and I shall live.

Psalm 118 Samech

I HATE the duplicitous heart:
but I have loved your law.
You are my helper and my protector;
and in your word I have greatly hoped.
Depart from me, you malignant people,
and I will keep God's commandments:
Uphold me according to your word, and I shall live;
and let me not be confounded in my expectation.
Help me and I shall be saved,
and I will delight always in your statutes.
You despise all who fall away from your laws;
for their thoughts are unjust.

I account as fickle all the sinners of the earth:
therefore I love your commandments.
Pierce my flesh through with your fear;
for I am afraid of your judgements.

Glory be...

Ant. Lord, uphold me according to your word, and I shall live.

Short reading
Mark 15:25-26

A ND IT was the third hour, when they crucified him. And the inscription of the charge against him was written over him: 'The King of the Jews'. And with him they crucified two thieves, one on his right hand and the other on his left.

Let us pray.

L OOK upon your family, Lord, for which our Lord Jesus Christ did not hesitate to give himself into the hands of murderers and undergo the torments of the cross. Through the same Jesus Christ our Lord. Amen.

℣. Let us bless the Lord.
℟. **Thanks be to God.**

Sext

℣. O God, ✠ come to my assistance.
℟. O Lord, be swift to my aid.
℣. Glory be to the Father, and to the Son, and to the Holy Spirit.
**℟. As it was in the beginning, is now and ever shall be,
world without end. Amen.**

O GOD of truth, O Lord of might,
Who orderest time and change aright,
And send'st the early morning ray,
And light'st the glow of perfect day:

Extinguish thou each sinful fire,
And banish every ill desire;
And while thou keep'st the body whole,
Shed forth thy peace upon the soul.

O Father, that we ask be done,
Through Jesus Christ, thine only Son;
Who, with the Holy Ghost and thee,
Doth live and reign eternally. Amen.

Rector potens, verax Deus

Ant. Lord, give me understanding and I will study your law.

Psalm 118 Ayin

I HAVE done justly and rightly:
do not betray me to my slanderers.
Uphold your servant for his good,
lest the proud calumniate me.
My eyes faint for your salvation
and for the word of your justice.
Deal with your servant according to your mercy
and teach me your commands.
I am your servant, give me understanding:
that I may know your testimonies.

It is time, O Lord, to act:
> for they have broken your law.
Therefore I love your command
> above gold and the topaz.
Therefore I direct my life to all your precepts:
> I hate all the ways of the liar.

Glory be...

Ant. Lord, give me understanding and I will study your law.

Short reading   *Luke 23:39-44*

ONE OF the robbers who were hanged blasphemed Jesus, saying, 'If you be the Christ save yourself and us!' But the other answered, saying, 'Do you not fear God, since you are under the same condemnation? And we indeed justly; for we receive the due reward of our deeds; but this man has done no evil.' And he said to Jesus, 'Lord, remember me when you shall come into your Kingdom.' And Jesus said to him, 'Truly, I say to you, this day you will be with me in paradise.' It was almost the sixth hour, and there was darkness over all the earth until the ninth hour.

Let us pray.

LOOK upon your family, Lord, for which our Lord Jesus Christ did not hesitate to give himself into the hands of murderers and undergo the torments of the cross. Through the same Jesus Christ our Lord. Amen.

℣. Let us bless the Lord.
℟. Thanks be to God.

∽   ∽   ∽

None

℣. O God, ✠ come to my assistance.
℟. O Lord, be swift to my aid.
℣. Glory be to the Father, and to the Son, and to the Holy Spirit.
**℟. As it was in the beginning, is now and ever shall be,
world without end. Amen.**

O GOD, Creation's secret force,
Thyself unmoved, all motion's source,
Who from the morn till evening ray
Through all its changes guid'st the day:

Grant us, when this short life is past,
The glorious evening that shall last;
That, by a holy death attained,
Eternal glory may be gained.

O Father, that we ask be done,
Through Jesus Christ, thine only Son;
Who, with the Holy Ghost and thee,
Doth live and reign eternally. Amen.

Rerum Deus tenax vigor

Ant. The Lord Jesus was obedient unto death on a cross.

Psalm 118 Pe

YOUR testimonies are wonderful:
therefore my soul has sought them.
The declaration of your words gives light
and understanding to little ones.
I open my mouth and gasp
because I long for your commandments.
Look upon me and have mercy on me,
according to the judgement of those that love you.
Direct my steps according to your word;
and let no iniquity have dominion over me.

Redeem me from the calumnies of men,
    that I may keep your commandments.
Make your face to shine on your servant
    and teach me your laws.
My eyes send forth streams of water
    because your law is not kept.

Glory be…

Ant. The Lord Jesus was obedient unto death on a cross.

Short reading   *Mark 15:34-39*

A ND at the ninth hour Jesus cried with a loud voice saying: *'Eloi, Eloi, lama sabachthani?'* Which is, when interpreted, 'My God, my God, why have you forsaken me?' And some of the bystanders hearing it said, 'Behold, he is calling on Elijah.' And one ran and filled a sponge full of vinegar, and putting it on a reed, gave it to him to drink, saying, 'Stay, let us see if Elijah will come to take him down.' And Jesus having cried with a loud voice, gave up his spirit. And the veil of the temple was rent in two, from the top to the bottom. And the centurion, who stood by him, seeing that he had cried out and given up his spirit, said, 'Indeed this man was the Son of God!'

Let us pray.

L OOK upon your family, Lord, for which our Lord Jesus Christ did not hesitate to give himself into the hands of murderers and undergo the torments of the cross. Through the same Jesus Christ our Lord. Amen.

℣. Let us bless the Lord.
℟. Thanks be to God.

∾   ∾   ∾

Vespers

℣. O God, ✠ come to my assistance.
℟. **O Lord, be swift to my aid.**
℣. Glory be to the Father, and to the Son, and to the Holy Spirit.
℟. **As it was in the beginning, is now and ever shall be,
world without end. Amen.**

W HEN I survey the wondrous cross
On which the Prince of glory died,
My richest gain I count as loss,
And pour contempt on all my pride.

Forbid it, Lord, that I should boast
Save in the death of Christ my God;
All the vain things that charm me most,
I sacrifice them to his blood.

See from his head, his hands, his feet,
Sorrow and love flow mingled down;
Did e'er such love and sorrow meet,
Or thorns compose so rich a crown?

His dying crimson like a robe
Spreads o'er his body on the tree;
Then I am dead to all the globe,
And all the globe is dead to me.

Were the whole realm of nature mine,
It were an offering far too small;
Love so amazing, so divine,
Demands my soul, my life, my all.

I. Watts

Ant. Cast your care on the Lord and he will sustain you.

Psalm 54

O GOD, let your ears be open to my prayer,
do not hide from my supplication,
be attentive to me and hear me.

I am grieved in my prayer,
I am troubled at the voice of the enemy,
at the clamour of the sinner;
for they have cast evil upon me,
and in fury they are set against me.

My heart is troubled within me,
   and the terror of death has fallen upon me,
Fear and trembling have come upon me
   and terror has covered me.

And I said: Who will give me wings like a dove
   that I may fly and be at rest?
So I would go flying far away
   and abide in the wilderness.

I have waited for him who saves me
   from the spirit of cowardice,
   and from the mighty storm.

Cast them down O Lord,
   and divide their tongues;
   for I see iniquity and contention in the city.

Day and night, they go round its walls.
   Inside it is full of trouble and injustice.
   Usury and deceit have not departed its streets.

For if it had been my enemy who reviled me,
   I would truly have borne with it.
If it had been one who hated me who spoke against me,
   I could perhaps have hidden myself from him.

But it was you, a man of my own heart,
   my confidant, my familiar companion!
We used to take sweet counsel together
   We walked together in the house of God as friends.

Let death come upon them!
   Let them go down alive into Hell!
For there is wickedness in their dwellings,
   right in the very midst of them!

But I have cried to God
   and the Lord will save me.
In the evening, morning, and at noon
   I will cry out and pray.

He will redeem my soul in peace
   from those who battle against me:
   for there were many with me.

God will hear
   and the Eternal One will humble them,
for they will not change;
   they will never fear God.

The betrayer has turned his hand
   against those who were at peace with him;
   he has defiled his covenant.
His words are softer than butter,
   while having war in his heart.
His words are smoother than oil,
   but truly they are wicked swords.

Cast your care upon the Lord
   and he will sustain you.
He will never suffer
   the just man to waver.

But you, O God, will bring them down
   into the pit of destruction.
Bloody and deceitful men
   shall not live out half their days.
But I will trust in you, O Lord.

Glory be…

Ant. Cast your care on the Lord and he will sustain you.

Short reading

Philippians 2:6-11

CHRIST Jesus, though being in the form of God, did not think equality with God a thing to be grasped, but emptied himself, taking the form of a servant, being made in the likeness of men and in habit found as a man. He humbled himself, becoming obedient unto death, even to the death of the cross. For this, God has also highly exalted him and given him a name which is above all names, that in the name of Jesus every knee should bow, those in Heaven, on earth and under the earth, and that every tongue should confess that the Lord Jesus Christ is in the glory of God the Father.

The Magnificat

Luke 1:46-55

MY ✠ SOUL magnifies the Lord,
   my spirit rejoices in God who is my Saviour,
   who has looked upon the humility of his handmaiden.

Behold, all generations from now
    will acknowledge me blessed,
For the mighty one has done great things for me:
    Holy is his name!
His mercy is from one generation to the next on those who fear him.
    Mighty is his arm!
He has scattered the proud in the imagination of their hearts,
    and has put down the powerful from their thrones,
    exalting those of humble degree.
The hungry he has filled with good things,
    but the rich he has dismissed with nothing.
Remembering his mercy, he has helped his servant Israel,
    as he promised to our fathers,
    to Abraham and to his posterity for ever more.

Glory be…

Intercessions   *Either these, or others at choice or need.*

For those unjustly deprived of freedom, *(pause for prayer)*
    ℟. **Hear us, O Lord.**
For those who lack the necessities of life, *(pause)* ℟.
For those who fight evil with good, *(pause)* ℟.
For an end to famine and war, *(pause)* ℟.
Lord, grant rest to those who have given their lives for justice or
    truth. *(pause)* ℟.

Lord, have mercy.
Christ, have mercy.
Lord, have mercy.

Our Father…

Let us pray.

L ORD, grant us the gift to be always contemplating what is
    right, and make us well-disposed to putting it into action, that
we who can do nothing without you may be worthy to live as you
wish. Through our Lord Jesus Christ, your Son, who lives and reigns
with you and the Holy Spirit, one God, world without end. Amen.

℣. Let us bless the Lord.
℟. **Thanks be to God.**

Compline

℣. O God, ✠ come to my assistance.
℟. O Lord, be swift to my aid.
℣. Glory be to the Father, and to the Son, and to the Holy Spirit.
**℟. As it was in the beginning, is now and ever shall be,
world without end. Amen.**

Examination of conscience, and act of penance.

B EFORE the ending of the day,
Creator of the world we pray
That with thy wonted favour thou
Wouldst be our guard and keeper now.

From all ill dreams defend our eyes,
From nightly fears and fantasies;
Tread under foot our ghostly foe,
That no pollution we may know.

O Father, that we ask be done,
Through Jesus Christ, thine only Son;
Who, with the Holy Ghost and thee,
Doth live and reign eternally. Amen.

Te lucis ante terminum

Ant. For your name's sake, O Lord, give me life.

Psalm 142

L ORD, hear my prayer:
give ear to my supplication in your truth:
Hear me in your justice.
And do not enter into judgement with your servant,
for in your sight no one living shall be justified.

For the enemy persecutes my soul;
he has brought down my life to the earth;
he has made me to dwell in darkness
like those who have died long ago.
My spirit is in anguish within me
my heart within me is troubled.

I remember the days of old:
    I meditate on all your deeds;
    I meditate on the works of your hands.

I stretch forth my hands towards you.
    My soul is like waterless earth for you.

Hear me speedily, O Lord;
    for my spirit has fainted away.
Do not turn your face away from me,
    lest I be like those who go down into the pit.

In the morning let me hear of your mercy,
    for in you have I hoped.
Make the way known to me where I should walk:
    for I have lifted up my soul to you.

Deliver me from my enemies, O Lord:
    to you I have fled.
Teach me to do your will,
    for you are my God.
Your good spirit shall lead me into the right land.

For your name's sake, O Lord,
    you will give me life in your justice.
You will bring my soul out of trouble
    and in your mercy you will destroy my enemies.
And you will cut off all those who afflict my soul,
    for I am your servant.

Glory be…

Ant. For your name's sake, O Lord, give me life.

Short reading
Isaiah 53:4-5

SURELY he has borne our infirmities and carried our sorrows; yet we thought of him as a leper, one struck by God, and afflicted. But he was wounded for our iniquities, he was bruised for our sins; upon him was the chastisement that gave us peace, and with his bruises we are healed.

The Nunc Dimittis

Luke 2:29-32

Ant. Save us, O Lord, while we wake, and watch over us as we
sleep, that we may pass the night with Christ and rest in peace.

L ORD, ✠ now let your servant depart in peace,
    according to your promise;
    for my eyes have seen your salvation
  which you have prepared in the presence of all peoples,
a light for revelation to the Gentiles,
    and for glory to your people Israel.

Glory be…

Ant. Save us, O Lord, while we wake, and watch over us as we
sleep, that we may pass the night with Christ and rest in peace.

Let us pray.

V ISIT this house, O Lord, we pray, and drive far from it the
  deadly power of the enemy. May your holy angels dwell
here instead, that we may be preserved in peace, with your blessing on us always. Through Christ our Lord. Amen.

Antiphon in honour of our Lady, pp.341ff.
or:

W E FLY to thy patronage, holy Mother of God.
  Despise not our petitions in our necessities
But deliver us from every evil,
O glorious and blessed Virgin!

SATURDAY

And feasts of our Lady

Vigils

℣. O Lord, open ✠ my lips.
℟. And my mouth shall declare your praise.

Antiphon: Blessed are you among women
and blessed is the fruit of your womb.

Psalm 97

SING to the Lord a new song
because he has done wonderful things.
His right hand has wrought for him salvation,
and his arm is holy.

The Lord has made known his salvation:
he has revealed his justice
in the sight of the Gentiles.

He has remembered his mercy and his truth
towards the house of Israel.
All the ends of the earth have seen
the salvation of our God.

Sing joyfully to God, all the earth;
make melody, rejoice and sing.
Sing praise to the Lord on the harp,
on the harp and with the voice of a psalm.

With long trumpets and with the sound of the cornet
make a joyful noise before the Lord our King.

Let the sea be moved and all its waves,
the world also, and those that dwell in it.
Let the rivers clap their hands,
the mountains rejoice together
at the presence of the Lord
For he comes to judge the earth.

He shall judge the world with justice,
and the people with equity.

Glory be...

Antiphon: Blessed are you among women
and blessed is the fruit of your womb.

℣. Grace is poured upon your lips;
℟. Therefore God has blessed you for ever.

First reading

One chapter from the scriptures.

Response to the reading

℣. Blessed are you, O Virgin Mary, who bore the Lord, the creator of the world.
**℟. You gave birth to your own Creator, and yet still remain
a virgin.**
℣. Hail Mary, full of grace; the Lord is with you.
**℟. You gave birth to your own Creator, and yet still remain
a virgin.**

Second reading

Spiritual reading.

Response to the reading

℣. How can I praise you, holy and immaculate Virgin?
℟. For you held him whom even the heavens cannot contain.
℣. Blessed are you among women, and blessed is the fruit of
your womb.
℟. For you held him whom even the heavens cannot contain.

Let us pray.

G RANT, O merciful God, support to our frailty; that we who
celebrate the memory of the holy Mother of God may, by
the help of her intercession, arise from our sins. Through Christ
our Lord. Amen.

℣. Let us bless the Lord.
℟. Thanks be to God.

∾   ∾   ∾

Lauds

℣. O God, ✠ come to my assistance.

℟. O Lord, be swift to my aid.

℣. Glory be to the Father, and to the Son, and to the Holy Spirit.

℟. As it was in the beginning, is now and ever shall be, world without end. Amen.

HAIL, thou star of ocean,
Portal of the sky;
Ever virgin Mother
Of the Lord most high.
Oh! by Gabriel's Ave
Utter'd long ago,
Eva's name reversing,
'Stablish peace below.

Break the captive's fetters,
Light on blindness pour,
All our ills expelling,
Every bliss implore.
Show thyself a mother;
Offer him our sighs,
Who for us incarnate
Did not thee despise.

Virgin of all virgins,
To thy shelter take us;
Gentlest of the gentle,
Chaste and gentle make us.
Still, as on we journey,
Help our weak endeavour;
Till with thee and Jesus
We rejoice for ever.

Through the highest Heaven,
To the almighty Three,
Father, Son and Spirit,
One same glory be.

Ave maris Stella

Ant. The angel Gabriel was sent to Mary,
a virgin espoused to Joseph.

Psalm 99

SING joyfully to God, all the earth.
　　Serve the Lord with gladness.
　　Come before his presence with exceeding joy.

Know that the Lord, he is God.
　　He made us, and we are his,
　　we are his people, and the sheep of his pasture.

Go within his gates with praise,
　　into his courts with hymns:
　　and give glory to him.

Bless his name, for the Lord is sweet,
　　his mercy endures for ever,
　　and his truth from generation to generation.

Glory be...

　　Ant. The angel Gabriel was sent to Mary,
　　　　a virgin espoused to Joseph.

Short reading *Isaiah 11:1-2*

THERE shall come forth a rod out of the root of Jesse, and
a flower shall rise up out of his root. And the Spirit of the
Lord shall rest upon him, the spirit of wisdom and of understanding, the spirit of counsel and of fortitude, the spirit of knowledge
and of godliness.

The Benedictus

Luke 1:68-79

BLESSED ✠ be the Lord, the God of Israel,
　　who has visited and redeemed his people,
　　and has lifted up a horn of salvation for us
in the family of his servant David.
For this he swore through the mouths of holy men:
　　those who were prophets, from the beginning:
There would be salvation from our foes,
　　and from the hand of all those who hate us;
to comfort our fathers,
　　and to honour his holy covenant,
which oath once he swore to Abraham, our father,
　　that he would grant us,

that freed from the hand of our enemies,
    and without fear, we may serve him,
    in holiness and justice in his very presence all our days.
And you, my son, will be named Prophet of the Most High;
    for you will go before the presence of the Lord
    to prepare his way,
to teachknowledge of salvation to his people
    that their sins may be forgiven,
    through the merciful heart of our God,
when the Daystar shall visit us from on high
    to enlighten those who sit in darkness
    and in the shadow of death,
    and guide our feet to the way of peace.

Glory be…

Intercessions   *Either these, or others at choice or need.*

Grant us ever greater love of your Son. *(pause for prayer)*
    R. Mary, pray for us to God.
Grant us the spirit of prayer and penance. *(pause)* **R.**
Help us to be better witnesses of your Son. *(pause)* **R.**
Cure our sick and give help to the needy. *(pause)* **R.**
Give us grace to imitate your purity. *(pause)* **R.**
Help us generously to do God's will, as you did. *(pause)* **R.**
Mary, help us to become saints. *(pause)* **R.**

Lord, have mercy.
Christ, have mercy.
Lord, have mercy.

Our Father…

Let us pray.

L ORD God, whose Son was pleased to take flesh in the womb
of the Blessed Virgin Mary at the angel's message, grant
that, as we venerate her as the Mother of God, so we may be
assisted by her intercession with you. Through the same Lord
Jesus Christ, your Son, who lives and reigns with you in the unity
of the Holy Spirit, one God for ever and ever. Amen.

℣. Let us bless the Lord.
R. Thanks be to God.

Terce

℣. O God, ✠ come to my assistance.
℟. O Lord, be swift to my aid.
℣. Glory be to the Father, and to the Son, and to the Holy Spirit.
**℟. As it was in the beginning, is now and ever shall be,
world without end. Amen.**

REMEMBER, O Creator Lord!
That in the Virgin's sacred womb
Thou wast conceived and of her flesh
Didst our mortality assume.

Mother of grace, O Mary blest!
To thee, sweet fount of love, we fly:
Shield us through life, and take us hence
To thy dear bosom when we die.

O Jesu, born of Virgin bright!
Immortal glory be to Thee;
Praise to the Father infinite,
And Holy Ghost eternally. Amen.

Memento, rerum Conditor

Ant. Mary said: 'Do whatever Jesus tells you.'

Psalm 120

I SHALL lift up my eyes to the hills.
From whence shall help come to me?
My help is from the Lord,
  who made Heaven and earth.

May he not let your foot be moved,
  nor he who keeps you slumber.
Behold, shall neither slumber nor sleep
  he who keeps watch over Israel.

The Lord is your keeper;
  the Lord is your protection on your right hand.

The sun shall not burn you by day,
    nor the moon by night.

The Lord will keep you from all evil;
    may the Lord keep your soul.
The Lord will keep your coming in and your going out
    from henceforth, now and for ever.

Glory be…

Ant. Mary said: 'Do whatever Jesus tells you.'

Short reading   *John 2:1-5*

A ND on the third day, there was a marriage at Cana of Galilee
   and the mother of Jesus was there; Jesus also was invited
with his disciples to the marriage. And when the wine failed, the
mother of Jesus said to him, 'They have no wine.' And Jesus said
to her, 'Woman, what is that to do with me and you? My hour is
not yet come.' His mother said to the servants, 'Whatever he
says to you, do.'

Let us pray.

O MERCIFUL God, support to our frailty, grant that we who
  celebrate the memory of the holy Mother of God may, by
the help of her intercession, arise from our iniquities. Through
the same Christ our Lord. Amen.

℣. Let us bless the Lord.
℟. Thanks be to God.

Sext

℣. O God, ✠ come to my assistance.
℟. O Lord, be swift to my aid.
℣. Glory be to the Father, and to the Son, and to the Holy Spirit.
**℟. As it was in the beginning, is now and ever shall be,
world without end. Amen.**

O QUEEN of all the virgin choir!
　　Enthroned above the starry sky,
Who with thy bosom's milk didst feed
Thy own Creator, Lord most high:

What man had lost in hapless Eve,
Thy sacred womb to man restores;
Thou to the wretched here beneath
Hast opened Heaven's eternal doors.

Hail, O refulgent Hall of light!
Hail, Gate sublime of Heaven's high King,
Through thee redeemed to endless life,
Thy praise let all the nations sing.

O Jesu! born of Virgin bright,
Immortal glory be to thee;
Praise to the Father infinite,
And Holy Ghost eternally. Amen.

O Gloriosa Virginum

Ant. The Virgin Mary bore the Son of the eternal Father.

Psalm 121

I REJOICED when they said to me:
　We shall go into the house of the Lord!
Our feet are standing within your courts,
　　O Jerusalem!

Jerusalem, built as a city
　　which is compact together,
is where the tribes go up,
　　the tribes of the Lord,

as was decreed for Israel,
to praise the name of the Lord.
There were set the seats for judgement,
seats for the house of David.

O pray for the peace of Jerusalem!
'Sureness for those who love you!
Peace be within your walls,
and abundance within your towers!'

For the sake of my brethren and my neighbours,
I will speak peace within you.
Because of the house of the Lord our God,
I will seek good things for you.

Glory be…

Ant. The Virgin Mary bore the Son of the eternal Father.

Short reading *Luke 1:26-38 passim*

THE angel Gabriel was sent from God to a virgin espoused to a man whose name was Joseph, of the house of David; and the virgin's name was Mary. And he came in to her and said, 'Hail, full of grace, the Lord is with you!' But she, having heard, was greatly troubled at his saying, and thought within herself what manner of greeting this could be. And the angel said to her, 'Fear not, Mary, for you have found grace with God. Behold, you will conceive in your womb and bring forth a son, and you shall call his name Jesus.' And Mary said, 'Behold the handmaid of the Lord; be it done to me according to your word.'

Let us pray.

POUR forth your grace, we beseech you, Lord, into our hearts, that we who, by the angel's message, have known the incarnation of Christ your Son may, by his passion and cross, be made partakers in his resurrection. Through the same Christ our Lord. Amen.

℣. Let us bless the Lord.
℟. **Thanks be to God.**

❧   ❧   ❧

None

℣. O God, ✠ come to my assistance.
℟. O Lord, be swift to my aid.
℣. Glory be to the Father, and to the Son, and to the Holy Spirit.
**℟. As it was in the beginning, is now and ever shall be,
world without end. Amen.**

> UNDER the world-redeeming rood
> The most afflicted Mother stood,
> Mingling her tears with her Son's blood;
> As that streamed down from every part,
> Of all his wounds she felt the smart:
> What pierced his body pierced her heart.
>
> *from the Stabat Mater*

Ant. Our help is in the name of the Lord, who made Heaven and earth.

Psalm 123

> IF IT had not been that the Lord was with us,
> let Israel now say,
> If it had not been that the Lord was with us,
> when men rose up against us,
> perhaps they would have swallowed us up alive.
>
> Our soul has passed through a torrent:
> Our soul has passed
> through the surging waters.
>
> Blessed be the Lord,
> who has not given us to be a prey to their teeth.
> Our soul has been delivered
> as a sparrow out of a snare of the fowlers.
> The snare is broken, and we are delivered.
>
> Our help is in the name of the Lord
> who made Heaven and earth.
>
> Glory be…

Ant. Our help is in the name of the Lord, who made Heaven and earth.

Short reading *John 19:25-27*

NOW THERE stood by the cross of Jesus his mother, and his mother's sister, Mary the wife of Cleophas, and Mary Magdalene. When Jesus therefore saw his mother, and the disciple whom he loved standing there, he said to his mother, 'Woman, behold your son.' After that, he said to the disciple, 'Behold your mother.' And from that hour the disciple took her as his own.

Let us pray.

O LORD Jesus Christ who out of infinite charity became, for the sake of sinful man, the scorn of men and the outcast of the people, and died for us on the cross to obtain our relief from eternal shame: grant us, we beseech, by the merits of your most sorrowful crucifixion, and by the glorious intercession of your most tender Mother, who stood beneath your cross, the spirit of perfect contrition for our sins, and of a holy death; who live and reign for ever and ever. Amen.

℣. Let us bless the Lord.
℟. Thanks be to God.

℘ ℘ ℘

First Vespers of Sunday

Sunday begins with the celebration of Vespers on Saturday evening

℣. O God, ✠ come to my assistance.
℟. O Lord, be swift to my aid.
℣. Glory be to the Father, and to the Son, and to the Holy Spirit.
**℟. As it was in the beginning, is now and ever shall be,
world without end. Amen.**

O GLADSOME light, O grace
Of God the Father's face,
The eternal splendour wearing;
Celestial, holy, blest,
Our Saviour Jesus Christ,
Joyful in thine appearing.

Now, ere day fadeth quite,
We see the evening light,
Our wonted hymn outpouring;
Father of might unknown,
Thee, his incarnate Son,
And Holy Spirit adoring.

To thee of right belongs
All praise of holy songs,
O Son of God, Lifegiver;
Thee, therefore, O Most High,
The world doth glorify,
And shall exalt for ever.

Φῶς ἱλαρόν

Ant. In the morning you will see his glory.

Psalm 67:1-7, 18-20, 22, 24-35

L ET GOD arise, and let his enemies be scattered;
let those that hate him flee from before his face!
As smoke vanishes, so let them vanish away:
　　as wax melts before the fire,
　　let the wicked perish at the presence of God!
But let the just feast and rejoice before God,
　　and be delighted with gladness.

Sing to God, sing a psalm to his name;
>make a way for him who ascends upon the west;
>The Lord is his name.
Father of the orphans and protector of widows
>is God in his holy place.
God gives the homeless a home to dwell in;
>he leads out the bound to prosperity;
>but the rebellious dwell in a parched land.

You have gone up on high,
>you have led captivity captive,
>and received gifts from men,
even among the rebellious,
>that the Lord God may dwell there.

Blessed be the Lord, day be day;
>God is our salvation,
>and will make our journey prosper.
Our God is a God of salvation;
>and to God, the Lord, belongs escape from death.
The Lord said, I will bring them back from Basan,
>I will bring them back from the depth of the sea.

They have seen your solemn processions, O God,
>the processions of my God, my King,
>who goes into the sanctuary.

Princes went before, joined with singers:
>in the midst of them, maidens playing on timbrels.
In the assembly, bless God the Lord,
>from the fountains of Israel.
There is Benjamin, a youth, in ecstasy,
>the princes of Juda are their leaders,
>the princes of Zabulon, the princes of Nepthali.

Command your strength, O God;
>Confirm, O God, what you have wrought in us.
From your temple in Jerusalem,
>kings shall offer gifts to you.

Rebuke the wild beasts that dwell among the reeds,
>the herd of bulls with the cattle of the nations.
Trample those who lust after silver,
>Scatter the nations who delight in war.

Ambassadors shall come from Egypt;
>Ethiopia shall soon stretch out her hands to God.
Sing to God, you kingdoms of the earth;
>sing praises to the Lord,

Sing to God who rises above the Heaven of heavens,
>the eastern heavens;
>>behold, he gives to his voice the voice of power.
Give glory to God, for the sake of Israel,
>his magnificence and his power is in the clouds.
God is wonderful in his saints:
>the God of Israel is the one
>who will give power and strength to his people.

Blessed be God!

Glory be…

Ant. In the morning you will see his glory.

Short reading

1 Corinthians 15:20-22

B UT NOW Christ is risen from the dead, the first fruits of those who sleep. For as by a man came death, so also by a man has come the resurrection of the dead. And as in Adam all die, so also in Christ all shall be made alive.

The Magnificat

Luke 1:46-55

M Y ✠ SOUL magnifies the Lord,
>my spirit rejoices in God who is my Saviour,
>who has looked upon the humility of his handmaiden.
Behold, all generations from now
>will acknowledge me blessed,
For the mighty one has done great things for me:
>Holy is his name!
His mercy is from one generation to the next on those who fear him.
>Mighty is his arm!
He has scattered the proud in the imagination of their hearts,
>and has put down the powerful from their thrones,
>exalting those of humble degree.

The hungry he has filled with good things,
  but the rich he has dismissed with nothing.
Remembering his mercy, he has helped his servant Israel,
  as he promised to our fathers,
  to Abraham and to his posterity for ever more.

Glory be…

Intercessions   *Either these, or others at choice or need.*

Lord, heal those who are sick in body. *(pause for prayer)* ℞. **Hear us, O Lord.**
Lord, heal those who are sick in mind. *(pause)* ℞.
Lord, give us greater devotion to your Mother. *(pause)* ℞.
Lord, grant rest to the dead. *(pause)* ℞.

Lord, have mercy.
Christ, have mercy.
Lord, have mercy.

Our Father…

Let us pray.

O GOD, as you gave joy to the world through the resurrection of your only Son Jesus Christ from the dead, grant that by the prayers of his Virgin Mother we may be freed from all sorrow and come to the fullness of joy in your Kingdom. Through the same Jesus Christ, your Son, who lives and reigns with you and the Holy Spirit, one God, world without end. Amen.

℣. Let us bless the Lord.
℞. **Thanks be to God.**

Compline

℣. O God, ✠ come to my assistance.
℟. O Lord, be swift to my aid.
℣. Glory be to the Father, and to the Son, and to the Holy Spirit.
**℟. As it was in the beginning, is now and ever shall be,
world without end. Amen.**

Examination of conscience, and act of penance.

B EFORE the ending of the day,
Creator of the world, we pray
That with thy wonted favour thou
Wouldst be our guard and keeper now.

From all ill dreams defend our eyes,
From nightly fears and fantasies;
Tread under foot our ghostly foe,
That no pollution we may know.

O Father, that we ask be done,
Through Jesus Christ, thine only Son;
Who, with the Holy Ghost and thee,
Doth live and reign eternally. Amen.

Te lucis ante terminum

Ant. Bless the Lord throughout the night.

Psalm 130

L ORD, my heart is not exalted,
nor are my eyes lofty;
Neither have I walked in great matters
nor in wonderful things above me.

But I have calmed and quieted my soul,
like a child that is weaned by its mother;
like a child that is quieted is my soul.
Let Israel hope in the Lord
from henceforth, now, and for ever.

Glory be...

Ant. Bless the Lord throughout the night.

Short reading *Revelation 22:4-5*

THEY shall see the Lord's face, and his name shall be on their foreheads. And night shall be no more; they shall not need the light of the lamp nor the light of the sun, for the Lord God shall enlighten them, and they shall reign for ever and ever.

The Nunc Dimittis
Luke 2:29-32

Ant. Save us, O Lord, while we wake, and watch over us as we sleep, that we may pass the night with Christ and rest in peace.

LORD, ✠ now let your servant depart in peace,
according to your promise;
for my eyes have seen your salvation
which you have prepared in the presence of all peoples,
a light for revelation to the Gentiles,
and for glory to your people Israel.

Glory be...

Ant. Save us, O Lord, while we wake, and watch over us as we sleep, that we may pass the night with Christ and rest in peace.

Let us pray.

VISIT this house, O Lord, we pray, and drive far from it the deadly power of the enemy. May your holy angels dwell here instead, that we may be preserved in peace, with your blessing on us always. Through Christ our Lord. Amen.

Antiphon in honour of our Lady, pp.341ff.
or:

WE FLY to thy patronage, holy Mother of God.
Despise not our petitions in our necessities
But deliver us from every evil,
O glorious and blessed Virgin.

ॐ　　ॐ　　ॐ

AN OFFICE FOR THE DEAD

Vigils

℣. O Lord, ✠ open my lips.
℟. And my mouth shall declare your praise.

Antiphon: Direct, O Lord God, my way in your sight.

Psalm 6

O LORD, rebuke me not in your indignation,
nor chastise me in your anger.
Have mercy on me, O Lord, for I am weak:
heal me, O Lord, for my bones are troubled.
My soul is troubled exceedingly:
and you, Lord, how long…?

Turn to me O Lord, and deliver my soul:
O save me for your mercy's sake.
For there is no one in death who remembers you
and in Hell, who shall praise you?

I have laboured in my groanings:
every night I wash my bed,
I water my couch with my tears.
My eye is troubled through grief:
I have grown old among my enemies.

Leave me, you workers of iniquity:
for the Lord has heard the sound of my weeping.
The Lord has heard my supplication:
The Lord has received my prayer.

So let all my enemies be ashamed
and very much troubled.
Let them be turned back,
and be ashamed very speedily.

Eternal rest grant unto them, O Lord,
and let perpetual light shine on them.

Antiphon: Direct, O Lord God, my way in your sight.

℣. May the Lord place them with the princes,
℟. **With the princes of his people.**

First reading

One chapter from the scriptures.

Response to the reading

℣. Out of the depths I cry to you, O Lord. Lord, hear my voice.
℟. **Remember me, O Lord, my life is but a breath.**
℣. Let your ears be attentive to the voice of my supplication.
℟. **Remember me, O Lord, my life is but a breath.**

Second reading

Spiritual reading.

Response to the reading

℣. Deliver us, O Lord from eternal death in that mighty day,
℟. **When you shall come in fire to judge the world.**
℣. Eternal rest grant to them, O Lord, and let perpetual light shine
on them,
℟. **When you shall come in fire to judge the world.**

*Collects for special categories of people, see p. 380
otherwise:*

Let us pray.

O LORD, whose nature it is to have mercy and spare, we
humbly beg your mercy on the souls of the faithful departed,
that through your mercy and our feeble prayers, they may attain
to that glory which they have always desired. Through Christ our
Lord. Amen.

℣. Let us bless the Lord.
℟. **Thanks be to God.**

ॐ   ॐ   ॐ

Lauds

℣. O God, ✠ come to my assistance.
℟. O Lord, be swift to my aid.
℣. Glory be to the Father, and to the Son, and to the Holy Spirit.
**℟. As it was in the beginning, is now and ever shall be,
  world without end. Amen.**

HELP, Lord, the souls that thou hast made,
  The souls to thee so dear,
In prison for the debt unpaid
Of sins committed here.

Those holy souls, they suffer on,
Resigned in heart and will,
Until thy high behest is done,
And justice has its fill.

For daily falls, for pardoned crime,
They joy to undergo
The shadow of thy cross sublime,
The remnant of thy woe.

O, by their patience of delay,
Their hope amid their pain,
Their sacred zeal to burn away
Disfigurement and stain;

O, by their fire of love, not less
In keenness than the flame,
O, by their very helplessness,
O, by thy own great name,

Good Jesu, help! sweet Jesu, aid
The souls to thee most dear,
In prison for the debt unpaid
Of sins committed here.

J.H.Newman

Ant. Lord, do not remember the sins of my youth.

Psalm 24

TO YOU, O Lord, I have lifted up my soul.
  In you, O Lord, I put my trust: let me not be ashamed.

Neither permit my enemies to laugh at me:
  for no one who hopes in you shall be confounded.
But let all those be confounded
  who do unjustly, without cause.

Show me, Lord, your ways,
  and teach me your paths.
Direct me in your truth, and teach me:
  for you are God my Saviour:
  I have waited for you all the day long.

Remember your compassion, O Lord,
  and your mercies which have been
  since the beginning of the world.

Do not remember the sins of my youth, nor my failings:
  but remember me according to your mercy,
  for the sake of your goodness, O Lord.

The Lord is sweet and upright:
  therefore he will lead sinners in the way.
He will guide the mild in judgement,
  he will teach the meek his ways.

All the ways of the Lord are mercy and truth,
  to those who keep his covenant and testimonies.
For your name's sake, Lord, pardon my sin:
  for it is great.
Who is the man who fears the Lord?
  He will instruct him in the way he has chosen.
His soul shall dwell in good things:
  and his descendents shall inherit the land.

The Lord is close to those who fear him:
  and his covenant shall be shown to them.
My eyes are ever on the Lord
  for it is he who plucks my feet out from the snare.

Look upon me and have mercy on me,
  for I am alone and poor.
The troubles of my heart have increased:
  deliver me from my difficulties.
See my abjectness and my labour:
  and forgive me all my sins.

Look at all my enemies! They are grown greater
    and hate me with an unjust hatred.
Keep my soul and deliver me:
    I shall not be ashamed, for I have hoped in you.
The innocent and the upright have adhered to me,
    because I have waited for you.

Deliver Israel, O Lord,
    from all his tribulations.

Eternal rest grant unto them, O Lord,
    and let perpetual light shine on them.

Ant. Lord, do not remember the sins of my youth.

Short reading   *Job 19:23-6*

W HO will grant that my words be written? Who will grant
    me that they be inscribed in a book? Or with an iron pen
on a plate of lead, or else be graven in flint? For I know that my
Redeemer lives, and on the last day I will rise out of the earth;
and I shall be clothed again with my skin, and in my flesh I shall
see my God.

The Benedictus

Luke 1:68-79

B LESSED ✠ be the Lord, the God of Israel,
    who has visited and redeemed his people,
    and has lifted up a horn of salvation for us
in the family of his servant David.
For this he swore through the mouths of holy men:
    those who were prophets, from the beginning:
There would be salvation from our foes,
    and from the hand of all those who hate us;
to comfort our fathers,
    and to honour his holy covenant,
which oath once he swore to Abraham, our father,
    that he would grant us,
that freed from the hand of our enemies,
    and without fear, we may serve him,
        in holiness and justice in his very presence all our days.

And you, my son, will be named Prophet of the Most High;
for you will go before the presence of the Lord
to prepare his way,
to teach knowledge of salvation to his people
that their sins may be forgiven,
through the merciful heart of our God,
when the Daystar shall visit us from on high
to enlighten those who sit in darkness
and in the shadow of death,
and guide our feet to the way of peace.

Eternal rest grant unto them, O Lord,
and let perpetual light shine on them.

Intercessions   *Either these, or others at choice or need.*

Grant rest to those we love who have died. *(pause for prayer)*
R̷. Lord, hear us in your love.
Give us greater faith in the resurrection. *(pause)* **R̷.**
Help us to face our own death with courage and faith. *(pause)* **R̷.**
Bless and strengthen those who work with the dying. *(pause)* **R̷.**

Lord, have mercy.
Christ, have mercy.
Lord, have mercy.

Our Father…

Collects for special categories of people, see p. 380
otherwise:

Let us pray.

O LORD, whose nature it is to have mercy and spare, we
humbly beg your mercy on the souls of the faithful departed,
that through your mercy and our feeble prayers, they may attain
to that glory which they have always desired. Through Christ our
Lord. Amen.

V̷. Let us bless the Lord.
R̷. Thanks be to God.

ʘ   ʘ   ʘ

Terce

℣. O God, ✠ come to my assistance.
℟. O Lord, be swift to my aid.
℣. Glory be to the Father, and to the Son, and to the Holy Spirit.
**℟. As it was in the beginning, is now and ever shall be,
    world without end. Amen.**

HEAR what the voice from Heaven proclaims
For all the pious dead:
Sweet is the savour of their names,
And soft their sleeping bed.

Far from this world of toil and strife,
In going to their Lord,
The labours of their mortal life
End in a large reward.

Isaac Watts alt.

Ant. The Lord keeps trust for ever.

Psalm 145

PRAISE the Lord, O my soul:
I will praise the Lord while I yet live,
I will sing to my God as long as I shall be.

Put not your trust in princes,
in the children of men,
in whom there is no salvation.
For when the breath of man goes forth,
he returns unto the earth;
and on that day all his thoughts shall perish.

But blessed is the one
who has the God of Jacob as his helper,
whose hope is in the Lord his God,
Who made the heavens and the earth,
the seas and all things that are in them,
Who keeps truth for ever,
who does justly for those that suffer wrong,
who gives food to the hungry.

The Lord looses those who are fettered;
   the Lord enlightens the blind.
The Lord lifts up those who are cast down,
   the Lord loves the just.

The Lord shelters the strangers,
   he supports the fatherless and the widow,
   but the ways of sinners he will destroy.
The Lord will reign for ever:
   your God, O Sion, for generation unto generation.

Eternal rest grant unto them, O Lord,
   and let perpetual light shine on them.

Ant. The Lord keeps trust for ever.

Short reading   *1 Thessalonians 4:12-14*

A ND we will not have you ignorant, brethren, concerning
those who are asleep, that you may not sorrow as others
who have no hope. For if we believe that Jesus died and rose
again, so, through Jesus, God will bring with him those who sleep.

Collects for special categories of people, see p.380
otherwise:

Let us pray.

O LORD, whose nature it is to have mercy and spare, we
humbly beg your mercy on the souls of the faithful departed,
that through your mercy and our feeble prayers, they may attain
to that glory which they have always desired. Through Christ our
Lord. Amen.

℣. Let us bless the Lord.
℟. Thanks be to God.

ༀ   ༀ   ༀ

Sext

℣. O God, ✠ come to my assistance.
℟. O Lord, be swift to my aid.
℣. Glory be to the Father, and to the Son, and to the Holy Spirit.
**℟. As it was in the beginning, is now and ever shall be,
    world without end. Amen.**

JESU, Son of Mary,
    Fount of life alone
Oft we hail thee present
On thine altar-throne.
Humbly we adore thee,
Lord of endless might,
In the mystic symbols
Veiled from earthly sight.

Often were they wounded
In the deadly strife;
Heal them, good Physician,
With the balm of life,
Every taint of evil,
Frailty and decay,
Good and gracious Saviour,
Cleanse and purge away.

Think, O Lord, in mercy
On the souls of those
Who, in faith gone from us,
Now in death repose.
Here 'mid stress and conflict
Toils can never cease;
There, the warfare ended,
Bid them rest in peace.

Rest eternal grant them,
After weary fight;
Shed on them the radiance
Of thy heavenly light.
Lead them onward, upward,
To the holy place,
Where thy saints made perfect
Gaze upon thy face.

Yesu Bin Mariamu

Ant. Lord, you have delivered my soul that it should not perish.

Isaiah 38:10-20

I SAID: In the midst of my days
    I shall go to the gates of the dead.
    I sought for the residue of my years.

I said: After all, I shall not see the Lord God
    in the land of the living!
So I shall behold man no more,
    among the inhabitants of the world.

My generation is now at an end,
    and it is rolled away from me,
    as a shepherd's tent.
My life is cut off, as by a weaver:
    while I was yet but beginning he cut me off.
From morning until night
    you will make an end of me.

I hoped until morning,
    but as a lion so has he broken all my bones,
and from morning till night
    you will make an end of me.

I will cry like a young swallow,
    I will groan like a dove:
    my eyes are weakened from looking upward.
Lord, I suffer violently:
    then answer me!

What shall I say, or what can be an answer,
    when he himself has done this?
I will recount to you all my years
    in the bitterness of my soul.

O Lord, if man's life be such,
    and if the life of my spirit be in such things as these,
    you must correct me and make me live.
For behold, when I am at peace
    is my bitterness most bitter.

But you have delivered my soul,
    that it should not perish:
    you have cast all my sins behind your back.
For Hell shall not acknowledge you,
    neither shall death praise you,
nor shall those who go down to the pit
    look for your truth.

The living, the living shall give praise to you,
    as I do this day:
the father shall make your truth known
    to his children.

O Lord, save me,
 and we will sing our psalms all the days of our life
 in the house of the Lord.

Eternal rest grant unto them, O Lord,
 and let perpetual light shine on them.

Ant. Lord, you have delivered my soul that it should not perish.

Short reading
Wisdom 1:13-15

FOR GOD has not made death, neither has he any pleasure in
the destruction of the living. For he created all things that
they might be, and he made the nations of the earth for health;
and there is no poison of destruction in them, nor Kingdom of
Hell upon earth. For justice is perpetual and immortal.

Collects for special categories of people, see p.380
otherwise:

Let us pray.

O LORD, whose nature it is to have mercy and spare, we
humbly beg your mercy on the souls of the faithful departed,
that through your mercy and our feeble prayers, they may attain
to that glory which they have always desired. Through Christ our
Lord. Amen.

℣. Let us bless the Lord.
℟. Thanks be to God.

None

℣. O God, ✠ come to my assistance.
℟. O Lord, be swift to my aid.
℣. Glory be to the Father, and to the Son, and to the Holy Spirit.
**℟. As it was in the beginning, is now and ever shall be,
world without end. Amen.**

O LORD, to whom the spirits live
　　Of all the faithful passed away,
Upon their path that brightness give
Which shineth to the perfect day.

O Light eternal, Jesu blest,
Shine on them all, and give them rest.

Direct us with thine arm of might
And bring us perfected with them
To dwell within thy city bright,
The heavenly Jerusalem.

O Light eternal, Jesu blest,
Shine on them all, and give them rest.

R.F. Littledale

Ant. Turn again, O Lord, and set my soul free.

Psalm 69

O GOD come to my assistance,
　　O Lord, make haste to help me.
Let them be confounded and ashamed
　　that seek my soul.

Let them be turned backward and blush for shame
　　that desire evils to me.
Let them be directly turned away in confusion
　　that say to me: It is well, it is well!

Let all that seek you rejoice
　　and be glad in you;
and let such as love your salvation say always:
　　The Lord be glorified!

But I am needy and poor:
O God, help me!
You are my helper and my deliverer;
O Lord, make no delay.

Eternal rest grant unto them, O Lord,
and let perpetual light shine on them.

Ant. Turn again, O Lord, and set my soul free.

Short reading

Isaiah 25:6-8

A ND the Lord of hosts will make for all peoples on this mountain a feast of fat things, a feast of wine, of fat things full of
marrow, of wine purified from the lees. And he will destroy on
this mountain the bond that ties all peoples, the web that is cast
over all nations. He will throw down death headlong for ever,
and the Lord God will wipe away tears from every face, and the
reproach of his people he shall take away from off the whole
earth; for the Lord has spoken it.

Collects for special categories of people, see p.380
otherwise:

Let us pray.

O LORD, whose nature it is to have mercy and spare, we
humbly beg your mercy on the souls of the faithful departed,
that through your mercy and our feeble prayers, they may attain
to that glory which they have always desired. Through Christ our
Lord. Amen.

℣. Let us bless the Lord.
℟. Thanks be to God.

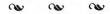

Vespers

℣. O God, ✠ come to my assistance.
℟. O Lord, be swift to my aid.
℣. Glory be to the Father, and to the Son, and to the Holy Spirit.
℟. As it was in the beginning, is now and ever shall be, world without end. Amen.

GIVE rest, O Christ,
to thy servants with thy saints:
where sorrow and pain are no more,
neither sighing, but life everlasting.

Thou only art immortal,
the Creator and maker of man,
and we are mortal, formed of the earth
and unto earth shall we return.

For so thou didst ordain
when thou createdst us, saying:
'Dust thou art and unto dust thou shalt return.'
All we go down to the dust;
but weeping o'er the grave we make our song:

Alleluia! Alleluia! Alleluia!

Kontakion of the Departed

Ant. You will turn, O God, and bring us to life.

Psalm 84

LORD, you have blessed your land,
you have reversed the captivity of Jacob.
You have forgiven the iniquity of your people,
you have covered all their sins.

You have mitigated all your anger,
you have turned away
from the wrath of your indignation.
Convert us, O God our Saviour,
and turn away your anger from us.

Will you be angry with us for ever:
will you extend your wrath
from generation to generation?

Will you not turn, O God, and bring us to life:
    and your people shall rejoice in you.
Show us, O Lord, your mercy,
    and grant us your salvation.

I will hear what the Lord has to say to me:
    for he will speak peace to his people,
and to his saints,
    and to those who are converted in the heart.

Surely, his salvation is near
    to those who fear him:
    that glory may dwell in our land.
Mercy and truth have met each other:
    justice and peace have kissed.
Truth has sprung out of the earth,
    and justice has looked down from Heaven.

For the Lord will bestow goodness,
    and our earth shall yield her fruit.
Justice shall walk before him,
    and shall set his steps on their way.

Eternal rest grant unto them, O Lord,
    and let perpetual light shine on them.

Ant. You will turn, O God, and bring us to life.

Short reading   *1 Corinthians 15:20-22*

B UT NOW Christ is risen from the dead, the first fruits
of those who sleep. For as by a man came death, so by a
man has come the resurrection of the dead. For as in Adam all
die, so also in Christ all shall be made alive.

The Magnificat

Luke 1:46-55

M Y ✠ SOUL magnifies the Lord,
    my spirit rejoices in God who is my Saviour,
    who has looked upon the humility of his handmaiden.
Behold, all generations from now
    will acknowledge me blessed,
For the mighty one has done great things for me:
    Holy is his name!

His mercy is from one generation to the next on those who fear him.
  Mighty is his arm!
He has scattered the proud in the imagination of their hearts,
  and has put down the powerful from their thrones,
  exalting those of humble degree.
The hungry he has filled with good things,
  but the rich he has dismissed with nothing.
Remembering his mercy, he has helped his servant Israel,
  as he promised to our fathers,
  to Abraham and to his posterity for ever more.

Eternal rest grant unto them, O Lord,
  and let perpetual light shine on them.

Intercessions   *Either these, or others at choice or need.*

Grant resurrection to those who sleep in death. *(Pause for prayer)*
  ℟. **Lord, bring us to life in your name.**
Give pardon and mercy to the dead in Purgatory. *(Pause)* ℟.
Give the gift of faith to those who have none. *(Pause)* ℟.
Grant rest to those we love *(N. & N.)* who have died. *(Pause)* ℟.

> Lord, have mercy.
> Christ, have mercy.
> Lord, have mercy.

> Our Father...

Collects for special categories of people, see p.380
otherwise:

Let us pray.

O LORD, whose nature it is to have mercy and spare, we
humbly beg your mercy on the souls of the faithful departed,
that through your mercy and our feeble prayers, they may attain
to that glory which they have always desired. Through Christ our
Lord. Amen.

> ℣. Let us bless the Lord.
> ℟. **Thanks be to God.**

∽   ∽   ∽

Compline

℣. O God, ✠ come to my assistance.
℟. O Lord, be swift to my aid.
℣. Glory be to the Father, and to the Son, and to the Holy Spirit.
**℟. As it was in the beginning, is now and ever shall be,
world without end. Amen.**

B EFORE the ending of the day,
Creator of the world, we pray
That with thy wonted favour thou
Wouldst be our guard and keeper now.

From all ill dreams defend our eyes,
From nightly fears and fantasies;
Tread under foot our ghostly foe,
That no pollution we may know.

O Father, that we ask be done,
Through Jesus Christ, thine only Son;
Who, with the Holy Ghost and thee,
Doth live and reign eternally. Amen.

Te lucis ante terminum

Ant. Into your hands, O Lord, I commend my spirit.

Psalm 129

O ut of the depths I have cried to you, O Lord:
Lord, hear my voice!
Let your ears be attentive to the voice of my supplication.

If you, O Lord, will mark iniquities,
Lord, who could stand it?
But with you is merciful forgiveness,
that we should revere you.

I have relied upon you, O Lord;
>my soul has relied on his word.
My soul has hoped in the Lord,
>more than watchman for the dawn.

More than watchman for the dawn
>let Israel hope in the Lord
Because with the Lord there is mercy
>and with him plentiful redemption.
And he shall redeem Israel
>from all its iniquities.

Eternal rest grant unto them, O Lord,
>and let perpetual light shine on them.

Ant. Into your hands, O Lord, I commend my spirit.

Short reading

Revelation 22:4-5

THEY shall see the Lord's face, and his name shall be on their foreheads. And night shall be no more; they shall not need the light of the lamp nor the light of the sun, for the Lord God shall enlighten them, and they shall reign for ever and ever.

The Nunc Dimittis

Luke 2:29-32

Ant. Save us, O Lord, while we wake, and watch over us as we sleep, that we may pass the night with Christ and rest in peace.

LORD, ✠ now let your servant depart in peace,
>according to your promise;
>for my eyes have seen your salvation
which you have prepared in the presence of all peoples,
a light for revelation to the Gentiles,
>and for glory to your people Israel.

Eternal rest grant unto them, O Lord,
>and let perpetual light shine on them.

Ant. Save us, O Lord, while we wake, and watch over us as we sleep, that we may pass the night with Christ and rest in peace.

Let us pray.

V ISIT this house, O Lord, we pray, and drive far from it the
    deadly power of the enemy. May your holy angels dwell
here instead, that we may be preserved in peace, with your blessing on us always. Through Christ our Lord. Amen.

Antiphon in honour of our Lady, pp.341ff.
or:

W E FLY to thy patronage, holy Mother of God.
    Despise not our petitions in our necessities
But deliver us from every evil,
O glorious and blessed Virgin.

ɷ   ɷ   ɷ

THE GREATER FEASTS OF SAINTS

Vigils

℣. O Lord, ✠ open my lips.
℞. And my mouth shall declare your praise.

Antiphon Blessed is the one whose will is the law of the Lord.

Psalm 1

BLESSED is the man who does not abide
in the council of the ungodly,
nor stand in the way of sinners,
nor sit in the company of scoffers,
but whose will is in the law of the Lord
and on his law meditates day and night.

And he shall be like a tree
which is planted near running waters,
which shall bring forth its fruit in due season,
and whose leaves shall not fall.
Whatsoever he shall do shall prosper.

Not so the wicked, not so,
but they shall be like the dust
which the wind drives from the face of the earth.
Therefore the wicked shall not rise again in judgement,
nor sinners in the council of the just.

For the Lord knows the way of the just,
and the way of the wicked shall perish.

Glory be…

Antiphon Blessed is the one whose will is the law of the Lord.

℣. The Lord shall lead them in a straight way,
℞. And show them the Kingdom of God.

First reading

One chapter from the scriptures.

Response to the reading

℣. Whoever is baptized in Christ has put on Christ;
℟. **You are all one in Christ Jesus.**
℣. Neither Jew nor Greek, neither male nor female;
℟. **You are all one in Christ Jesus.**

Second reading

Spiritual reading.

Response to the reading

℣. You are light in the Lord: walk as children of the light;
℟. **And the fruit of the light is goodness, justice and truth.**
℣. You are the light of the world: let your light shine!
℟. **And the fruit of the light is goodness, justice and truth.**

Let us pray.

O GOD, who alone are holy, and without whom nothing is good, by the intercession of Saint N. grant that we may, by imitating *his/her* virtues become like *him/her,* whose feast we celebrate with joy. Through Christ our Lord. Amen.

℣. Let us bless the Lord.
℟. **Thanks be to God.**

Lauds

℣. O God, ✠ come to my assistance.
℟. **O Lord, be swift to my aid.**
℣. Glory be to the Father, and to the Son, and to the Holy Spirit.
℟. **As it was in the beginning, is now and ever shall be, world without end. Amen.**

FOR ALL the Saints, who from their labours rest,
Who thee by faith before the world confessed
Thy name, O Jesus, be for ever blest.
   Alleluya!

O may thy soldiers, faithful, true and bold,
Fight as the Saints who nobly fought of old,
And win, with them, the victor's crown of gold.
   Alleluya!

O blest communion! fellowship divine!
We feebly struggle, they in glory shine;
Yet all are one in thee, for all are thine.
   Alleluya!

But lo! there breaks a yet more glorious day;
The Saints triumphant rise in bright array:
The King of Glory passes on his way.
   Alleluya!

From earth's wide bounds, from ocean's farthest coast,
Through gates of pearl streams in the countless host,
Singing to Father, Son and Holy Ghost.
   Alleluya!

W.W. How

Ant. The saints shall rejoice in glory.

Psalm 149

SING to the Lord a new song,
let his praise be sung in the assembly of the saints!

Let Israel rejoice in him that made her,
  and let the children of Sion be joyful in their King.
Let them praise his name in choir,
  and sing to him with timbrel and psaltery.

For the Lord is well pleased with his people:
  he will exalt the meek with salvation.
The saints shall rejoice in their glory,
  they shall be joyful in their beds.

The high praises of God shall be in their mouth:
  and two-edged swords in their hands,
To execute judgement upon the nations,
  chastisements among the people!

To bind their kings with fetters,
  and their nobles with manacles of iron.
To bring upon them the judgement that is written:
  this glory is for all his saints.

Glory be...

> *Ant.* The saints shall rejoice in glory.

Short reading *Romans 12:1-2*

I BESEECH you therefore, brethren, by the mercy of God, that you present your bodies as a living sacrifice, holy and pleasing to God, your reasonable service. Do not be conformed to this world but be reformed by newness of mind, that you may prove what is the good and acceptable and perfect will of God.

The Benedictus

Luke 1:68-79

B LESSED ✠ be the Lord, the God of Israel,
  who has visited and redeemed his people,
  and has lifted up a horn of salvation for us
in the family of his servant David.
For this he swore through the mouths of holy men:
  those who were prophets, from the beginning:
There would be salvation from our foes,
  and from the hand of all those who hate us;
to comfort our fathers,
  and to honour his holy covenant,

which oath once he swore to Abraham, our father,
    that he would grant us,
that freed from the hand of our enemies,
    and without fear, we may serve him,
        in holiness and justice in his very presence all our days.
And you, my son, will be named Prophet of the Most High;
    for you will go before the presence of the Lord
        ᵢto prepare his way,
to teach knowledge of salvation to his people
    that their sins may be forgiven,
        through the merciful heart of our God,
when the Daystar shall visit us from on high
    to enlighten those who sit in darkness
    and in the shadow of death,
        and guide our feet to the way of peace.

Glory be...

Intercessions   *Either these, or others at choice or need.*

Grant that we may come to share in the glory of your saints,
(pause for prayer) ℟. **Lord, may your saints intercede for us.**
Grant that we be heroic in our faith, hope and love. *(pause)* ℟.
May we faithfully meditate on your word, as your saints did.
    (pause) ℟.
Grant that those who invoke the protection of Saint N. may experience *his/her* help. *(pause)* ℟.

Lord, have mercy.
Christ, have mercy.
Lord, have mercy.

Our Father...

Let us pray.

O GOD, who alone are holy, and without whom nothing is good, by the intercession of Saint N. grant that we may, by imitating *his/her* virtues become like *him/her,* whose feast we celebrate with joy. Through Christ our Lord. Amen.

℣. Let us bless the Lord.
℟. **Thanks be to God.**

∾   ∾   ∾

Terce

℣. O God, ✠ come to my assistance.
℞. O Lord, be swift to my aid.
℣. Glory be to the Father, and to the Son, and to the Holy Spirit.
**℞. As it was in the beginning, is now and ever shall be,
world without end. Amen.**

COME, Holy Ghost, with God the Son
And God the Father, ever one;
Shed forth thy grace within our breast
And dwell with us a ready guest.

By every power, by heart and tongue,
By act and deed, thy praise be sung;
Inflame with perfect love each sense
That others' souls may kindle thence.

O Father, that we ask be done,
Through Jesus Christ, thine only Son;
Who, with the Holy Ghost and thee,
Doth live and reign eternally. Amen.

Nunc nobis, Sancte Spiritus

Ant. Blessed is the man who fears the Lord.

Psalm 111

BLESSED is the man who fears the Lord;
    he will delight greatly in his commandments.
His posterity shall be mighty upon earth;
    the generation of the righteous shall be blessed.
Glory and wealth shall be in his house;
    and his justice remains for ever and ever.
For the righteous he is like a lamp risen up in darkness;
    he is merciful, compassionate and just.
Happy is the man who shows pity and lends,
    who orders his affairs with care;
    he shall stand firm for ever.
The just one shall be in everlasting remembrance;
    No evil tidings shall he fear.

His heart is ever ready to hope in the Lord;
>His heart is strong: he shall not be moved
>until he sees the destruction of his enemies.
He has given, given freely to the poor:
>his justice remains for ever and ever:
>his horn shall be raised in glory.
The wicked shall see and be angry,
>he shall gnash his teeth and pine away:
>the desire of the wicked shall perish.

Glory be…

Ant. Blessed is the man who fears the Lord.

Short reading
1 Samuel 16:7

A ND the Lord said to Samuel, 'Do not look on his face nor on the height of his stature…; for the Lord does not see as man sees; man looks on the appearance, but the Lord beholds the heart.'

Let us pray.

O GOD, who alone are holy, and without whom nothing is good, by the intercession of Saint N. grant that we may, by imitating *his/her* virtues become like *him/her,* whose feast we celebrate with joy. Through Christ our Lord. Amen.

℣. Let us bless the Lord.
℟. Thanks be to God.

∾   ∾   ∾

Sext

℣. O God, ✠ come to my assistance.
℟. O Lord, be swift to my aid.
℣. Glory be to the Father, and to the Son, and to the Holy Spirit.
**℟. As it was in the beginning, is now and ever shall be,
world without end. Amen.**

O GOD of truth, O Lord of might,
Who orderest time and change aright,
And send'st the early morning ray,
And light'st the glow of perfect day:

Extinguish thou each sinful fire,
And banish every ill desire;
And while thou keep'st the body whole,
Shed forth thy peace upon the soul.

O Father, that we ask be done,
Through Jesus Christ, thine only Son;
Who, with the Holy Ghost and thee,
Doth live and reign eternally. Amen.

Rector potens, verax Deus

Ant. The Lord has given food to those who fear him.

Psalm 110

I WILL praise you, Lord, with my whole heart
in the council of the just, and in the congregation.
Great are the works of the Lord:
to be studied by all who love them.
His work is praise and magnificence:
his justice continues for ever and ever.
He has remembered his wonderful works,
being a merciful and gracious Lord:
he has given food to those who fear him.
He will always be mindful of his covenant,
he will show to his people the power of his works,
that he may give them the inheritance of the nations.

The works of his hands are truth and justice,
> All his commands are faithful, firm for ever more,
> made in truth and equity.
He has sent redemption to his people:
> he has commanded his covenant for ever.
Holy and terrible is his name:
> the fear of the Lord is the beginning of wisdom,
Well understood by all who observe it:
> his praise endures for ever and ever.

Glory be…

Ant. The Lord has given food to those who fear him.

Short reading

Isaiah 66:1-2

T HUS says the Lord: 'Heaven is my throne and the earth is my footstool; what is the house which you will build for me, and what is this place of my rest? My hand has made all these things, and so all these things are mine, says the Lord. But whom will I respect? The one that is poor and little, contrite in spirit, and who trembles at my word.'

Let us pray.

O GOD, who alone are holy, and without whom nothing is good, by the intercession of Saint N. grant that we may, by imitating *his/her* virtues become like *him/her,* whose feast we celebrate with joy. Through Christ our Lord. Amen.

℣. Let us bless the Lord.
℟. Thanks be to God.

None

℣. O God, ✠ come to my assistance.
℟. **O Lord, be swift to my aid.**
℣. Glory be to the Father, and to the Son, and to the Holy Spirit.
℟. **As it was in the beginning, is now and ever shall be,**
    world without end. Amen.

O GOD, Creation's secret force,
  Thyself unmoved, all motion's source,
Who from the morn till evening ray
Through all its changes guid'st the day:

Grant us, when this short life is past,
The glorious evening that shall last;
That, by a holy death attained,
Eternal glory may be gained.

O Father, that we ask be done,
Through Jesus Christ, thine only Son;
Who, with the Holy Ghost and thee,
Doth live and reign eternally. Amen.

Rerum Deus tenax vigor

Ant. The just shall dwell in the tent of the Lord.

Psalm 14

L ORD, who shall dwell in your tent?
  Or who shall rest on your holy hill?
He that walks without blemish,
    He whose works are just.
He that speaks truth in his heart,
    and has not used deceit with his tongue,
nor has done evil to his neighbour,
    nor taken up a quarrel with his friend.
In his sight, malignancy is brought to nothing,
    but he glorifies those who fear the Lord.

He keeps his oaths to his neighbours, though it hurt him,
    he does not put his money to usury
    not take bribes against the innocent.
Whoever does these things shall stand firm for ever more.

Glory be...

Ant. The just shall dwell in the tent of the Lord.

Short reading   *Philippians 4:8-9*

FOR THE rest, brethren, whatever is true, whatever modest, whatever just, whatever holy, whatever lovely, whatever of good repute, if there is any virtue, if there is anything worthy of praise, think on these things. The things which you have learned and received and heard and seen in me, do; and the God of peace shall be with you.

Let us pray.

O GOD, who alone are holy, and without whom nothing is good, by the intercession of Saint N. grant that we may, by imitating *his/her* virtues become like *him/her,* whose feast we celebrate with joy. Through Christ our Lord. Amen.

        ℣. Let us bless the Lord.
        ℞. Thanks be to God.

Vespers

℣. O God, ✠ come to my assistance.
℟. **O Lord, be swift to my aid.**
℣. Glory be to the Father, and to the Son, and to the Holy Spirit.
℟. **As it was in the beginning, is now and ever shall be, world without end. Amen.**

G IVE me the wings of faith to rise
    Within the veil, and see
The saints above, how great their joys,
    How bright their glories be.

Once they were mourning here below,
    And wet their couch with tears;
They wrestled hard, as we do now,
    With sins, and doubts, and fears.

I ask them whence their victory came;
    They, with united breath,
Ascribe their conquest to the Lamb,
    Their triumph to his death.

Our glorious Leader claims our praise
    For his own pattern given;
While the long cloud of witnesses
    Show the same path to Heaven.

Isaac Watts

Ant. Let every spirit praise the Lord.

Psalm 150

P RAISE the Lord in his holy place:
    praise him in the firmament of his power.
Praise him for his mighty acts,
    praise him according to the excellence of his greatness.

Praise him with the sound of trumpet,
    praise him with psaltery and harp.
Praise him with timbrel and choir,
    praise him with strings and organs.

Praise him on well-sounding cymbals,
praise him on cymbals of joy.

Let everything that breathes praise the Lord!

Glory be...

Ant. Let every spirit praise the Lord.

Short reading   *Romans 8:28-30*

WE KNOW that to those who love God, all things work together for good, to such as, according to his purpose, are
called to be saints. For those whom he foreknew he also predestined to be conformed to the image of his Son, in order that he
might be the first-born among many brethren. And those whom
he predestined he also called; and those whom he called he also
justified; and those whom he justified he also glorified.

The Magnificat

Luke 1:46-55

MY ✠ SOUL magnifies the Lord,
my spirit rejoices in God who is my Saviour,
who has looked upon the humility of his handmaiden.
Behold, all generations from now
will acknowledge me blessed,
For the mighty one has done great things for me:
Holy is his name!
His mercy is from one generation to the next on those who fear him.
Mighty is his arm!
He has scattered the proud in the imagination of their hearts,
and has put down the powerful from their thrones,
exalting those of humble degree.
The hungry he has filled with good things,
but the rich he has dismissed with nothing.
Remembering his mercy, he has helped his servant Israel,
as he promised to our fathers,
to Abraham and to his posterity for ever more.

Glory be...

Intercessions.   *Either these, or others at choice or need.*

Grant us strength to pursue holiness of life. *(pause for prayer)* ℟.
  Lord, make us holy as you are holy.
Make us more effective witnesses to your Kingdom. *(pause)* ℟.
Send us more saints, Lord, to tell us of your Kingdom. *(pause)* ℟.
Admit to the company of your saints those we love who have
  died. *(pause)* ℟.

Lord, have mercy.
Christ, have mercy.
Lord, have mercy.

Our Father…

Let us pray.

O GOD, who alone are holy, and without whom nothing
  is good, by the intercession of Saint N. grant that we may,
by imitating *his/her* virtues become like *him/her,* whose feast we
celebrate with joy. Through Christ our Lord. Amen.

℣. Let us bless the Lord.
℟. **Thanks be to God.**

COMPLINE
all as on Sunday, p.19

DEVOTIONS

THE SEVEN PENITENTIAL PSALMS

These seven psalms have long been used by the Christian to express penitence at any time that it seems appropriate: before or after Confession, for instance, or on the days of penance: Fridays and the whole season of Lent. They are given here in the traditional Douai-Challoner version.

Antiphon: Remember not, O Lord, our offences, nor those of our parents, and take not revenge of our sins.

Psalm 6

Domine, ne in furore

O Lord, rebuke me not in thine indignation,
   nor chastise me in thy wrath.
   Have mercy on me, O Lord, for I am weak;
heal me, O Lord, for my bones are troubled.
And my soul is troubled exceedingly;
   but thou, O Lord, how long ?
Turn to me, O Lord, and deliver my soul:
   oh, save me for thy mercy's sake.
For there is no one in death that is mindful of thee;
   and who shall acknowledge thee in hell ?
I have laboured in my groanings;
   every night I will wash my bed,
   I will water my couch with my tears.
Mine eyes are troubled through indignation;
   I have grown old amongst all mine enemies.
Depart from me, all ye workers of iniquity;
   for the Lord hath heard the voice of my weeping.
The Lord hath heard my supplication;
   the Lord hath received my prayer.
Let all mine enemies be ashamed,
   and be very much troubled;
   let them be turned back
   and be ashamed very speedily.

Glory be…

Psalm 21

Beati quorum

B lessed are they whose iniquities are forgiven,
and whose sins are covered.
Blessed is the man to whom the Lord hath not imputed sin,
and in whose spirit there is no guile.
Because I was silent, my bones grew old;
whilst I cried out all the day long.
For day and night thy hand was heavy upon me;
I am turned in mine anguish, whilst the thorn is fastened.
I have acknowledged my sin to thee;
and mine injustice I have not concealed.
I said, I will confess against myself mine injustice to the Lord;
and thou hast forgiven the wickedness of my sin.
For this shall every one that is holy pray to thee:
in a seasonable time.
And yet in a flood of many waters,
they shall not come nigh unto him.
Thou art my refuge from the trouble which hath encompassed me;
my joy, deliver me from them that surround me.
I will give thee understanding,
and I will instruct thee in this way in which thou shalt go:
I will fix mine eyes upon thee.
Do not become like the horse and the mule,
which have no understanding.
With bit and bridle bind fast their jaws,
who come not near unto thee.
Many are the scourges of the sinner;
but mercy shall encompass him that hopeth in the Lord.
Be glad in the Lord, and rejoice, ye just;
and glory, all ye right of heart.

Glory be…

Psalm 37

Domine, ne in furore

R ebuke me not, O Lord, in thine indignation;
nor chastise me in thy wrath.

For thine arrows are fastened in me,
  and thy hand hath been strong upon me.
There is no health in my flesh, because of thy wrath;
  there is no peace for my bones, because of my sins.
For mine iniquities are gone over my head;
  and as a heavy burden, are become heavy upon me.
My sores are putrefied and corrupted,
  because of my foolishness.
I am become miserable, and am bowed down even to the end:
  I walked sorrowful all the day long.
For my loins are filled with illusions;
  and there is no health in my flesh.
I am afflicted and humbled exceedingly;
  I roared with the groaning of my heart.
Lord, all my desire is before thee;
  and my groaning is not hidden from thee.
My heart is troubled, my strength hath left me;
  and the light of mine eyes itself is not with me.
My friends and my neighbours have drawn near,
  and have stood against me.
And they that were near me stood afar off;
  and they that sought my soul used violence.
And they that sought evils to me spoke vain things;
  and studied deceits all the day long.
But I, as a deaf man, heard not;
  and was as a dumb man, not opening his mouth.
And I became as a man that heareth not;
  and that hath no reproofs in his mouth.
For in thee, O Lord, have I hoped:
  thou wilt hear me, O Lord my God.
For I said, lest at any time mine enemies rejoice over me;
  and whilst my feet are moved,
    they speak great things against me.
For I am ready for scourges;
  and my sorrow is continually before me.
For I will declare mine iniquity;
  and I will think for my sin.
But mine enemies live, and are stronger than I;
  and they that hate me wrongfully are multiplied.
They that render evil for good have detracted me,
  because I followed goodness.

Forsake me not, O Lord my God:
>   do not thou depart from me.
Attend unto my help,
>   O Lord, the God of my salvation.

Glory be…

Psalm 50

Miserere

Have mercy on me, O God, according to thy great mercy;
and according to the multitude of thy tender mercies
>   blot out mine iniquity.
Wash me yet more from mine iniquity,
>   and cleanse me from my sin.
For I know mine iniquity,
>   and my sin is always before me.
To thee only have I sinned,
>   and have done evil before thee;
that thou mayest be justified in thy words,
>   and mayest overcome when thou art judged.
For behold I was conceived in iniquities;
>   and in sins did my mother conceive me.
For behold, thou hast loved truth;
>   the uncertain and hidden things of thy wisdom
>   thou hast made manifest to me.
Thou shalt sprinkle me with hyssop, and I shall be cleansed;
>   thou shalt wash me, and I shall be made whiter than snow.
To my hearing thou shalt give joy and gladness;
>   and the bones that have been humbled shall rejoice.
Turn away thy face from my sins,
>   and blot out all mine iniquities.
Create a clean heart in me, O God,
>   and renew a right spirit within me.
Cast me not away from thy face,
>   and take not thy Holy Spirit from me.
Restore unto me the joy of thy saving mercy,
>   and strengthen me with a perfect spirit.
I will teach the unjust thy ways;
>   and the wicked shall be converted to thee.

Deliver me from the guilt of blood,
 O God, thou God of my salvation;
 and my tongue shall extol thy justice.
O Lord, thou wilt open my lips;
 and my mouth shall declare thy praise.
For if thou hadst desired sacrifice,
 I would indeed have given it;
 with burnt-offerings thou wilt not be delighted.
A sacrifice to God is an afflicted spirit:
 a contrite and humble heart, O God, thou wilt not despise.
Deal favourably, O Lord, in thy good will with Sion,
 that the walls of Jerusalem may be built up.
Then shalt thou accept the sacrifice of justice,
 oblations, and whole burnt-offerings;
 then shall they lay calves upon thine altar.

Glory be…

Psalm 101

Domine, exaudi

Hear, O Lord, my prayer,
 and let my cry come unto thee.
Turn not away thy face from me;
 in the day when I am in trouble,
 incline thine ear to me.
In whatever day I shall call upon thee,
 hear me speedily.
For my days are vanished like smoke;
 and my bones are grown dry like fuel for the fire.
I am smitten as grass, and my heart is withered,
 because I forgot to eat my bread.
Through the voice of my groaning,
 my bone hath cleaved to my flesh.
I am become like a pelican of the wilderness;
 I am like a night raven in the house.
I have watched and am become as a sparrow,
 all alone on the house top.
All the day long mine enemies reproached me,
 and they that praised me did swear against me.
For I did eat ashes like bread,
 and mingled my drink with weeping.

Because of thine anger and indignation;
    for having lifted me up thou hast thrown me down.
My days have declined like a shadow,
    and I am withered like grass.
But thou, O Lord, endurest for ever;
    and thy remembrance to all generations.
Thou shalt arise and have mercy on Sion;
    for it is time to have mercy on it, yes, the time is come.
For the stones thereof have pleased thy servants,
    and they shall have pity on the earth thereof.
And the Gentiles shall fear thy name, Lord,
    and all the kings of the earth thy glory.
For the Lord hath built up Sion;
    and he shall be seen in his glory.
He hath had regard to the prayer of the humble;
    and he hath not despised their petition.
Let these things be written unto another generation;
    and the people that shall be created shall praise the Lord.
Because he hath looked forth from his high sanctuary;
    from heaven the Lord hath looked upon the earth.
That he might hear the groans of them that are in fetters;
    that he might release the children of the slain.
That they may declare the Name of the Lord in Sion,
    and his praise in Jerusalem.
When the people assemble together,
    and kings, to serve the Lord,
    he answered them in the way of his strength.
Declare unto me
    the fewness of my days.
Call me not away in the midst of my days;
    thy years are unto generation and generation.
In the beginning, O Lord, thou foundedst the earth;
    and the heavens are the works of thy hands.
They shall perish, but thou remainest;
    and all of them shall grow old like a garment.
And as a vesture thou shalt change them,
    and they shall be changed;
but thou art always the self-same,
    and thy years shall not fail.
The children of thy servants shall continue,
    and their seed shall be directed for ever.

Glory be…

Psalm 129

De profundis

O ut of the depths I have cried to thee, O Lord:
Lord, hear my voice.
Let thine ears be attentive
to the voice of my supplication.
If thou, O Lord, shalt observe iniquities:
Lord, who shall endure it?
For with thee there is merciful forgiveness:
and by reason of thy law
I have waited for thee, O Lord.
My soul hath relied on his word:
my soul hath hoped in the Lord.
From the morning watch even until night,
let Israel hope in the Lord.
Because with the Lord there is mercy,
and with him plentiful redemption.
And he shall redeem Israel
from all his iniquities.

Glory be...

Psalm 142

Domine, exaudi

H ear, O Lord, my prayer;
give ear to my supplication in thy truth;
hear me in thy justice.
And enter not into judgment with thy servant:
for in thy sight no man living shall be justified.
For the enemy hath persecuted my soul;
he hath brought down my life to the earth.
He hath made me to dwell in darkness,
as those that have been dead of old;
and my spirit is in anguish within me,
my heart within me is troubled.
I remembered the days of old,
I meditated on all thy works;
I mused upon the works of thy hands.

I stretched forth my hands to thee;
> my soul is as earth without water unto thee.

Hear me speedily, O Lord;
> my spirit hath fainted away.

Turn not away thy face from me,
> lest I be like unto them that go down into the pit.

Cause me to hear thy mercy in the morning,
> for in thee have I hoped.

Make the way known to me wherein I should walk;
> for I have lifted up my soul to thee.

Deliver me from mine enemies, O Lord;
> to thee have I fled:
> teach me to do thy will, for thou art my God.

Thy good spirit shall lead me into the right land;
> for thy Name's sake, O Lord,
> Thou wilt quicken me in thy justice.

Thou wilt bring my soul out of trouble;
> and in thy mercy thou wilt destroy mine enemies.

And thou wilt cut off all them that afflict my soul;
> for I am thy servant.

Glory be…

Antiphon: Remember not, O Lord, our offences, nor those of our parents, and take not revenge of our sins.

THE GREAT LITANY *OF* SAINTS

THE Great Litany is associated with some of the most important events in the Christian life: at baptism, at deathbed, at priestly ordination. It is also traditionally sung in procession through the fields on the Rogation days, these being the Monday, Tuesday and Wednesday before Ascension Day.

Kýrie eléison.	*Kýrie eléison.*	Lord, have mercy,	*Lord, have mercy.*
Christe eléison.	*Christe eléison.*	Christ have mercy,	*Christ...*
Kýrie eléison.	*Kýrie eléison.*	Lord have mercy,	*Lord ...*

Pater de cælis Deus,
miserére nobis.
Fili Redémptor mundi Deus,
miserére nobis.
Spíritus Sancte Deus,
miserére nobis.
Sancta Trínitas, unus Deus,
miserére nobis.

God the Father of heaven,
have mercy on us.
God the Son, redeemer of the world,
have mercy on us.
God the Holy Spirit,
have mercy on us.
Holy Trinity, one God,
have mercy on us.

Sancta María,	*ora pro nobis.*	Holy Mary,	*pray for us.*
Sancta Dei Génitrix,	*ora pro nobis.*	Holy Mother of God,	*pray for us.*
Sancta Virgo vírginum,	*ora pro nobis.*	Holy Virgin of virgins,	*pray for us.*
Sancti Míchael, Gábriel et Ráphael,	*orate pro nobis.*	Saints Michael, Gabriel and Raphael,	*pray for us.*
Omnes sancti Angeli,	*orate pro nobis.*	All holy Angels,	*pray for us.*

Sancte Abraham,	*ora*	Holy Abraham,	*pray*
Sancte Móyses,	*ora*	Holy Moses,	*pray*
Sancte Elía,	*ora*	Holy Elijah,	*pray*
Sancte Ioánnes Baptísta,	*ora*	Saint John the Baptist,	*pray*
Sancte Ioseph,	*ora*	Saint Joseph,	*pray*
Omnes sancti patriárchæ et prophétæ,	*orate*	All holy patriarchs and prophets,	*pray*

Sancti Petre et Paule,	*orate*	Saints Peter and Paul,	*pray*
Sancte Andréa,	*ora*	Saint Andrew,	*pray*
Sancti Ioánnes et Iacóbe,	*orate*	Saints James and John,	*pray*
Sancte Thoma,	*ora*	Saint Thomas,	*pray*
Sancte Matthǽe,	*ora*	Saint Matthew,	*pray*
Omnes sancti Apóstoli,	*orate*	All holy Apostles,	*pray*
Sancte Luca,	*ora*	Saint Luke,	*pray*

Sancte Marce,	*ora*	Saint Mark,	*pray*
Sancte Bárnaba,	*ora*	Saint Barnabas,	*pray*
Sancta María Magdaléna,	*ora*	Saint Mary Magdalen,	*pray*
Omnes sancti discípuli Dómini,		All holy disciples of the Lord,	
	orate		*pray*
Sancte Stéphane,	*ora*	Saint Stephen,	*pray*
Sancte Ignáti Antiochéne,	*ora*	Saint Ignatius of Antioch,	*pray*
Sancte Polycárpe,	*ora*	Saint Polycarp,	*pray*
Sancte Iustíne,	*ora*	Saint Justin,	*pray*
Sancte Laurénti,	*ora*	Saint Laurence,	*pray*
Sancte Cypriáne,	*ora*	Saint Cyprian,	*pray*
Sancte Bonifáti,	*ora*	Saint Boniface,	*pray*
Sancte Stansláe,	*ora*	Saint Stanislaus,	*pray*
Sancte Thoma Becket,	*ora*	Saint Thomas Becket,	*pray*
Sancti Ioánnes Fisher et Thoma		Saints John Fisher and Thomas	
More,	*orate*	More,	*pray*
Sancte Paule Miki,	*ora*	Saint Paul Miki,	*pray*
Sancti Ioánnes de Brébeuf et Isaac		Saints John de Brébeuf and Isaac	
Jogues,	*orate*	Jogues,	*pray*
Sancte Petre Chanel,	*ora*	Saint Peter Chanel,	*pray*
Sancte Cárole Lwánga,	*ora*	Saint Charles Lwanga,	*pray*
Sanctæ Perpétua et Felícitas,	*orate*	Saints Perpetua and Felicity,	*pray*
Sancta Agnes,	*ora*	Saint Agnes,	*pray*
Sancta María Gorétti,	*ora*	Saint Maria Goretti,	*pray*
Omnes sancti mártyres,	*orate*	All holy martyrs,	*pray*
Sancti Leo et Gregóri,	*orate*	Saints Leo and Gregory,	*pray*
Sancte Ambrósi,	*ora*	Saint Ambrose,	*pray*
Sancte Hierónyme,	*ora*	Saint Jerome,	*pray*
Sancte Augustíne,	*ora*	Saint Augustine,	*pray*
Sancte Athanási,	*ora*	Saint Athanasius,	*pray*
Sancti Basíli et Gregóri		Saints Basil and Gregory	
Nazianzéne,	*orate*	Nazienzen,	*pray*
Sancte Ioánnes Chrysóstome,	*ora*	Saint John Chrysostom,	*pray*
Sancte Martíne,	*ora*	Saint Martin,	*pray*
Sancte Patríci,	*ora*	Saint Patrick,	*pray*
Sancti Cyrílle et Methódi,	*orate*	Saints Cyril and Methodius,	*pray*
Sancte Cárole Borroméo,	*ora*	Saint Charles Borromeo,	*pray*
Sancte Francísce de Sales,	*ora*	Saint Francis de Sales,	*pray*
Sancte Pie Décime,	*ora*	Saint Pius the Tenth,	*pray*
Sancte Antóni,	*ora*	Saint Anthony,	*pray*
Sancte Benedícte,	*ora*	Saint Benedict,	*pray*
Sancte Bernárde,	*ora*	Saint Bernard,	*pray*
Sancti Francísce et Domínice,	*orate*	Saints Francis and Dominic,	*pray*
Sancte Thoma de Aquíno,	*ora*	Saint Thomas Aquinas,	*pray*
Sancte Ignáti de Lóyola,	*ora*	Saint Ignatius of Loyola,	*pray*

Sancte Francísce Xávier,	*ora*	Saint Francis Xavier,	*pray*
Sancte Vincénti de Paul,	*ora*	Saint Vincent de Paul,	*pray*
Sancte Ioánnes María Viánney,	*ora*	Saint John Mary Vianney,	*pray*
Sancte Ioánnes Bosco,	*ora*	Saint John Bosco,	*pray*
Sancta Catharína Senénsis,	*ora*	Saint Catherine of Siena,	*pray*
Sancta Terésia de Avila,	*ora*	Saint Teresa of Avila,	*pray*
Sancta Rosa de Lima,	*ora*	Saint Rose of Lima,	*pray*

Sancte Ludovíce,	*ora*	Saint Louis,	*pray*
Sancta Mónica,	*ora*	Saint Monica,	*pray*
Sancta Elísabetha Hungáriæ,	*ora*	Saint Elizabeth of Hungary,	*pray*
Omnes Sancti et Sanctæ Dei,	*orate*	All holy saints of God,	*pray*

Propítius esto,
    líbera nos, Dómine.

Be merciful: *Lord, deliver us.*

Ab omni malo,
    líbera nos, Dómine.

From all evil,   *Lord, deliver us.*

Ab omni peccáto,   *líbera*

From all sin,   *Lord, deliver us.*

Ab insídiis diáboli,   *líbera*

From the snares of the devil,
    Lord, deliver us.

Ab ira et ódio et omni mala
voluntáte,   *líbera*

From anger, hate and all ill-will,
    Lord, deliver us.

A morte perpétua,   *líbera*

From everlasting death,   *Lord,*

Per incarnatiónem tuam,   *líbera*

By your incarnation,   *Lord,*

Per nativitátem tuam,   *líbera*

By your nativity, *Lord, deliver us.*

Per baptísmum et sanctum
ieiúnium tuum,   *líbera*

By your baptism and holy fast,
    Lord, deliver us.

Per crucem et passiónem tuam,
    líbera

By your cross and passion,
    Lord, deliver us.

Per mortem et sepultúram tuam,
    líbera

By your death and burial,
    Lord, deliver us.

Per sanctam resurrectiónem tuam,
    líbera

By your holy resurrection,
    Lord, deliver us.

Per admirábilem ascensiónem
tuam,   *líbera*

By your wonderful ascension,
    Lord, deliver us.

Per effusiónem Spíritus Sancti,
    líbera

By your pouring out of the Holy
Spirit,   *Lord, deliver us.*

Per gloriósum advéntum tuum,
    líbera

By your glorious second coming,
    Lord, deliver us.

Christe, Fili Dei vivi,
    miserére nobis.

Christ, Son of the living God,
    have mercy on us.

Qui in hunc mundum venísti,
    miserére

Who came into this world,
    have mercy on us.

Qui in cruce pependísti, *miserére*

Who hung upon the cross,
    have mercy on us.

Qui mortem propter nos accepísti,
miserére
Qui in sepúlcro iacuísti, *miserére*

Qui a mórtuis resurrexísti,
miserére
Qui in cælos ascendísti, *miserére*

Qui Spíritum Sanctum in Apóstolos misísti, *miserére*
Qui sedes ad déxteram Patris,
miserére
Qui ventúrus es iudicáre vivos et mórtuos, *miserére*

Ut nobis parcas,
te rogámus, audi nos.
Ut ad veram pæniténtiam nos perdúcere dignéris, *te rogámus*
Ut nosmetípsos in tuo sancto servítio confortáre et conserváre dignéris, *te rogámus*
Ut ómnibus benefactóribus nostris sempitérna bona retríbuas,
te rogámus
Ut fructus terræ dare et conserváre dignéris, *te rogámus*
Ut nobis indúlgeas, *te rogámus*

Ut mentes nostras ad cæléstia desidéria érigas, *te rogámus*
Ut ánimas nostras, fratrum, propinquórum et benefactórum nostrórum ab ætérna damnatióne erípias, *te rogámus*
Ut ómnibus fidélibus defúnctis réquiem ætérnam donáre dignéris,
te rogámus
Ut mundum a peste, fame et bello serváre dignéris, *te rogámus*
Ut cunctis pópulis pacem et veram concórdiam donáre dignéris,
te rogámus
Ut Ecclésiam tuam sanctam régere et conserváre dignéris, *te rogámus*

Who accepted death for our sakes,
have mercy on us.
Who lay buried in the tomb,
have mercy on us.
Who arose from death, *have mercy*

Who ascended to heaven,
have mercy on us.
Who sent the Holy Spirit upon the Apostles, *have mercy on us.*
Who are seated at the right hand of the Father, *have mercy on us.*
Who will come to judge the living and the dead, *have mercy on us.*

That you might spare us,
we beseech you to hear us.
That you might draw us to true penitence, *we beseech*
That you might confirm us in your holy service, *we beseech*

That you might grant all our benefactors eternal reward, *we beseech*

That you might grant us the fruits of the earth, *we beseech*
That you might be patient with us,
we beseech

That you might lift our minds to heavenly things, *we beseech*
That you might free the our souls, and those of our neighbours and benefactors from eternal damnation, *we beseech*
That you might give rest to all the faithful departed, *we beseech*

That you might keep the world from disease, famine and war, *we beseech*
That you might grant to all people peace and true concord, *we beseech*

That you might be pleased to govern and keep your holy Church,
we beseech

Ut domnum apostólicum et omnes ecclesiásticos órdines in sancta religióne conserváre dignéris,
te rogámus

Ut ómnibus in Christum credéntibus unitátem largíri dignéris,   *te rogámus*

Ut omnes hómines ad Evangélii lumen perdúcere dignéris,
te rogámus, audi nos.

That you might be pleased to keep the Pope and all in Holy Orders true in holy religion,   *we beseech*

That you might grant unity to all who believe in Christ, *we beseech*

That you might lead all people to the light of the Gospel,
we beseech you to hear us.

Agnus Dei, qui tollis peccáta mundi,   *miserére nobis.*
Agnus Dei, qui tollis peccáta mundi,   *miserére nobis.*
Agnus Dei, qui tollis peccáta mundi,   *miserére nobis.*

Lamb of God, you take away the sins of the world; *have mercy on us.*
Lamb of God, you take away the sins of the world; *have mercy on us.*
Lamb of God, you take away the sins of the world; *have mercy on us.*

Christe, audi nos.
Christe, audi nos.
Christe, exáudi nos.
Christe, exáudi nos.

Christ, hear us.
Christ, hear us.
Christ, graciously hear us.
Christ, graciously hear us.

Kýrie eléison.
Christe eléison.
Kýrie eléison.

Lord, have mercy.
Christ, have mercy.
Lord, have mercy.

Orémus.

Let us pray.

D EUS, refúgium nostrum et virtus, adésto piis Ecclésiæ tuæ précibus, auctor ipse pietátis, et præsta, ut, quod fidéliter pétimus, efficáciter consequámur. Per Christum Dóminum nostrum.
Amen.

O GOD, our refuge and strength, author of all holiness, hear the holy prayers of your Church, and grant what we faithfully ask. Through Christ our Lord.
Amen.

THE LITANY OF LORETO

T HIS is the best known litany in honour of our Lady, sung during the Middle Ages at the shrine of Loreto. Among many titles of devotion, the litany borrows images from the Old Testament, particularly those involving the manifestations of God, applying them by way of analogy to Mary, who is Theotokos, the God-Bearer.

Kýrie eléison.	*Kýrie eléison.*	Lord, have mercy.	*Lord, have mercy.*
Christe eléison.	*Christe eléison.*	Christ, have mercy.	*Christ, have mercy.*
Kýrie eléison.	*Kýrie eléison.*	Lord, have mercy.	*Lord, have mercy.*

Pater de cælis Deus,
          miserére nobis.
Fili Redémptor mundi Deus,
          miserére nobis.
Spíritus Sancte Deus,
          miserére nobis.
Sancta Trínitas, unus Deus,
          miserére nobis.

God the Father of heaven,
          have mercy on us.
God the Son, redeemer of the
    world,   *have mercy on us.*
God the Holy Spirit,
          have mercy on us.
Holy Trinity, one God,
          have mercy on us.

Sancta María,	*ora pro nobis.*	Holy Mary,	*pray for us.*
Sancta Dei Génitrix,		Holy Mother of God,	*pray*
	ora pro nobis.		
Sancta Virgo vírginum,		Holy Virgin of virgins,	*pray*
Mater Christi,	*ora*	Mother of Christ,	*pray*
Mater divínæ grátiæ,	*ora*	Mother of divine grace,	*pray*
Mater puríssima,	*ora*	Mother most pure,	*pray*
Mater castíssima,	*ora*	Mother most chaste,	*pray*
Mater invioláta,	*ora*	Mother inviolate,	*pray*
Mater intemeráta,	*ora*	Mother undefiled,	*pray*
Mater amábilis,	*ora*	Mother most amiable,	*pray*
Mater admirábilis,	*ora*	Mother most admirable,	*pray*
Mater boni consílii,	*ora*	Mother of good counsel,	*pray*
Mater Creatóris,	*ora*	Mother of our Creator,	*pray*
Mater Salvatóris,	*ora*	Mother of our Saviour,	*pray*
Mater Ecclésiæ,	*ora*	Mother of the Church,	*pray*
Mater Família,	*ora*	Mother of the Family,	*pray*
Virgo prudentíssima,	*ora*	Virgin most prudent,	*pray*
Virgo veneránda,	*ora*	Virgin most venerable,	*pray*
Virgo prædicánda,	*ora*	Virgin most renowned,	*pray*
Virgo potens,	*ora*	Virgin most powerful,	*pray*
Virgo clemens,	*ora*	Virgin most merciful,	*pray*
Virgo fidélis,	*ora*	Virgin most faithful,	*pray*
Spéculum iustítiæ,	*ora*	Mirror of justice,	*pray*
Sedes sapiéntiæ,	*ora*	Seat of wisdom,	*pray*
Causa nostræ lætítiæ,	*ora*	Cause of our joy,	*pray*
Vas spirituále,	*ora*	Spiritual vessel,	*pray*
Vas honorábile,	*ora*	Vessel of honour,	*pray*
Vas insígne devotiónis,	*ora*	Vessel of singular devotion,	*pray*
Rosa mýstica,	*ora*	Mystical rose,	*pray*

Turris Davídica,	*ora*	Tower of David,	*pray*
Turris ebúrnea,	*ora*	Tower of ivory,	*pray*
Domus áurea,	*ora*	House of gold,	*pray*
Fœderis arca,	*ora*	Ark of the covenant,	*pray*
Iánua cæli,	*ora*	Gate of heaven,	*pray*
Stella matutína,	*ora*	Morning star,	*pray*
Salus infirmórum,	*ora*	Health of the sick,	*pray*
Refúgium peccatórum,	*ora*	Refuge of sinners,	*pray*
Consolátrix afflictórum,	*ora*	Comforter of the afflicted,	*pray*
Auxílium Christianórum,	*ora*	Help of Christians,	*pray*
Regína angelórum,	*ora*	Queen of angels,	*pray*
Regína patriarchárum,	*ora*	Queen of patriarchs,	*pray*
Regína prophetárum,	*ora*	Queen of prophets,	*pray*
Regína apostolórum,	*ora*	Queen of apostles,	*pray*
Regína mártyrum,	*ora*	Queen of martyrs,	*pray*
Regína confessórum,	*ora*	Queen of confessors,	*pray*
Regína vírginum,	*ora*	Queen of virgins,	*pray*
Regína sanctórum ómnium,	*ora*	Queen of all saints,	*pray*

Regina sine labe origináli concépta, *ora* — Queen conceived without original sin, *pray*

Regína sacratíssimi Rosárii, *ora* — Queen of the most holy Rosary, *pray*

Regína pacis, *ora* — Queen of peace, *pray*

Agnus Dei, qui tollis peccáta mundi, *parce nobis, Dómine.* — Lamb of God, you take away the sins of the world, *spare us, O Lord.*

Agnus Dei, qui tollis peccáta mundi, *exáudi nos, Dómine.* — Lamb of God, you take away the sins of the world, *graciously hear us, O Lord.*

Agnus Dei, qui tollis peccáta mundi, *miserére nobis.* — Lamb of God, you take away the sins of the world, *have mercy on us.*

Christe, audi nos.
Christe, audi nos.
Christ, hear us.
Christ, hear us.

Christe, exáudi nos.
Christe, exáudi nos.
Christ, graciously hear us.
Christ, graciously hear us.

℣. Ora pro nobis, sancta Dei Génitrix.
℟. Ut digni efficiámur promissiónibus Christi.

℣. Pray for us, O holy Mother of God.
℟. That we may be made worthy of the promises of Christ.

Orémus.

Let us pray.

GRATIAM tuam, quǽsumus, Dómine, méntibus nostris infúnde: ut qui, Angelo nuntiánte, Christi Fílii tui incarnatiónem cognóvimus, per passiónem eius et crucem ad resurrectiónis glóriam perducámur. Per eúndem Christum Dóminum nostrum. Amen.

POUR forth, we beseech thee, O Lord, thy grace into our hearts; that we, to whom the incarnation of Christ, thy Son, was made known by the message of an angel, may, by his passion and cross, be brought to the glory of his resurrection. Through the same Christ our Lord. Amen.

LITANY OF THE SACRED HEART OF JESUS

Lord, have mercy.	*Lord, have mercy.*
Christ, have mercy.	*Christ, have mercy.*
Lord, have mercy.	*Lord, have mercy.*
Christ, hear us.	*Christ, graciously hear us.*
God the Father of heaven,	*Have mercy on us.*
God the Son, Redeemer of the world,	*Have mercy on us.*
God the Holy Ghost,	*Have mercy on us.*
Holy Trinity, one God,	*Have mercy on us.*
Heart of Jesus, Son of the eternal Father,	*Have mercy on us.*
Heart of Jesus, formed by the Holy Ghost in the womb of the Virgin Mother,	*Have mercy on us.*
Heart of Jesus, united hypostatically to the Word of God,	*Have mercy on us.*
Heart of Jesus, infinite in majesty,	*Have mercy on us.*
Heart of Jesus, holy temple of God,	*Have mercy on us.*
Heart of Jesus, tabernacle of the Most High,	*Have mercy on us.*
Heart of Jesus, house of God, and gate of heaven,	*Have mercy on us.*
Heart of Jesus, glowing furnace of charity,	*Have mercy on us.*
Heart of Jesus, abode of justice and love,	*Have mercy on us.*
Heart of Jesus, full of kindness and love,	*Have mercy on us.*
Heart of Jesus, abyss of all virtues,	*Have mercy on us.*
Heart of Jesus, most worthy of all praise,	*Have mercy on us.*
Heart of Jesus, King and centre of all hearts,	*Have mercy on us.*
Heart of Jesus, wherein are all the treasures of wisdom and knowledge,	*Have mercy on us.*
Heart of Jesus, wherein abides the fullness of the Godhead,	*Have mercy on us.*
Heart of Jesus, in which the Father was well pleased,	*Have mercy on us.*
Heart of Jesus, of whose fullness we have all received,	*Have mercy on us.*
Heart of Jesus, desire of the eternal hills,	*Have mercy on us.*
Heart of Jesus, patient and abounding in mercy,	*Have mercy on us.*
Heart of Jesus, rich unto all that call upon thee,	*Have mercy on us.*
Heart of Jesus, source of life and holiness,	*Have mercy on us.*
Heart of Jesus, atonement for our iniquities,	*Have mercy on us.*
Heart of Jesus, glutted with reproaches,	*Have mercy on us.*
Heart of Jesus, bruised for our sins,	*Have mercy on us.*
Heart of Jesus, made obedient unto death,	*Have mercy on us.*
Heart of Jesus, pierced by the lance,	*Have mercy on us.*

Heart of Jesus, source of all consolation,	*Have mercy on us.*
Heart of Jesus, our life and resurrection,	*Have mercy on us.*
Heart of Jesus, our peace and reconciliation,	*Have mercy on us.*
Heart of Jesus, victim of sin,	*Have mercy on us.*
Heart of Jesus, salvation of all who trust in thee,	*Have mercy on us.*
Heart of Jesus, hope of all who die in thee,	*Have mercy on us.*
Heart of Jesus, delight of all the saints,	*Have mercy on us.*

Lamb of God, who takest away the sins of the world, *Spare us, O Lord.*
Lamb of God, who takest away the sins of the world,

Graciously hear us, O Lord.
Lamb of God, who takest away the sins of the world, *Have mercy on us.*

℣. Jesus, meek and humble of heart,
℟. **Make our hearts like unto thy Heart.**

Let us pray.

A LMIGHTY and everlasting God, look upon the Heart of thy well-beloved Son, and upon the praise and satisfaction which he rendered to thee on behalf of sinners; and, being thus appeased, grant them the pardon which they seek from thy mercy, in the name of the same Jesus Christ, thy Son, who lives and reigns with thee for ever and ever. Amen.

DEVOTIONS

FOR THE

SACRAMENTS

DEVOTIONS FOR MASS

BEFORE MASS

Prayer of St Ambrose

LORD Jesus Christ, I approach your banquet table in fear and trembling, for I am a sinner, and dare not rely on my own worth but only on your goodness and mercy. I am defiled by many sins in body and soul, and by my unguarded thoughts and words. Gracious God of majesty and awe, I seek your protection, I look for your healing; poor troubled sinner that I am, I appeal to you, the fountain of all mercy. I cannot bear your judgment, but I trust in your salvation. Lord, I show my wounds to you and uncover my shame before you. I know my sins are many and great, and they fill me with fear, but I hope in your mercies, for they cannot be numbered. Lord Jesus Christ, eternal king, God and man, crucified for mankind, look upon me with mercy and hear my prayer, for I trust in you. Have mercy on me, full of sorrow and sin, for the depth of your compassion never ends. Praise to you, saving sacrifice, offered on the wood of the cross for me and for all mankind. Praise to the noble and precious blood, flowing from the wounds of my crucified Lord Jesus Christ and washing away the sins of the whole world. Remember, Lord, your creature, whom you have redeemed with your blood. I repent my sins, and I long to put right what I have done. Merciful Father, take away all my offences and sins; purify me in body and soul, and make me worthy to taste the holy of holies. May your body and blood, which I intend to receive, although I am unworthy, be for me the remission of my sins, the washing away of my guilt, the end of my evil thoughts, and the rebirth of my better instincts. May it incite me to do the works pleasing to you and profitable to my health in body and soul, and be a firm defence against the wiles of my enemies. Amen.

∿

JESUS, my God and my all, my soul longs for you. My heart yearns to receive you in Holy Communion. Come, bread of heaven and food of angels, to nourish my soul and to rejoice my heart. Come, most lovable friend of my soul, to inflame me with such love that I may never again be separated from you.

Prayer of St Thomas Aquinas

ALMIGHTY and ever-living God, I approach the sacrament of your only-begotten son, our Lord Jesus Christ. I come sick to the doctor of life, unclean to the fountain of mercy, blind to the radiance of eternal light, and poor and needy to the Lord of heaven and earth. Lord, in your great generosity, heal my sickness, wash away my defilement, enlighten my blindness, enrich my poverty, and clothe my nakedness. May I receive the bread of angels, the King of kings and Lord of lords, with humble reverence, with the purity and faith, the repentance and love, and the determined purpose that will help to bring me to salvation. May I receive the sacrament of the Lord's body and blood, and its reality and power. Kind God, may I receive the body of your only-begotten Son, our Lord Jesus Christ, born from the womb of the Virgin Mary, and so be received into his mystical body and numbered among his members. Loving Father, as on my earthly pilgrimage I now receive your beloved Son under the veil of a sacrament, may I one day see him face to face in glory, who lives and reigns with you for ever. Amen.

Collect for purity

O GOD to whom all hearts are open, and from whom nothing lies hidden, cleanse, we pray, the thoughts of our hearts by the inspiration of your Holy Spirit, that we may come to love you perfectly and worthily praise your holy name. Through Christ our Lord. Amen.

BEHOLD, O my loving Saviour, I present myself before your holy altar, to assist at the divine sacrifice. Give me all the grace you wish me to derive from it, and take away, I beg, all that impedes that grace. fill my heart with love for you who have not hesitated to give yourself for me on the altar of the cross.

GRANT me, O God, a warm heart, an open ear and a ready tongue to assist at this holy Mass. May my participation be wholehearted, and may my humble prayer ascend like incense in your sight, O most high, and be joined with the worship of your angels.

The Bidding of the Bedes

*This prayer, here somewhat modernized, comes from the ancient rites
used in England before the Reformation, sometimes read at the sermon
time, or at the rood screen before High Mass.*

LET us offer now a special prayer to God Almighty, and to the
Glorious Virgin, his Mother, our Lady Saint Mary, and to
all saints, for the peace and welfare of holy Church; for our Holy
Father, the Pope, for our Right Reverend Father, the Bishop of
this diocese; for the clergy of this church and all that have the
charge of souls, as well as for all religious men and women, that
God grant them each in their degree so well to do that it may
bring glory to God and salvation to souls.

We pray for our Sovereign, and for all that rule in the land,
that God may give them counsel so to do, that it may be to his
praise and the welfare of the realm.

We pray now especially for all the faithful of this diocese; for
all toilers both on land and sea, that God keep them safe in soul
and in body and also in goods; for all of good life, that God main-
tain them therein and give them an increase of goodness; and for
all those that are bound in debt, or in deadly sin, that God of his
great mercy soon lead them out.

And that these prayers may be heard and brought about the
sooner, let everyone here present now say one *Pater Noster* and
an *Ave Maria.*

Now let us offer a prayer to our Blessed Lady, Saint Mary,
and to all the saints in heaven for all the people of this parish,
wherever they may be, especially for all those that are sick, that
God of his goodness send them release of pain and turn them to
the way that is most to his pleasure and the welfare of their souls.

Let us pray especially for all those that have made the celebration of this Mass possible, through their offerings and contri-
butions to God and to this holy church, that God reward them
with everlasting bliss, and we pray for those that do not do so,
that God soon bring them to amendment.

Let us likewise pray for all those that serve or sing in this
church; for those that give or bequeath of their goods to it; for
those that find any ornament, vestment or vessel, candle or lamp,
for the worship of God, or of any of his saints in this place, for
those who founded this church, and for those who have main-
tained it.

For all these people, and for all here present, and for all that have need of prayer, let everyone now hail our Lady with an *Ave*.

And now let us pray for all the souls that await God's mercy in the purification of Purgatory, especially for the souls of our parents, kinsfolk and friends; for all those whose bones are buried in this parish, and for all souls for whom we are bound to pray, that God of his great mercy release them from their pain, if it be his blessed will.

And that our prayers may somewhat stand them in stead, every one of your charity help them heartily with a *Pater Noster* and an *Ave Maria*.

∾

LET us, who mystically represent the Cherubim, singing the thrice-holy hymn to the life-giving Trinity, cast away from us all earthly care; that we may receive the King of all, surrounded by the angelic hosts. Alleluia, Alleluia, Alleluia. Lift up your hands to the Sanctuary, and bless the Lord.

Liturgy of St John Chrysostom

PREPARATION FOR COMMUNION

I BELIEVE, O Lord, and acknowledge, that you are Christ, the Son of the living God, who came into the world to save sinners, of whom I am the greatest. I believe that what I receive is indeed your very own pure Body and precious Blood. So I pray you: have mercy on me, and forgive my sins, intentional and unintentional, which I have committed whether by word or by deed, knowingly and unknowingly: and so make me worthy without condemnation to partake of your most pure Mysteries, that my sins may be forgiven, and bring eternal life. Amen.

Liturgy of St John Chrysostom

∾

MY FATHER and my God, help me to make a worthy communion: restore in me the image of Jesus your Son which I have lost, that, with Thomas the doubter, I too may acknowledge him as my Lord and my God, whom I am about to receive today.

O SON of God, take me today as a partaker at your mystical banquet: for I will not tell your enemies your secrets, nor will I kiss you as Judas did, but like the just thief I appeal to you: *Remember me, O Lord, when you come into your kingdom.*

Liturgy of St John Chrysostom

∾

O HOLY Lord, almighty Father, eternal God, grant me worthily to receive this most holy Body and Blood of your Son our Lord Jesus Christ that I may thereby receive forgiveness of all my sins, and be filled with your Holy Spirit, and posess your peace; for you are the only God, and there is no other beside you, whose kingdom and glorious reign lasts for ever and ever. Amen.

Sarum

∾

O GOD, weaken, cast away, and forgive my sins, as many as I have committed, knowingly and unknowingly, whether by word or by deed: O forgive them all, kind lover of man; and by the prayers of your most pure and ever Virgin Mother, make me worthy, without condemnation, to receive your blessed and most pure Body, for the healing of soul and body alike. For yours is the kingdom, the power, and the glory: Father, and Son, and Holy Spirit, now, and always, and for ever and ever. Amen.

Let the partaking of your holy Mysteries be to me not for judgment or condemnation, O Lord, but for the healing of both soul and body.

Liturgy of St John Chrysostom

∾

O GOD the Father, fount and source of all goodness, who, moved by your loving-kindness, willed your only-begotten Son to descend for us to this base world and to take flesh, that same which I, unworthy one, will soon receive: I worship you, I glorify you, I praise you with utter dedication of my mind and heart, and beg you not to abandon us your servants, but rather forgive us our sins, that so we may be enabled to serve you, the only living and true God with a clean heart and a chaste body. Through the same Christ our Lord. Amen.

Sarum

HAIL for evermore, most holy flesh of Christ, to me before all and above all the highest source of joy. The body of our Lord Jesus Christ be to me, a sinner, the way and the life. In the name of the Father, Son and Holy Spirit. Amen.

And hail for evermore, heavenly drink, to me before all and above all the highest source of joy. The body and blood of our Lord Jesus Christ be to me a perpetual healing to everlasting life. Amen. In the name of the Father, Son and Holy Spirit. Amen.

Sarum

THANKSGIVING
AFTER COMMUNION

I THANK you, Holy Lord, almighty Father, eternal God, for refreshing me with the most sacred Body and Blood of your Son our Lord Jesus Christ, and I pray that this Sacrament of our salvation of which I, an unworthy sinner, have partaken, does not judge or condemn me as I deserve, but be beneficial to the preservation of my body, and the keeping of my soul unto everlasting life. Amen.

Sarum

WELCOME to my heart, Lord Jesus. Take me and renew me, transform and mould me into your image. Let the memory and grace of this communion remain with me for today and throughout life. Amen.

O DIVINE Lord! Thou hast at length satisfied the earnest desires of my heart. I possess thee, I embrace thee; O make me entirely thine. Indeed I am not worthy to receive thee under my roof: say but the word and I shall truly be healed.

Other devotions, see p. 208

AFTER MASS

Placeat Tibi Sancta Trinitas

MAY this Mass be pleasing to you, O Holy Trinity; may it be a source of grace to the priest who has said it, to us who have heard it and to all those for whom we have offered it. Amen.

∾

Prayer of St Thomas Aquinas after Mass

LORD, Father, all-powerful and ever-living God, I thank you, for even though I am a sinner, your unprofitable servant, not because of my worth but in the kindness of your mercy, you have fed me with the precious body and blood of your Son, our Lord Jesus Christ. I pray that this holy communion may bring me not condemnation and punishment, but forgiveness and salvation. May it be a helmet of faith and a shield of good will. May it purify me from evil ways and put an end to my evil passions. May it bring me charity and patience, humility and obedience, and growth in the power to do good. May it be my strong defence against all my enemies, visible and invisible, and the perfect calming of all my evil impulses, bodily and spiritual. May it unite me more closely to you, the one true God, and lead me safely through death to everlasting happiness with you. And I pray that you will lead me, a sinner, to the banquet where you, with your Son and Holy Spirit, are true and perfect light, total fulfilment, everlasting joy, gladness without end, and perfect happiness to your saints. Grant this through Christ our Lord. Amen.

∾

Prayer of St Bonaventure

PIERCE, O most sweet Lord Jesus, my inmost soul with the most joyous and healthful wound of your love, with true, serene, and most holy apostolic charity, that my soul may ever languish and melt with love and longing for you, that it may yearn for you and faint for your courts, and long to be dissolved and to be with you. Grant that my soul may hunger after you, the bread of angels, the refreshment of holy souls, our daily and

supersubstantial bread, having all sweetness and savour and every
delight of taste, upon whom the angels desire to look, and may
my inmost soul be filled with the sweetness of your savour; may
it ever thirst after you, the fountain of life, the fountain of wisdom and knowledge, the fountain of eternal light, the torrent of
pleasure, the richness of the house of God; may it ever compass
you, seek you, find you, run to you, attain you, meditate upon
you, speak of you, and do all things to the praise and glory of
your name, with humility and discretion, with love and delight,
with ease and affection, and with perseverance unto the end; may
you alone be ever my hope, my entire assurance, my riches, my
delight, my pleasure, my joy, my rest and tranquillity, my peace,
my sweetness, my fragrance, my sweet savour, my food, my refreshment, my refuge, my help, my wisdom, my portion, my possession and my treasure, in whom may my mind and my heart be
fixed and firm and rooted immovably henceforth and for ever. Amen.

W E THANK you, Lord, lover of humanity, benefactor of
our souls, that you have made us worthy today to partake
of your heavenly and undying Sacraments. Straighten out our
path; strengthen us in your devotion; protect us; give strength to
our steps, through the prayers and intercession of the glorious
Mother of God and ever-Virgin Mary, and of all your Saints.

Liturgy of St John Chrysostom

Anima Christi

S OUL of Christ, be my sanctification;
Body of Christ, be my salvation;
Blood of Christ, fill all my veins;
Water of Christ's side, wash out my stains;
Passion of Christ, my comfort be;
O good Jesu, listen to me;
In thy wounds I fain would hide,
Ne'er to be parted from Thy side;
Guard me, should the foe assail me;
Call me when my life shall fail me;
Bid me come to Thee above,
With Thy saints to sing Thy love,
World without end.

tr. J.H. Newman

DEVOTIONS FOR THE SACRAMENT OF PENANCE

BEFORE CONFESSION

LORD, be merciful to me a sinner! All I have comes from you: my home, my family, my food, my clothing, even my life, and I have repaid your goodness with my sins. Deeply I regret my ingratitude, and I beg grace to make some amends, beginning with this Sacrament of Penance. Help me to unburden myself of anything that stands between us and to be truly sorry. My Jesus, mercy! Mary, help!

HEAVENLY and forgiving Father: see here before you your prodigal child! I have squandered your wonderful gifts of grace, and can expect nothing more from your already overflowing goodness. But here I am, begging once more for your forgiveness. Treat me as one of your hired servants. I deserve nothing more.

BATTER my heart, three-person'd God; for, you
As yet but knock, breathe, shine, and seek to mend;
That I may rise, and stand, o'erthrow me, and bend
Your force, to break, blow, burn and make me new.
I, like an usurped town, to another due,
Labour to admit you, but O, to no end,

Reason, your viceroy in me, me should defend,
But is captiv'd, and proves weak or untrue.
Yet dearly I love you, and would be loved fain,
But am betroth'd unto your enemy:
Divorce me, untie, or break that knot again,
Take me to you, imprison me, for I
Except you enthrall me, never shall be free,
Nor ever chaste, except you ravish me.

John Donne

L ORD Jesus Christ, whose arms were extended on the cross
out of love for me, here I am, acknowledging that it was I
who drove those nails into your hands and feet by my sins. Help
me truly to cleanse my soul in this sacrament of Confession, hid-
ing nothing from you who were hung naked on the cross for me,
and with true sorrow together with a resolute determination never
to repeat my faults.

C OME, Holy Spirit, and reveal me truly to myself. Show me
the truth: let me see myself as you see me. Show me my
soul in all its disfigurement that I may take it to be healed and
made beautiful again as once you made it in baptism.

O GOD, who opened the eyes of the blind, open the eyes of
my heart, so as to drive from me all the darkness of wickedness and vice, the very appearance of defilement, that I may raise
up my eyes on high towards the beauty of your holy glory.

Coptic Liturgy of St Mark

Quærens me sedísti lassus,   You sought me to exhaustion,
Redimísti crucem passus;   And redeemed me with your cross;
Tantus labor non sit cassus.   Let not such a labour be in vain!

From the Dies Iræ

ACTS OF CONTRITION

O MY GOD, because you are so good, I am very sorry that I have sinned against you, and with the help of your grace I will not sin again.

Traditional

❧

O MY GOD, I am sorry and beg pardon for all my sins, and detest them above all things, because they deserve your dreadful punishments, because they have crucified my loving Saviour Jesus Christ, and, most of all, because they offend your infinite goodness: and I firmly resolve, by the help of your grace, never to offend you again and carefully to avoid the occasions of sin. Amen.

❧

O MY GOD, who are infinitely good and always hate sin, I beg pardon from my heart for all my offences against you. I detest them all and am heartily sorry for them because they offend your infinite goodness: and I firmly resolve, by the help of your grace, never more to offend you and carefully to avoid the occasions of sin. Amen.

❧

O MY GOD, I love you with my whole heart and above all things. I am heartily sorry that I have offended you. May I never offend you more. O may I love you without ceasing, and make it my delight to do in all things your most holy will. Amen.

Traditional

❧

MY GOD, I am sorry for my sins with all my heart. In choosing to do wrong and failing to do good, I have sinned against you whom I should love above all things. I firmly intend, with your help, to do penance, to sin no more, and to avoid whatever leads me to sin. Our Saviour Jesus Christ suffered and died for us. In his name, my God, have mercy. Amen.

J ESUS, you knew all my miseries before your eyes were fixed on me and yet you did not turn away from my wretchedness; rather, because of it, you loved me with a love more sweet and tender. Jesus, I beg pardon for having corresponded so little to your love; Jesus, I beg of you to forgive and to purify my actions in your divine blood; Jesus, I am deeply grieved at having offended you because you are infinitely holy; Jesus, I repent with heartfelt sorrow, and I promise to do all in my power to avoid these faults in the future.

Revealed to Sr Josepha Menendez, adapted by Rex Baker

AFTER CONFESSION

B LESS the Lord, O my soul, and all that is within me, bless his holy name!
Bless the Lord, O my soul, and never forget all his goodness!
For the Lord is kindly, long-suffering and of great mercy.
Bless the Lord, O my soul, and all that is within me, bless his holy name!
　　Blessed are you, O Lord!

Liturgy of St John Chrysostom

M Y ✠ SOUL magnifies the Lord,
my spirit rejoices in God who is my Saviour,
　　who has looked upon the humility of his handmaiden.
Behold, all generations from now
　　will acknowledge me blessed,
For the mighty one has done great things for me:
　　Holy is his name!
His mercy is from one generation to the next on those who fear him.
　　Mighty is his arm!
He has scattered the proud in the imagination of their hearts,
　　and has put down the powerful from their thrones,
　　exalting those of humble degree.
The hungry he has filled with good things,
　　but the rich he has dismissed with nothing.
Remembering his mercy, he has helped his servant Israel,
　　as he promised to our fathers,
　　to Abraham and to his posterity for evermore.
Glory be…

Luke 1:46-55

A Prayer to the Holy Spirit, the Life of the Soul

MY GOD, I adore you, Eternal Paraclete, the light and the life of my soul. You might have been content with merely giving me good suggestions, inspiring grace and helping from without. But in your infinite compassion you have from the first entered into my soul, and taken possession of it. You will go from me, if I sin, and I shall be left to my own miserable self. God forbid, I will use what you have given me; I will call on you when tried and tempted. Through you I will never forsake you.

J.H. Newman

O HOW late have I loved you, O love for ever ancient and for ever new, how late have I loved you!

St Augustine

PUBLIC
DEVOTIONS

BENEDICTION
OF THE
BLESSED SACRAMENT

*As the Blessed Sacrament is exposed on the altar,
this, or another Eucharistic hymn is sung.*

O SALUTARIS Hóstia
　Quæ Cæli pandis óstium
Bella præmunt hostília,
Da robur, fer auxílium.

O SAVING victim, opening wide
　The gate of heav'n to man below,
Our foes press on from every side,
Thine aid supply, thy strength bestow.

Uni, trinóque Dómino
Sit sempitérna glória,
Qui vitam sine término
Nobis donet in pátria.
Amen.

To thy great name be endless praise,
Immortal Godhead, one in three,
O grant us endless length of days
In our true native land with thee.
Amen.

At this point there may be prayers or readings.

TANTUM ergo Sacraméntum
　Venerémur cérnui.　*(all bow)*
Et antíquum documéntum
Novo cedat rítui.
Præstet fides suppleméntum
Sénsuum deféctui.

DOWN in adoration falling,
　Lo! the sacred Host we hail;
Lo, o'er ancient forms departing,
Newer rites of grace prevail;
Faith, for all defects supplying
Where the feeble senses fail.

Genitóri, genitóque
Laus et iubilátio:
Salus, honor, virtus quoque
Sit et benedíctio:
Procedénti ab utróque
Compar sit laudátio.
Amen.

To the everlasting Father,
And the Son who reigns on high
With the Holy Ghost proceeding
Forth from each eternally,
Be salvation, honour, blessing.
Might and endless majesty.
Amen.

℣. Panem de cælis præstitísti
　　eis.
℟. **Omne delectaméntum in
　　se habéntem.**

℣. You gave them manna from
　　heaven.
℟. **And very sweet it was to the
　　taste.**

The following, or another collect in English is now sung or said:

Orémus.

D EUS, qui nobis sub sacraménto mirábili passiónis tuæ memóriam reliquísti: tríbue quǽsumus, ita nos córporis et sánguinis tui sacra mystéria venerári; ut redemptiónis tuæ fructum in nobis iúgiter sentiámus. Qui vivis et regnas in sǽcula sæculórum. Amen.

Let us pray.

O GOD, who in this wonderful sacrament left us a memorial of your passion, grant that as we venerate this holy mystery of your body and blood, we may come to experience the effects of your redemption, who live and reign for ever and ever. Amen.

The priest raises the Sacred Host in blessing.
The following Divine Praises *may at some point be said:*

B LESSED be God
Blessed be his holy name
Blessed be Jesus Christ, true God and true Man
Blessed be the name of Jesus
Blessed be his most Sacred Heart
Blessed be his most Precious Blood
Blessed be Jesus in the most holy Sacrament of the altar
Blessed be the Holy Spirit, the Paraclete
Blessed be the great Mother of God, Mary most holy
Blessed be her holy and immaculate conception
Blessed be her glorious assumption
Blessed be the name of Mary, Virgin and Mother
Blessed be St Joseph, her spouse most chaste
Blessed be God in his angels and in his saints

Finally, as the Blessed Sacrament is returned to the tabernacle
the following, or another hymn is sung.

Ant. Adorémus in ætérnum sanctíssimum Sacraméntum.

Ant. Let us adore for ever the most holy Sacrament.

Psalm 116

L AUDATE Dóminum, omnes gentes, Laudáte eum, omnes pópuli.

P RAISE the Lord, all you nations, Praise him, all you peoples.

Quóniam confirmáta est super nos misericórdia eius, Et véritas Dómini manet in ætérnum.

For his mercy has been shown forth towards us, And the Lord keeps his word for ever.

Glória Patri et Fílio et Spirítui Sancto. Sicut erat in princípio et nunc et semper, et in sǽcula sæculórum. Amen.

Glory be to the Father, and to the Son, and to the Holy Spirit. As it was in the beginning, is now and ever shall be, world without end. Amen.

Ant. Adorémus in ætérnum sanctíssimum sacraméntum.

Ant. Let us adore for ever the most holy Sacrament.

Or, in some places is sung three times:

O SACRAMENT most holy, O Sacrament divine! All praise and all thanksgiving be every moment thine!

PRIVATE DEVOTIONS
BEFORE THE
BLESSED SACRAMENT

A quarter of an hour before the Blessed Sacrament

TO PLEASE me, my dear child, it is not necessary to know much; all that is required is to love me much, to be deeply sorry for ever having offended me, and desirous of being ever faithful to me in future.

Speak to me now as you would to your dearest friend. Tell me all that now fills your mind and heart. Are there any you wish to commend to me? Tell me their names, and tell me what you would wish me to do for them. Do not fear, ask for much; I love generous hearts, which, forgetting themselves, wish well to others.

Speak to me of the poor you wish to comfort; tell me of the sick that you would wish to see relieved. Ask of me something for those who have been unkind to you, or who have crossed you. Ask much for them all; commend them with all your heart to me.

And ask me many graces for yourself. Are there not many and many you would wish to name, that would make you happier to yourself, more useful and pleasing to others, more worthy of the love of me, the dearest Lord, Master and Spouse of your soul? Tell me the whole list of the favours you want of me. Tell me them with humility, knowing how poor you are without them, how unable to gain them by yourself; ask for them with much love, that they may make you more pleasing to me.

With all a child's simplicity, tell me how self-seeking you are, how proud, vain, irritable, how cowardly in sacrifice, how lazy in work, uncertain in your good resolutions, and then ask me to bless and crown your efforts. Poor child, fear not, blush not at the sight of so many failings; there are Saints in Heaven who had the faults you have; they came to me lovingly, they prayed earnestly to me, and my grace has made them good and holy in my sight.

You should be mine, body and soul: fear not, therefore, to ask of me gifts of body and mind, health, judgment, memory, and success—ask for them for my sake: that God may be glorified in all things. I can grant everything, and never refuse to give what may make a soul dearer to me and better able to fulfil the will of God.

Have you no plans for the future which occupy, perhaps distress, your mind? Tell me your hopes, your fears. Is it about your future state? your position among my creatures? some good you wish to bring to others? In what shall I help and bless your good will?

And for me you must have—have you not? some zeal, some wish to do good to the souls of others. Some, perhaps, who love and care for you, have ceased, almost, to know or care for me. Shall I give you strength, wisdom and tact, to bring these poor ones close to my Heart again? Have you failed in the past? tell me how you acted; I will show you why you did not gain all you expected; rely on me, I will help you, and will guide you to lead others to me.

And what crosses have you, my dear child? Have they been many and heavy ones? Has some one caused you pain? some one wounded your self-love? slighted you? injured you? Lay your head upon my breast, and tell me how you suffered. Have you felt that some have been ungrateful to you, and unfeeling towards you? Tell me all, and in the warmth of my Heart you will find strength to forgive and even to forget that they have ever wished to pain you.

And what fears have you, my child? My providence shall comfort you; my love sustain you. I am never away from you, never can abandon you. Are some growing cold in the interest and love they had for you? Pray to me for them; I will restore them to you if it be better for you and your sanctification.

Have you not some happiness to make known to me? What has happened, since you came to me last, to console you, to gladden and give you joy? What was it? a mark of true friendship you received? a success unexpected and almost unhoped for? a fear suddenly taken away from you? and did you remember the while, that in all it was my will, my love, that brought all that your heart has been so glad to have? It was my hand, my dear child, that guided and prepared all for you. Look to me now, my child, and say, 'Dear Jesus, I thank you.'

You will soon leave me now; what promises can you make me? Let them be sincere ones, humble ones, full of love and desire to please me. Tell me how carefully you will avoid every occasion of sin, drive from you all that leads to harm, and shun the world—the great deceiver of souls.

Promise me to be kind to the poor; loving for my sake, to friends; forgiving to your enemies, and charitable to all, not in word alone and actions, but in your very thoughts. When you have little love for your neighbour, whom you see, you are forgetting me who am hidden from you.

Love all my saints; seek the help of your holy patrons. I love to glorify them by giving you much through them. Love, above all, my own sweet glorious Mother—she is your mother; O love her, speak to her often, and she will bring you to me, and for her sake I will love and bless you more each day.

Return soon to me again, but come with your heart empty of the world, for I have many more favours to give, more than you can know of; bring your heart so that I may fill it with many gifts of my love.

My peace be with you.

A Simple Prayer Book

∾

A Prayer to the five wounds

The anonymous writer plays on the old word for beloved: leman, and the lemon, that bitter fruit.

JESUS Christ, my Leman sweet,
  That diedest on the bitter tree,
With all my might I thee beseech
For thy deep woundès two and three,
That as firmly may thy love
Into mine heart fixèd be
As was the spear into thine Heart
When thou sufferedst death for me.
My Jesu sweet, who died on Rood,
For the love of me,—
And boughtest me with thy Blood,
Have then mercy upon me;
And should me hinder any thing
From my love of thee,
Should it be dear, it shall be loathed;
So take it away from me. Amen.

Vernon Manuscript

∾

O MOST loving Jesus, to what an excess thy love has gone! Of thy own flesh and most precious blood thou hast prepared for me a divine banquet, in which thou givest me thy whole self. What could have moved thee to this transport of love? Nothing else, surely, than thy most loving heart. O adorable heart of my Jesus, furnace of divine love, receive into thy sacred wound my soul, that I may learn in that school of charity how to love my God, who has given me such wonderful proofs of his love. Amen.

∞

An Act of Spiritual Communion

I believe in you, O my Jesus, present in the most holy Sacrament of the Altar; I love you above all things; and I desire to receive you into my soul. Since I cannot now receive you sacramentally, come at least spiritually into my heart. I embrace you and I unite myself to you, as if you were already there. Permit me never to be separated from you.

∞

O Godhead Hid

HOW infinitely, indescribably, wonderful
is your presence, O Lord, in the Sacred Host.
What I see looks just like a white disc.
I feel it, smooth and so very ordinary:
I taste it and experience the flavour of bread.
Yet, you Lord, Truth itself, have said
'This is my Body.'
Never once in my life have I doubted that.
I thank you for the gift of faith.
'Than Truth's own word there is no truer token.'
Those standing beneath the cross to which you were nailed
saw your human Body; poor, weak, suffering.
But your Godhead remained so hidden.
Now, even your Body is concealed too.
I believe, Lord; help my unbelief.
I bow down in wonder before your humility.
Immeasurable greatness hidden under the semblance
     of the commonest of foods.
Your human Body is here, Jesus,
glorified but still bearing the wounds of your Passion,

wounds you endured for love of me.
Yes, Lord, you died for me.
You continue to offer yourself for me.
Through your dying I am able to live.
But you also give me yourself to feed my soul.
I believe that when I was baptised I was born again.
I received a wonderful new life,
a sharing in the life of the Divine Trinity,
a life that is indeed divine.
You, Lord, in your wonderful providence
feed everything according to its nature.
You feed the divine life of my soul
with divine food, your own very Self.
O mystery of mysteries, O mystery of faith.
I need your own gift to begin to understand it all.
How I long to cry out to the whole wide world,
'Why are you starving?
Why do you refuse the food that is God?'
Lord, I do believe.
Increase my faith. Move me to share it.

Francis Canon Ripley

❧

A morning prayer before the Blessed Sacrament

LORD Jesus, present before me in the Sacrament of the Altar, help me to cast out from my mind all thoughts of which you do not approve and from my heart all emotions which you do not encourage. Enable me to spend my entire day as a co-worker with you, carrying out the tasks that you have entrusted to me.

Be with me at every moment of this day: during the long hours of work, that I may never tire or slacken from your service; during my conversations, that they not become for me occasions of meanness toward others; during the moments of worry and stress, that I may remain patient and spiritually calm; during periods of fatigue and illness, that I may avoid self-pity and think of others; during times of temptation, and that I may take refuge in your grace.

Help me to remain generous and loyal to you this day, and so be able to offer it all up to you with its successes which I have achieved by your help and its failures which have occurred through my own fault. Let me come to the wonderful realization that life is most real when it is lived with you as the guest of my soul.

OUR MOST dear Saviour Christ, which after the finishing of the old paschal sacrifice hast instituted the new sacrament of thine own blessed body and blood for a memorial of thy bitter passion, give us such true faith therein, and such fervent devotion thereto, that our souls may take fruitful spiritual food thereby.

St Thomas More

IT SEEMS white, and is red;
It is quick, and seems dead;
It is flesh, and seems bread;
It is one and seems two;
It is God's body and no more.

Early English

O DIVINE Jesus, alone in so many tabernacles throughout the world without visitor or worshipper: I offer you my own heart. May its every beat be a prayer of love for you. In your love you are ever watching me: you never sleep, and like the father of the prodigal son, you are always looking out for returning sinners. O loving Jesus, O lonely Jesus, may my heart be a lamp, the light of which shall burn and comfort you alone in time and in eternity. Amen.

THE GREAT CREEDS

The Apostles' Creed

I BELIEVE in God the Father Almighty, Creator of heaven and earth; and in Jesus Christ his only Son our Lord; who was conceived by the Holy Ghost, born of the Virgin Mary, suffered under Pontius Pilate, was crucified, dead, and buried; he descended into hell; the third day he rose again from the dead; he ascended into heaven, sitteth at the right hand of God the Father Almighty; from thence he shall come to judge the living and the dead. I believe in the Holy Ghost; the holy Catholic Church; the communion of saints; the forgiveness of sins; the resurrection of the body, and life everlasting. Amen.

⧼

The Nicene Creed

I BELIEVE in one God, the Father Almighty, Maker of heaven and earth, and of all things visible and invisible. And in one Lord Jesus Christ, the only-begotten Son of God, born of the Father before all ages; God of God; Light of Light; true God; begotten, not made, consubstantial with the Father, by whom all things were made. Who, for us men, and for our salvation, came down from heaven; and was incarnate by the Holy Ghost, of the Virgin Mary; and was made man. He was crucified also for us, suffered under Pontius Pilate, and was buried. And the third day he rose again, according to the scriptures, and ascended into heaven, sitting at the right hand of the Father; and he shall come again with glory, to judge both the living and the dead; of whose kingdom there shall be no end.

And I believe in the Holy Ghost, the Lord and giver of life, who proceedeth from the Father and the Son; who together with the Father and the Son is adored and glorified; who spake by the Prophets. And one holy Catholic and Apostolic Church. I confess one baptism for the remission of sins. And I look for the resurrection of the dead, and the life of the world to come. Amen.

The Athanasian Creed

W HOSOEVER will be saved, before all things it is necessary that he hold the Catholic faith. Which faith, except every one do keep entire and inviolate, without doubt he shall perish everlastingly.*

Now the Catholic faith is this: that we worship one God in Trinity, and Trinity in Unity. Neither confounding the Persons, nor dividing the Substance. For one is the Person of the Father; another of the Son, another of the Holy Ghost.

But the Godhead of the Father, and of the Son, and of the Holy Ghost, is all one, the glory equal, the majesty co-eternal.

Such as the Father is, such is the Son, and such is the Holy Ghost. The Father is uncreated, the Son is uncreated, and the Holy Ghost is uncreated. The Father is incomprehensible, the Son is incomprehensible, and the Holy Ghost is incomprehensible. The Father is eternal, the Son is eternal, and the Holy Ghost is eternal.

And yet they are not three Eternals, but one Eternal. As also they are not three Uncreateds, nor three Incomprehensibles; but one Uncreated and one Incomprehensible. In like manner the Father is Almighty, the Son is Almighty, and the Holy Ghost is Almighty.

And yet they are not three Almighties, but one Almighty. So the Father is God, the Son is God, and the Holy Ghost is God; and yet they are not three Gods, but one God. So likewise the Father is Lord, the Son is Lord, and the Holy Ghost is Lord; and yet they are not three Lords, but one Lord.

For as we are compelled by Christian truth to acknowledge each Person by Himself to be God and Lord: We are forbidden by the Catholic religion to say there are three Gods, or three Lords.

The Father is made of no one, neither created nor begotten. The Son is from the Father alone, neither made nor created, but begotten. The Holy Ghost is from the Father and the Son, not made, nor created, nor begotten, but proceeding.

So there is one Father, not three Fathers; one Son, not three Sons; and one Holy Ghost, not three Holy Ghosts.

* The Church has always been anxious that this condemnation be not misunderstood. It applies only to those who wilfully and knowingly reject what is contained in this creed. So it does not condemn anyone honestly seeking after truth, or those who have been brought up not believing the faith.

And in this Trinity there is nothing before or after, nothing greater or less; but the whole three Persons are co-eternal to one another, and co-equal. So that in all things, as it hath been already said above, the Unity is to be worshipped in Trinity, and the Trinity in Unity. He, therefore, that would be saved, must thus think of the Trinity.

Furthermore, it is necessary to everlasting salvation, that he also believe rightly the Incarnation of our Lord Jesus Christ. Now the right faith is, that we believe and confess that our Lord Jesus Christ, the Son of God, is both God and Man. He is God of the substance of His Father, begotten before the world; and He is man of the substance of His Mother, born in the world; Perfect God, and perfect man, subsisting of a rational soul and human flesh. Equal to the Father according to His Godhead, and less than the Father according to His manhood. Who, although He be both God and Man, yet He is not two but one Christ. One, not by the conversion of the Godhead into flesh, but by the taking of the manhood unto God. One altogether, not by confusion of substance, but by unity of person. For as the rational soul and the flesh is one man, so God and Man is one Christ.

Who suffered for our salvation, descended to hell, rose again the third day from the dead. He ascended into heaven: He sitteth at the right hand of God the Father Almighty; from thence He shall come to judge the living and the dead. At whose coming all men have to rise again in their bodies, and shall give an account of their own works. And they that have done good shall go into life everlasting; and they that have done evil, into everlasting fire.

This is the Catholic faith, which, except a man believe faithfully and steadfastly, he cannot be saved.

Glory be to the Father, and to the Son, and the Holy Ghost.

As it was in the beginning, is now, and ever shall be, world without end. Amen.

STATIONS OF THE CROSS

SHORTER FORM

W*HEN there is not a lot of time, it suffices to spend only a moment before each station. The following are suggestions for prayers one might like to use at each pause.*

E TERNAL Father, I offer you the blood, the passion, the death of Jesus, and the sorrows of the Blessed Virgin, for the remission of my sins, the deliverance of the souls in Purgatory, the wants of our Holy Mother the Church, and the conversion of sinners.

Pope Pius IX

∾

E TERNAL Father, I offer you the precious blood of Jesus in reparation for my sins, and for the needs of the holy Church. My Jesus, mercy!

Pope Pius VII

∾

My sweetest Jesus, be not to me a Judge but a Saviour!

St Jerome Emiliani

∾

Viva! Viva! Gesù

G lory be to Jesus,
Who, in bitter pains,
Poured for me the life-blood
From his sacred veins.

∾

O LORD Jesus Christ, holy, immortal God, have mercy upon us all, and upon all people; purify us with your holy blood, forgive us with your holy blood, save us with your holy blood now and for ever. Amen.

TO WHAT excess, O my Saviour, hast thou loved me! O Jesus, crucified for my salvation, save me!

∾

Quærens me sedísti lassus,   You sought me to exhaustion,
Redemísti crucem passus;   And redeemed me with your cross;
Tantus labor non sit cassus.   Let not such a labour be in vain!

from the Dies Iræ

LONGER STATIONS OF THE CROSS

A NY *devotions may be used: the following selection is provided as a simple resource for a group or an individual to use as desired. Using it* all *is not to be recommended. At each station, at some point an act of love is usually made, such as:*

I LOVE thee, Jesus, my love above all things. I repent with my whole heart for having offended thee. Never permit me to separate myself from thee again; grant that I may love thee always, and then do with me as thou wilt.

There may be other devotions, such as the Our Father, the Hail Mary or Glory be, or prayers for the holy souls in Purgatory.

ᕡ   ᕡ   ᕡ

AT THE HIGH ALTAR

In the name of the Father, the Son ✠ and the Holy Spirit. Amen.

A reading from the first letter of St John

T HAT which we have seen and have heard, we declare to you, that you too may have fellowship with us, and our fellowship may be with the Father and with his Son Jesus Christ. And these things we write to you that you may rejoice, and your joy may be full. And this is the declaration which we have heard from him and now we declare it to you: God is light, and in him is no darkness at all.

If we say that we have fellowship with him, and walk in darkness, we lie, and do not do the truth. But if we walk in the light, as he also is in the light, we have fellowship with one another, and the blood of Jesus Christ cleanses us from all sin.

If we say that we have no sin, we deceive ourselves, and the truth is not in us. If we confess our sins, he is faithful and just, to forgive our sins, and to cleanse us from all iniquity. If we say that we have not sinned, we make him a liar, and his word is not in us. My little children, I write these things to you, that you may not sin. But if anyone does sin, we have an advocate with the Father: Jesus Christ the just. He is the propitiation for our sins; and not for ours only, but also for those of the whole world.

1 John 1:3-2:2

HEAVENLY Father, who did not spare your only Son, but freely gave him up for the life of the world, be present with us here as we prepare to remember your Son's terrible sufferings, undergone for our salvation. Do not let such labour go in vain, but touch our hearts, that we may be moved to sincere repentance for those sins which made our redeemer undergo such a sorrowful sacrifice.

O JESUS, our adorable Saviour, behold us prostrate at thy feet, imploring thy mercy for ourselves and for the souls of all the faithful departed. Vouchsafe to apply to us the infinite merits of thy Passion, on which we are about to meditate. Grant that while we trace this path of sighs and tears, our hearts may be so touched with contrition and repentance that we may be ready to embrace with joy all the crosses and sufferings and humiliations of this our life and pilgrimage.

Challoner

O JESUS Christ, my Lord, with what great love didst thou pass over the painful road which led thee to death; and I, how often have I abandoned thee! But now I love thee with my whole soul, and because I love thee, I am sincerely sorry for having offended thee. My Jesus, pardon me, and permit me to accompany thee in this journey. Thou art going to die for love of me, and it is my wish also, O my dearest Redeemer, to die for love of thee. O yes, my Jesus, in thy love I wish to live; in thy love I wish to die.

St Alphonsus Liguori

THE FIRST STATION
Jesus is condemned to death

℣. We adore thee, O Christ, and we bless thee,
℟. **Because by thy holy cross thou hast redeemed the world.**

Consider how Jesus, after having been scourged and crowned with thorns, was unjustly condemned by Pilate to die on the cross.

A reading from the Gospel according to St Matthew

PILATE saw that he was achieving nothing, but rather that a riot was breaking out, so taking water, he washed his hands before the people, saying 'I am innocent of the blood of this just man: you do what you wish.' And all the people answered, saying: 'His blood be upon us and upon our children'. Then he released Barabbas to them, and having scourged Jesus, gave him to them to be crucified.

Matthew 27:24-26

LEAVING the house of Caiaphas, and dragged before Pilate and Herod, mocked, beaten, and spat upon, his back torn with scourges, his head crowned with thorns, Jesus, who on the last day will judge the world, is himself condemned by unjust judges to a death of ignominy and torture.

Jesus is condemned to *death*. His death-warrant is signed, and who signed it but I, when I committed my first mortal sins? My first mortal sins, when I fell away from the state of grace into which thou didst place me by baptism; these it was that were thy death-warrant, O Lord. The Innocent suffered for the guilty. Those sins of mine were the voices which cried out, 'let him be crucified.' That willingness and delight of heart with which I committed them was the consent which Pilate gave to this clamorous multitude. And the hardness of heart which followed upon them, my disgust, my despair, my proud impatience, my obstinate resolve to sin on, the love of sin which took possession of me—what were these contrary and impetuous feelings but the blows and the blasphemies with which the fierce soldiers and the populace received thee, thus carrying out the sentence which Pilate had pronounced?

J.H. Newman

Iudas, mercátor péssimus ósculo pétiit Dóminum: ille ut agnus ínnocens non negávit Iudæ ósculum: * Denariórum número Christum Iudæis trádidit. V̅. Mélius illi erat, si natus non fuísset. * Denariórum número Christum Iudæis trádidit.

Judas, wretched trader, betrayed the Lord with a kiss. The Lord, as an innocent lamb, would not refuse Judas' kiss. * He betrayed Christ for a few miserable coins. V̅. Would that he had never been born! *He betrayed Christ for a few miserable coins.

Tenebræ response

BEHOLD our Lord and our God, mocked, scourged, crowned with thorns and condemned to death for the sins which we have committed!

Holy God!
Holy, mighty one!
Holy, immortal one!
Have mercy on us!

IT WAS for us that thou didst suffer, O blessed Jesus; it was for our sins thou wast condemned to die. Oh, grant that we may detest them from the bottom of our hearts, and by this repentance obtain thy mercy and pardon.

Challoner

Stabat Mater dolorósa
Iuxta crucem lacrymósa
Dum pendébat Fílius.

At the cross her station keeping
Stood the mournful Mother weeping
Close to Jesus to the last.

THE SECOND STATION
Jesus is made to bear his cross

℣. We adore thee, O Christ, and we bless thee,
℟. Because by thy holy cross thou hast redeemed the world.

Consider how Jesus, in making this journey with the cross on his shoulders, thought of us, and offered for us to his Father the death he was about to undergo.

A reading from the Gospel according to St Matthew

THEN the soldiers of the governor, taking Jesus into the hall, gathered around him, stripped him, dressed him in a scarlet cloak, plaited a crown out of thorns and placed it on his head, with a reed in his right hand. They knelt before him and mocked him, saying 'Hail, King of the Jews.' And spitting upon him, they took the reed and struck him about the head with it. And after they had mocked him, they took off the cloak from him, and made him put on his own garments, and led him away to crucify him.

Matthew 27:27-31

A STRONG, and therefore heavy Cross, for it is strong enough to bear him on it when he arrives at Calvary, is placed upon his torn shoulders. He receives it gently and meekly, nay, with gladness of heart, for it is to be the salvation of mankind.

True; but recollect, that heavy Cross is the weight of our sins. As it fell upon his neck and shoulders, it came down with a shock. Alas! what a sudden, heavy weight have I laid upon thee, O Jesus. And, though in the calm and clear foresight of thy mind—for thou seest all things—thou wast fully prepared for it, yet thy feeble frame tottered under it when it dropped down upon thee. Ah! how great a misery is it that I have lifted up my hand against my God. How could I ever fancy he would forgive me, unless he had himself told us that he underwent his bitter passion in order that he might forgive us. I acknowledge, O Jesus, in the anguish and agony of my heart, that it was my sins that struck thee on the face, that bruised thy sacred arms, that tore thy flesh with iron rods, that nailed thee to the Cross, and let thee slowly die upon it.

J.H. Newman

Tamquam ad latrónem exístis cum gládiis et fústibus comprehéndere me: * Cotídie apud vos eram in templo docens et non me tenuístis: et ecce flagellátum dúcitis ad crucifigéndum. ℣. Cumque iniecíssent manus in Iesum, et tenuíssent eum, dixit ad eos: * Cotídie apud vos eram in templo docens et non me tenuístis: et ecce flagellátum dúcitis ad crucifigéndum.

As if I were a criminal, you surround me with swords and clubs. * Day by day I taught in the temple and you never laid hands on me: yet now you scourge me and lead me out to my crucifixion. ℣. And when they laid hands on Jesus and held him, he said to them: * Day by day I taught in the temple and you never laid hands on me: yet now you scourge me and lead me out to my crucifixion.

∾

D EAR Lord, the thought that you have commanded me to take up my cross and follow in your footsteps frightens me when I consider just where those footsteps led. Give me courage, I beg, and a cheerful spirit just when the road seems darkest.

∾

B EHOLD our Lord and our God, led willingly to a cruel death for the sins which we have committed!

Holy God!
Holy, mighty one!
Holy, immortal one!
Have mercy on us!

∾

O JESUS, grant us, by virtue of thy cross, to embrace with meekness and cheerful submission the difficulties of our state, and to be ever ready to take up our cross and follow thee.

Challoner

∾

Cuius ánimam geméntem
Contristátam et doléntem
Pertransívit gládius.

Through her heart his sorrow sharing
All his bitter anguish bearing
Now at length the sword had passed.

THE THIRD STATION
Jesus falls the first time under his cross

℣. We adore thee, O Christ, and we bless thee,
℟. Because by thy holy cross thou hast redeemed the world.

Consider this first fall of Jesus under his cross. His flesh was torn by the scourges, his head was crowned with thorns, he had lost a great quantity of blood. He was so weakened he could scarcely walk, and yet he had to carry this great load upon his shoulders. The soldiers struck him rudely, and thus he fell several times.

∽

A reading from the prophet Isaiah

SURELY it is our sins that he has carried: our sorrows that he has borne, and we have thought of him as if he were a leper, as though he had been struck by God and afflicted. But he was wounded for our iniquities, he was bruised for our sins: the chastisement of our peace was upon him, and by his bruises we are healed. All we like sheep have gone astray, every one has turned aside into his own way; and the Lord has laid on him the iniquity of us all. He was offered because it was his own will, and he did not even open his mouth; he was led as a sheep to the slaughter and as a lamb to the shearer: not even opening his mouth.

Isaiah 53:4-7

∽

SATAN fell from heaven in the beginning; by the just sentence of his Creator he fell, against whom he had rebelled. And when he had succeeded in gaining man to join him in his rebellion, and his Maker came to save him, then his brief hour of triumph came, and he made the most of it. When the Holiest had taken flesh, and was in his power, then in his revenge and malice he determined, as he himself had been struck down by the almighty arm, to strike in turn a heavy blow at him who struck him. Therefore it was that Jesus fell down so suddenly.

O dear Lord, by this thy first fall raise us all out of sin, who have so miserably fallen under its power.

J.H. Newman

Animam meam diléctam trádidi in manus iniquórum, et facta est mihi heréditas mea sicut leo in silva: dedit contra me voces adversárius, dicens: Congregámini, et properáte ad devorándum illum: posuérunt me in desérto solitúdinis, et luxit super me omnis terra: * Quia non est invéntus qui me agnósceret, et fáceret bene. ℣. Insurrexérunt in me viri absque misericórdia, et non pepercérunt ánimæ meæ: * Quia non est invéntus qui me agnósceret, et fáceret bene.

The soul that I loved I betrayed into the hands of the wicked, and my inheritance has turned on me like a lion in the jungle; my adversary cries against me: 'Let us band together and destroy him'; they have abandoned me as if in a lonely desert, and the whole world mourns. * And there is not one who recognizes me, or who will show me kindness. ℣. Merciless men have risen against me, they will not spare me: * And there is not one who recognizes me, or who will show me kindness.

B EHOLD our Lord and our God, crushed to the ground for the sins which we have committed!

Holy God!
Holy, mighty one!
Holy, immortal one!
Have mercy on us!

O JESUS, who for our sins didst bear the heavy burden of the cross, and fall under its weight, may the thoughts of thy sufferings make us watchful over ourselves, and save us from any grievous fall into sin.

Challoner

O quam tristis et afflícta
Fuit illa benedícta
Mater Unigéniti!

Oh, how sad and sore distressed
Was that Mother highly blessed,
Of the sole-begotten One!

THE FOURTH STATION
Jesus meets his afflicted mother

℣. We adore thee, O Christ, and we bless thee,
℟. **Because by thy holy cross thou hast redeemed the world.**

*Consider the meeting of the Son and the Mother which took place
on this journey. Their looks became like so many arrows, to wound
those hearts which loved each other so tenderly.*

A reading from the Gospel according to St Luke

AND Simeon...said to Mary: Behold, this child is set for the
fall and for the resurrection of many in Israel, and for a sign
which shall be contradicted; and a sword shall pierce your own
soul, that out of many hearts thoughts may be revealed.

Luke 1:34-35

A reading from the book of Lamentations

TO WHAT can I compare you, or to what can I liken you, daughter of Jerusalem? How am I to understand you, that I may
comfort you, O Virgin daughter of Sion? For great as the sea is
your sorrow: who, then, can heal you?

Lamentations 2:13

THERE is no part of the history of Jesus but Mary has her part
in it. There are those who profess to be his servants, who
think that her work was ended when she bore him, and after that
she had nothing to do but disappear and be forgotten. But we, O
Lord, thy children of the Catholic Church, do not think so of thy
Mother. She brought the tender infant into the temple, she lifted
him up in her arms when the wise men came to adore him. She fled
with him to Egypt, she took him up to Jerusalem when he was
twelve years old. He lived with her at Nazareth for thirty years.
She was with him at the marriage-feast. Even when he had left her
to preach, she hovered about him. And now she shows herself as
he toils along the Sacred Way with his Cross on his shoulders.

Sweet Mother, let us ever think of thee when we think of Jesus; and when we pray to him, ever aid us by thy powerful intercession.

J.H. Newman

Caligavérunt óculi mei a fletu meo: quia elongátus est a me, qui consolabátur me: Vidéte, omnes pópuli, * Si est dolor símilis sicut dolor meus. ℣. O vos omnes, qui transítis per viam, atténdite, et vidéte. * Si est dolor símilis sicut dolor meus.

My eyes are worn out with weeping: those who could console me are far away: Look, everybody: * Is there any sorrow like to my sorrow? ℣. O all you passers-by: look, then, and see: * Is there any sorrow like to my sorrow?

∽

B EHOLD our Lord and our God suffering, and see the sorrow that our sins have given his holy Mother!

Holy God!
Holy, mighty one!
Holy, immortal one!
Have mercy on us!

∽

O JESUS, by the compassion which thou didst feel for thy Mother, have compassion on us, and give us a share in her intercession. O Mary, most afflicted Mother! intercede for us, that, though the sufferings of thy Son, we may be delivered from the wrath to come.

Challoner

∽

Quæ mœrébat et dolébat Pia Mater, dum vidébat Nati pœnas ínclyti.

Christ above in torment hangs; She beneath beholds the pangs Of her dying glorious Son.

∽   ∽   ∽

THE FIFTH STATION
Simon of Cyrene helps Jesus to carry his cross

℣. We adore thee, O Christ, and we bless thee,
℟. Because by thy holy cross thou hast redeemed the world.

*Consider how his executioners, seeing that at each step Jesus
was on the point of expiring, and fearing that he would die on the
way, whereas they wished him to die the ignominious death of the
cross, constrained Simon the Cyrenian to carry the cross behind
our Lord.*

∾

A reading from the Gospel according to St Mark

AND they forced one Simon, a Cyrenian, who passed by,
coming in from the country, the father of Alexander and
Rufus, to take up his cross.

Mark 15:21

A reading from the Gospel according to St Luke

JESUS said to all: If anyone will come after me, let him deny
himself, and take up his cross daily, and follow me. For whoever wishes to save his life shall lose it, whereas he that loses his
life for my sake shall save it. How is it an advantage for a man to
gain the whole world and yet lose himself: throw himself away?

Luke 9:23-25

∾

JESUS could bear his cross alone, did he so will; but he per-
mits Simon to help him, in order to remind us that we must take
part in his sufferings, and have a fellowship in his work. His merit
is infinite, yet he condescends to let his people add their merit to it.
The sanctity of the Blessed Virgin, the blood of the martyrs, the
prayers and penances of the saints, the good deeds of all the faithful take part in that work which, nevertheless, is perfect without
them. He saves us by his blood, but it is through and with ourselves that he saves us. Dear Lord, teach us to suffer with thee,
make it pleasant to us to suffer for thy sake, and sanctify all our
sufferings by the merits of thy own.

J.H. Newman

Sicut ovis ad occisiónem ductus est, et dum male tracterétur, non apéruit os suum: tráditus est ad mortem, * Ut vivificáret pópulum suum. ℣. Trádidit in mortem ánimam suam, et inter scelerátos reputátus est. * Ut vivificáret pópulum suum.

He was led as a lamb before his killers, and when he was badly treated he did not open his mouth: he was betrayed unto death, * that he might give life to his people. ℣. He was betrayed unto death, and reputed among the wicked, * that he might give life to his people.

❧

BEHOLD our Lord and our God, exhausted and able no more to carry his cross, and all for the sins which we have committed!

Holy God!
Holy, mighty one!
Holy, immortal one!
Have mercy on us!

❧

O LORD Jesus, may it be our privilege also to bear thy cross; may we glory in nothing else. By it may the world be crucified unto us, and we unto the world; may we never shrink from sufferings, but rather rejoice if we may be counted worthy to suffer for thy name's sake.

Challoner

❧

Quis est homo qui non fleret, Matrem Christi si vidéret In tanto supplício?

Is there one who would not weep, Whelmed in miseries so deep Christ's dear Mother to behold?

❧   ❧   ❧

THE SIXTH STATION
Veronica wipes the face of Jesus

℣. We adore thee, O Christ, and we bless thee,
℟. **Because by thy holy cross thou hast redeemed the world.**

Consider how the holy woman named Veronica, seeing Jesus so ill-used, and his face bathed in sweat and blood, presented him with a towel, with which he wiped his adorable face, leaving on it the impression of his holy countenance.

∾

A reading from the prophet Isaiah

THERE is no beauty in him, nor comeliness; we have seen him, and there was no sightliness, that we should desire him: despised, and the most abject of men, a man of sorrows, and acquainted with grief, and his look was as if it were hidden away and despised, so we esteemed him worthless. But surely it is *our* infirmities that he has borne; *our* sorrows that he has carried, and we have thought of him as we would a leper, and as one struck by God and afflicted. But it was for our iniquities that he was wounded, and it was for our sins that he was bruised, and by his bruises we are healed.

Isaiah 53: 2-5

A reading from the second letter of St Paul to the Corinthians

BUT WE all, beholding the glory of the Lord with open face, are transformed into the same image from glory to glory as by the Spirit of the Lord.

2 Corinthians 3:18

∾

MY MOST beloved Jesus! Thy face was beautiful before, but in this journey it has lost all its beauty, and wounds and blood have disfigured it. Alas! my soul also was once beautiful, when it received thy grace in baptism; but I have disfigured it since by my sins. Thou alone, my Redeemer, canst restore it to its former beauty. Do this by thy passion, O Jesus.

St Alphonsus Liguori

Tradidérunt me in manus impiórum, et inter iníquos proiecérunt me, et non pepercérunt ánimæ meæ: congregáti sunt advérsum me fortes: * Et sicut gigántes stetérunt contra me. ℣. Aliéni insurrexérunt advérsum me, et fortes quæsiérunt ánimam meam. * Et sicut gigántes stetérunt contra me.

They betrayed me into the hands of the unholy, and cast me down among the wicked: they would not even spare my soul: I am surrounded by violent men who seek to harm me: * like giants they threaten me. ℣. Strange men have risen against me, and the violent seek to take my life: * like giants they threaten me.

❧

B EHOLD the face of the Lord, wounded and made repulsive for the sins which we have committed!

Holy God!
Holy, mighty one!
Holy, immortal one!
Have mercy on us!

❧

O SACRED Head, surrounded
By crown of piercing thorn!
O bleeding head, so wounded,
Reviled, and put to scorn!
Death's pallid hue comes o'er thee,
The glow of life decays;
Yet angel hosts adore thee,
And tremble as they gaze.

❧

O MY Jesus, look upon us with mercy; turn your face towards each of us as you turned to Veronica, not that we may see your face with our earthly eyes, for surely we cannot deserve this privilege; but turn towards our hearts, we pray, so that keeping you in our remembrance, we may for ever draw from you, the source of power, strength for our daily battles. Amen.

Pope Pius IX

Quis non posset contristári,
Christi Matrem contemplári
Doléntem cum Fílio?

Can the human heart refrain
From partaking in her pain
In that Mother's pain untold.

THE SEVENTH STATION
Jesus falls the second time

℣. We adore thee, O Christ, and we bless thee,
℟. **Because by thy holy cross thou hast redeemed the world.**

Consider the second fall of Jesus under the cross; a fall which renews the pain of his head and members.

ༀ

A reading from the prophet Isaiah

FOR THE wickedness of my people have I struck him; he has done no iniquity, neither was there any deceit in his mouth. And the Lord was pleased to crush him in weakness.

Because his soul has laboured, he shall see and be filled: by his knowledge shall this my servant justify many, and he shall bear their iniquities. Therefore I will distribute to him whole armies, and he shall divide the spoils of the strong, because he handed over his soul to death, and was reputed with the wicked, and he has borne the sins of many, and he has prayed for transgressors.

Isaiah 52:8-12 passim

ༀ

WHAT streams of precious blood poured forth from the veins of our Blessed Lord when laden with the heavy cross on the sad way to Calvary! The very streets and ways of Jerusalem, through which he passed, were watered with it. This he did for the scandals, literally, the stumbling blocks, which his own followers had laid in the path of others by their own bad example, their infidelities. How many people have I led astray by my lukewarmness, my thoughtlessness, my lack of devotion? My God, may I henceforth make smooth your path before you into people's hearts by my fidelity.

ༀ

LORD God, so awful are the crimes of the world that even after receiving supernatural help and Simon's assistance, you fell again because of the weight of sin. Dear Lord, my falls will be for quite a different reason—where you did fall from weakness of the body, my failures are from weakness of the flesh; but whether through laziness or malice, I pray that your example may encourage me to rise. Lord, I mean to go on; I seem to have shaken

off the cross as being quite beyond my strength, but, Lord, I want
to take it up again and go ahead with you.

Dom Hubert van Zeller

Omnes amíci mei dereli-
quérunt me, et prævaluérunt
insidiántes mihi: trádidit me
quam diligébam: * Et
terribílibus óculis plaga
crudéli percuti-éntes, acéto
potábant me. ℣. Inter iníquos
proiecérunt me, et non
pepercérunt ánimæ meæ. * Et
terribílibus óculis plaga
crudéli percutiéntes, acéto
potábant me.

All my friends abandoned me,
and those who laid a snare for me
have triumphed over me: the one
whom I loved has betrayed me: *
And glaring at me, wounding me
with cruel blows, they gave me
vinegar to drink. ℣. They cast me
down among the wicked, and they
did not spare my soul.* And glaring at me, wounding me with
cruel blows, they gave me vinegar
to drink.

B EHOLD our Lord and our God, crushed to the ground a second time for the sins which we have committed!

Holy God!
Holy, mighty one!
Holy, immortal one!
Have mercy on us!

O JESUS! falling again under the burden of our sins, and of
thy sufferings for our sins, how often have we grieved thee
by our repeated falls into sin! Oh, may we rather die than ever
offend thee again!

Challoner

Pro peccátis suæ gentis
Vidit Iesum in torméntis
Et flagéllis súbditum.

Bruised, derided, cursed, defiled,
She beheld her tender Child
All with bloody scourges rent.

THE EIGHTH STATION
Jesus speaks to the daughters of Jerusalem

℣. We adore thee, O Christ, and we bless thee,
℞. **Because by thy holy cross thou hast redeemed the world.**

*Consider how these women wept with compassion at seeing Jesus
in such a pitiable state, streaming with blood as he walked along.
'My children,' said he, 'weep not for me, but for yourselves and
for your children.'*

A reading from the Gospel according to St Luke

THERE followed Jesus a great multitude of people, and
women who wailed and lamented for him. But Jesus, turning
to them, said: 'Daughters of Jerusalem, do not weep over me, but
weep for yourselves and for your children; for behold, the days
shall come when they will say: Blessed are the barren, and the
wombs that have not borne, and the breasts that have not given
suck. Then they shall begin to say to the mountains: Fall upon us,
and to the hills: Cover us.'

Luke 23:27-30

A reading from the book of Lamentations

MY EYES have failed with weeping, my soul is in torment,
my heart is poured out upon the earth for the destruction of
the daughter of my people, when the children and the infants faint
away in the streets of the city.

Lamentations 2:11

EVER since the prophecy of old time, that the Saviour of man
was to be born of a woman of the stock of Abraham, the
Jewish women had desired to bear him. Yet, now that he was
really come, how different, as the Gospel tells us, was the event
from what they had expected. He said to them 'that the days were
coming when they should say Blessed are the barren, and the
wombs that have not borne, and the breasts which have not given
suck.'

Ah, Lord, we know not what is good for us, and what is bad. We
cannot foretell the future, nor do we know when thou comest to visit
us, in what form thou wilt come. And therefore we leave it all to thee.
Do thou thy good pleasure to us and in us. Let us ever look at thee,

and do thou look upon us, and give us the grace of thy bitter cross and Passion, and console us in thy own way and at thy own time.

J.H.Newman

Plange quasi virgo, plebs mea: ululáte, pastóres, in cínere et cilício, * Quia venit dies Dómini magna, et amára valde. ℣. Accíngite vos, sacerdótes, et plángite, minístri altáris, aspérgite vos cínere. * Quia venit dies Dómini magna, et amára valde.

Cry like a virgin, my people: grieve, you shepherds, in sackcloth and ashes, * For the great day of the Lord is coming, and it will be very bitter. ℣. Gird yourselves up, you priests, and weep, you that serve at the altar; sprinkle yourselves with ashes * For the great day of the Lord is coming, and it will be very bitter.

❧

B EHOLD our Lord and our God, suffering bitterly for the sins which we have committed, but yet placing his children first!

Holy God!
Holy, mighty one!
Holy, immortal one!
Have mercy on us!

❧

O LORD Jesus, we mourn, and we will mourn both for thee and for ourselves; for thy suffering, and for our sins which caused them. Oh, teach us so to mourn that we may be comforted, and escape those dreadful judgements prepared for all who reject or neglect thee in this life.

Challoner

❧

Vidit suum dulcem Natum
Moriéndo desolátum,
Dum emísit spíritum.

For the sins of his own nation,
Saw him hang in desolation
Till his spirit forth he sent.

 ❧ ❧ ❧

THE NINTH STATION
Jesus falls the third time

℣. We adore thee, O Christ, and we bless thee,
℟. **Because by thy holy cross thou hast redeemed the world.**

*Consider the third fall of Jesus Christ. His weakness was extreme,
and the cruelty of his executioners excessive, who tried to hasten
his steps when he could scarcely move.*

∾

A reading from the book of Psalms

I LIE fallen to the pavement: give me life according to your
word. I have declared my ways, and you have heard me: teach
me your justifications, and I will contemplate your wondrous
works. My soul lies leaden through heaviness: give me strength
according to your word.

Psalm 118: 25-28

∾

JESUS had now arrived almost at the summit of Calvary, but
before he reached the spot where he was to be crucified, his
strength again fails him, and he falls the third time, to be again
dragged up and goaded onward by the brutal soldiers.

Challoner

∾

MY DEAREST Jesus: how often have I, too, fallen again
and again. How often have I thought that I could never
arise and carry on. And here I see before me a reminder that in
the greatest extremes, you persevered, urged on by your desire to
let the will of your heavenly Father be done. Give me, dearest Lord,
some share of this same perseverance: to labour on despite the
wounds, to toil and not to seek for rest until I, too, have done the
will of him who is my Father, thanks to your heroic sacrifice.

∾

Dixérunt ímpii apud se, non
recte cogitántes: Circum-
veniámus iustum, quóniam

The wicked say among themselves, not thinking rightly: Let
us surround the just man, for he

contrárius est opéribus nostris: promíttit se sciéntiam Dei habére, Fílium Dei se nóminat, et gloriátur patrem se habére Deum: * Videámus si sermónes illíus veri sunt: et si est vere Fílius Dei, líberet eum de mánibus nostris: mortis turpíssima condemnémus eum. ℣. Tamquam nugáces æstimáti sumus ab illo, et ábstinet se a viis nostris tamquam ab immundítiis: et præfert novíssima iustórum. * Videámus si sermónes illíus veri sunt: et si est vere Fílius Dei, líberet eum de mánibus nostris: mortis turpíssima condemnémus eum.

is opposed to what we want to do: he claims to have knowledge of God. He calls himself the Son of God, and glories in pretending that he has God for his Father: * Let us see if his words are true, for if he truly is the Son of God, God will free him from our hands: we will condemn him to a most horrible death. ℣. He reckons us as worthless, and keeps away from us as though we were unclean, and behaves as if the final end of the just were happy. * Let us see if his words are true, for if he truly is the Son of God, God will free him from our hands: we will condemn him to a most horrible death.

❧

B EHOLD our Lord and our God, crushed to the ground yet a third time for the sins which we have committed!

Holy God!
Holy, mighty one!
Holy, immortal one!
Have mercy on us!

❧

O LORD Jesus, we entreat thee, by the merits of this thy third most painful fall, to pardon our frequent relapses and our long continuance in sin; and may the thought of these thy sufferings make us to hate our sins more and more.

Challoner

❧

Eia Mater, fons amóris,
Me sentíre vim dolóris
Fac, ut tecum lúgeam.

O thou Mother! fount of love!
Touch my spirit from above,
Make my heart with thine accord.

❧   ❧   ❧

THE TENTH STATION

Jesus is stripped of his garments

℣. We adore thee, O Christ, and we bless thee,
℟. Because by thy holy cross thou hast redeemed the world.

*Consider the violence with which Jesus was stripped by his ex-
ecutioners. As his inner garments adhered to his torn flesh, they
dragged them off so roughly that the skin came with them. Com-
passionate your Saviour thus cruelly treated.*

∽

A reading from the Gospel according to St Matthew

A ND they came to the place that is called Golgotha which is
the place of Calvary. And they gave him wine to drink mingled with gall. And when he had tasted, he would not drink. And
after they had crucified him, they divided his garments, casting
lots, that what the prophet had spoken might be fulfilled: *They
divided my garments among them, and upon my vesture they cast
lots.* And they sat and watched him.

Matthew 27:33-36

∽

L ORD, I see in this Station the complete offering of yourself.
see this offering as an invitation to me: 'Give me yourself,'
you say, 'not only what you *have,* but what you *are.*' Lord God,
I am nearing Calvary with you: teach me to strip myself of all
that is not of God, until at last I stand beside your cross offered
entirely to you. Only in this way can I be worthy of the final
sacrifice of my own life to you.

Dom Hubert Van Zeller

∽

J ESUS would give up everything of this world before he left it.
He exercised the most perfect poverty. Even when he left the
holy house of Nazareth and went out to preach, he had nowhere
to lay his head. He lived on the poorest food, and on what was
given to him by those who loved and served him. And therefore
he chose a death in which not even his clothes were left to him.
He parted with what seemed most necessary, and even a part of
him, by the law of human nature since the fall.

Grant us in like manner, O dear Lord, to care nothing for anything on earth, and to bear the loss of all things, and to endure even shame, reproach, contempt and mockery, rather than that you shall be ashamed of us at the last day.

J.H.Newman

❧

Ierúsalem, surge, et éxue te véstibus iucunditátis: indúere cínere et cilício, * Quia in te occísus est Salvátor Israel. ℣. Deduc quasi torréntem lácrimas per diem et noctem, et non táceat pupílla óculi tui. * Quia in te occísus est Salvátor Israel.

Jerusalem, arise, and cast off your garments of joy: put on sackcloth and ashes, * For in your midst has been killed the Saviour of Israel. ℣. Let your tears run down by day and night, and give your eyes no rest, * For in your midst has been killed the Saviour of Israel.

❧

BEHOLD our Lord and our God, publicly stripped naked and humiliated for the sins which we have committed!

Holy God!
Holy, mighty one!
Holy, immortal one!
Have mercy on us!

❧

O LORD Jesus, thou didst endure this shame for our most shameful deeds. Strip us, we beseech thee, of all false shame, conceit, and pride, and make us so to humble ourselves voluntarily in this life, that we may escape everlasting ignominy in the world to come.

Challoner

❧

Fac ut árdeat cor meum
In amándo Christum Deum,
Ut sibi compláceam.

Make me feel as thou hast felt,
Make my soul to glow and melt
With the love of Christ my Lord.

❧ ❧ ❧

THE ELEVENTH STATION
Jesus is nailed to the cross

℣. We adore thee, O Christ, and we bless thee,
℞. **Because by thy holy cross thou hast redeemed the world.**

Consider how Jesus, having been placed upon the cross, extended his hands, and offered to his eternal Father the sacrifice of his life for our salvation. Those barbarians fastened him with nails, and then, securing the cross, allowed him to die with anguish on this infamous gibbet.

A reading from the Gospel according to St Mark

IT WAS the third hour when they crucified him. And the inscription of his crime was written: THE KING OF THE JEWS. With him they crucified two thieves, one on his right hand and the other on his left. Thus the scripture was fulfilled which says: *And with the wicked he was reputed.* And those who passed by blasphemed at him, saying: Ha! It was you that was going to destroy the temple in three days and build it up again! Save yourself and come down from the cross, then! In the same manner, the chief priests and scribes also mocked him to each other: He saved others, but he cannot save himself.

Mark 15:25-31

O CHRIST Jesus, I adore you, because you were lifted up from the earth in order to draw all things to yourself. For with your arms outstretched on the cross, I see you as though you were reaching out to embrace us, and I hear you cry: Come to me, all you who labour and are burdened and I will receive and refresh you. O Lord, if I am too sluggish in coming to you, draw me, O Jesus, with the cords of your love which you have shown in being willingly nailed to a cross. Let it be my supreme and only delight to know and seek Jesus, and him crucified. Far be it from me to glory, save in the cross of my Lord Jesus Christ.

O eternal Father, behold, this is your beloved Son in whom you are well pleased. Look upon the face of your anointed one, and turn away your face from my sins, for which your only begotten Son humbled himself, being made obedient even to the death of the cross. Behold: he is our advocate with you, and the propitiation for our sins, for he has himself borne our sins in his body on the tree, and by his stripes we are healed. The voice of the blood of your Son cries to you from the earth, not for vengeance, but for pardon. Let his passion and death be to us a remedy for and remission of our sins, we beg. Let the pains and wounds of his body become medicine to heal our souls' infirmity.

Ténebræ factæ sunt, dum crucifixíssent Jesum Judǽi, et circa horam nonam exclamávit Jesus voce magna: Deus meus, ut quid me derelequísti? * Et inclináto cápite, emísit spíritum. ℣. Exclámans Jesus voce magna, ait: Pater, in manus tuas comméndo spíritum meum. * Et inclináto cápite, emísit spíritum.

And there was darkness when the Jews crucified Jesus, and around the ninth hour, Jesus cried out with a loud voice: My God, why have you deserted me? * And with bowed head, he gave up his spirit. ℣. Jesus cried out with a loud voice: Father, into your hands I commend my spirit. * And with bowed head, he gave up his spirit.

B EHOLD our Lord and our God, cruelly nailed to a cross for the sins which we have committed!

Holy God!
Holy, mighty one!
Holy, immortal one!
Have mercy on us!

O JESUS, nailed to the cross, fasten our hearts there also, that they may be united to thee until death shall strike us with its fatal blow, and with our last breath we shall have yielded up our souls to thee.

Challoner

Sancta Mater, istud agas, Crucifíxi fige plagas Cordi meo válide.

Holy Mother, pierce me through; In my heart each wound renew, Of my Saviour crucified.

THE TWELFTH STATION
Jesus dies upon the cross for our salvation

℣. We adore thee, O Christ, and we bless thee,
℟. **Because by thy holy cross thou hast redeemed the world.**

*Consider how Jesus, after three hours' agony on the cross, being
consumed with anguish, abandoned himself to the weight of his
body, bowed his head, and died.*

A reading from the Gospel according to St Mark

AND when the sixth hour came, there was darkness over the
whole earth until the ninth hour. And at the ninth hour,
Jesus cried out with a loud voice, saying *Eloi, Eloi, lama
sabacthani?* Which is, interpreted: My God, my God, why have
you forsaken me? Some of the bystanders, hearing this, said: Listen: he is calling on Elijah. One ran and filled a sponge with vinegar, and putting it on a reed, gave it to him to drink, saying: let
us see if Elijah will come to take him down. But Jesus, having
cried out with a loud voice, gave up the spirit.

And the veil of the temple was torn in two, from top to bottom. The centurion who stood beside him, seeing that having
cried out in this manner he had given up the spirit, said: Indeed
this man was the Son of God.

Mark 15:33-39

CONSUMMATUM EST. It is completed: it has come to a
full end. The mystery of God's love towards us is accomplished. The price is paid, and we are redeemed. The eternal Father determined not to pardon us without a price, in order to show
especial favour. He condescended to make us valuable to him, as
we set a price for what we buy. He might have saved us without
a price—by the mere *fiat* of his will. But to show his love for us
he took a price which, if there was to be a price set upon us at all,
if there was any price at all to be taken for the guilt of our sins,
could be nothing short of the death of his Son in our nature.

O my God and Father: you have valued us so much as to pay
the highest of all possible prices for our sinful souls—help us to
love and choose you above all things as the one necessary and
one only good.

J.H. Newman

Ecce quómodo móritur iustus, et nemo pércipit corde: et viri iusti tollúntur, et nemo consíderat; a fácie iniquitátis sublátus est iustus: * Et erit in pace memória eius. ℣. Tamquam agnus coram tondénte se obmútuit, et non apéruit os suum: de angústia, et de iudício sublátus est. * Et erit in pace memória eius.

Behold how the righteous dies, and nobody notices: the just man is taken away, and nobody cares: the righteous is taken away by iniquity * and his memory will be in peace. ℣ Like a lamb before its shearers he was silent, and he did not open his mouth: in violence and by force of law was he taken * and his memory will be in peace.

❧

BEHOLD our Lord and our God, willingly butchered in our place for the sins which we have committed!

Holy God!
Holy, mighty one!
Holy, immortal one!
Have mercy on us!

❧

O JESUS, we devoutly embrace that honoured cross where thou didst love us even unto death. In that death we place all our confidence. Henceforth let us live only for thee; and in dying for thee let us die loving thee, and in thy sacred arms.

Challoner

❧

Tui nati vulneráti
Tam dignáti pro me pati
Pœnas mecum dívide.

Let me share with thee his pain
Who for all my sins was slain
Who for me in torments died.

❧　　❧　　❧

THE THIRTEENTH STATION

Jesus is taken down from the cross

℣. We adore thee, O Christ, and we bless thee,
℞. **Because by thy holy cross thou hast redeemed the world.**

*Consider how, after our Lord had expired, two of his disciples,
Joseph and Nicodemus, took him down from the cross, and placed
him in the arms of his afflicted Mother, who received him with
unutterable tenderness and pressed him to her bosom.*

A reading from the Gospel according to St John

THE Jews, because it was the Passover, being unwilling that
the bodies should remain on the cross during the Sabbath day—
for that was a great Sabbath day—requested of Pilate that their legs
might be broken and that they might be taken away. The soldiers
therefore came and they broke the legs of the first, and of the other
that was crucified with him. But after they came to Jesus, when
they saw that he was already dead, they did not break his legs. Instead, one of the soldiers with a spear opened his side, and immediately there came out blood and water. And he that saw it has given
testimony, and his testimony is true. And he knows that he speaks
the truth, that you also may believe. For these things were done so
that the scripture might be fulfilled: *you shall not break a bone of
him.* And again, another scripture says: *they shall look on him whom
they pierced.* After these things, Joseph of Arimathea, who was a
disciple of Jesus, but secretly for fear of the Jews, made a request of
Pilate that he might take away the body of Jesus. And Pilate gave
him leave. He came therefore and took away the body of Jesus.

John 19:31-38

HE IS your property now, O Virgin Mother, once again, for
he and the world have met and parted. He went out from you
to do his Father's work—and he has done and suffered it. Satan and
bad men have no longer any claim upon him—too long has he been
in their arms. He has not been in your arms, O Mother of God, since
he was a child—but now, you have a claim upon him, when the
world has done its worst. We rejoice in this great mystery. He has
been hidden in your womb, he has lain on your bosom, he has been
carried in your arms—and now that he is dead, he is placed upon
your lap. Virgin Mother of God, pray for us.

J.H. Newman

Recéssit pastor noster, fons aquæ vivæ, ad cuius tránsitum sol obscurátus est: * Nam et ille captus est, qui captívum tenébat primum hóminem: hódie portas mortis et seras páriter Salvátor noster disrúpit. ℣. Destrúxit quidem claustra inférni, et subvértit poténtias diáboli. * Nam et ille captus est, qui captívum tenébat primum hóminem: hódie portas mortis et seras páriter Salvátor noster disrúpit.

Our shepherd is gone, the fount of living waters, at whose passing the very sun was darkened: * For the one who held the first man prisoner is himself taken: today our Saviour has broken the gates of death and its portals. ℣. He has destroyed the eternal prison, and undermined the power of the devil; * for the one who held the first man prisoner is himself taken: today our Saviour has broken the gates of death and its portals.

❧

BEHOLD our Lord and our God, dead in the arms of his grieving Mother for the sins which we have committed!

Holy God!
Holy, mighty one!
Holy, immortal one!
Have mercy on us!

❧

O THOU whose grief was boundless as an ocean that hath no limits, Mary, Mother of God, grant us a share in thy most holy sorrow for the sufferings of thy Son, and have compassion on our infirmities. Accept us as thy children with thy beloved disciple. Show thyself a mother unto us; and may he, through thee, receive our prayer, who for us vouchsafed to be thy Son.

Challoner

❧

Fac me tecum pie flere
Crucifíxo condolére
Donec ego víxero.

Let me mingle tears with thee
Mourning him who mourn'd for me
All the days that I may live.

THE FOURTEENTH STATION
Jesus is laid in the tomb

℣. We adore thee, O Christ, and we bless thee,
℟. **Because by thy holy cross thou hast redeemed the world.**

Consider how the disciples carried the body of Jesus to bury it, accompanied by his holy Mother, who arranged it in the sepulchre with her own hands. Then they closed the tomb, and all withdrew.

∾

A reading from the Gospel according to St John

JOSEPH of Arimathea...took away the body of Jesus, and Nicodemus also came—he was the one who first came to Jesus at night, secretly, for fear of the Jews—bringing a mixture of myrrh and aloes, about a hundred pounds' weight. So they took the body of Jesus and bound it in linen cloths with the spices, according to the manner that Jews observe at a burial. Now there was a garden in the place where he was crucified, and in the garden a new sepulchre where no-one had yet been laid. Since it was the Jewish Passover, and because the sepulchre was near at hand, they laid Jesus there.

John 19:39-42

∾

JESUS, when he was nearest to his everlasting triumph, seemed to be farthest from triumphing. When he was nearest to entering upon his kingdom, and exercising all power in heaven and earth, he was lying dead in a cave of the rock. He was wrapped round in burying clothes, and confined within a sepulchre of stone, where he was soon to have a glorified spiritual body, which could penetrate all substances, go to and fro quicker than thought, and was about to ascend on high.

Make us to trust in you, O Jesus, that you will display in us a similar providence. Make us sure, O Lord, that the greater is our distress, the nearer we are to you. The more men scorn us, the more you honour us. The more men insult us, the higher you will exalt us. The more they forget us, the more you keep us in mind. The more they abandon us, the closer you will bring us to yourself.

J.H. Newman

Sepúlto Dómino, signátum est monuméntum, volvéntes lápidem ad óstium monuménti: * Ponéntes mílites, qui custodírent illum. ℣. Accedéntes príncipes sacerdótum ad Pilátum, petiérunt illum. * Ponéntes mílites, qui custodírent illum.

When the Lord was buried, they sealed the place, rolling a stone over the doorway: * And they posted soldiers who kept watch over him. ℣. The high priests went to Pilate to petition him: * And they posted soldiers who kept watch over him.

B EHOLD our Lord and our God, laid in the tomb for the sins which we have committed!

Holy God!
Holy, mighty one!
Holy, immortal one!
Have mercy on us!

W E TOO, O God, shall descend into the grave whenever it shall please thee, as it shall please thee, and wheresoever it shall please thee. Let thy just decrees be fulfilled; let our sinful bodies return to their parent dust, but do thou, in thy great mercy, receive our immortal souls, and when our bodies have risen again place them likewise in thy kingdom, that we may love and bless thee for ever. Amen.

Challoner

Iuxta crucem tecum stare
Et me tibi sociáre
In planctu desídero.

By the cross with thee to stay
There with thee to weep and pray
Is all I ask of thee to give.

THE FIFTEENTH STATION

(Where it is customary)

Jesus rises gloriously from the tomb

℣. We adore thee, O Christ, and we bless thee,
℟. Because by thy holy cross thou hast redeemed the world.

Consider how on the third day our Blessed Saviour, treading death underfoot, rose gloriously from the sepulchre where he had been laid and appeared to his Mother and his beloved disciples.

∾

A reading from the Gospel according to St Matthew

AND at the end of the Sabbath, when it began to dawn, beginning the first day of the week, Mary Magdalen and the other Mary came to see the sepulchre. And behold, there was a great earthquake, for an angel of the Lord had descended from heaven, and as he came, he rolled back the stone, and sat upon it. His countenance was like lightning and his garments as snow. And for fear of him, the guards were struck with terror, and became like dead men. And the angel spoke, and said to the women: Do not fear: for I know that you seek Jesus who was crucified. He is not here, for he is risen, as he had said. Come, and see the place where the Lord was laid. And go quickly: tell his disciples that he is risen; and behold he will go before you into Galilee; there you shall see him. So, I have foretold it to you. And they went out quickly from the sepulchre with fear but great joy, running to tell his disciples. And behold, Jesus met them saying: Hail! And they came up and took hold of his feet and adored him. Then Jesus said to them: Fear not. Go, tell my brethren that they should go into Galilee; there they shall see me.

Matthew 28:1-10

∾

THE longed-for redemption is come; the end to which we have looked forward is here. What greater and better thing can we do than to proclaim the power of the risen Lord? This Jesus bursting the bolts of hell, has raised for us the glorious banner of his Resurrection, and returning from the grave, he bears mankind aloft to the wondering stars, mankind which of old was over-thrown by the enemy's malice. O mystical and worshipful trans-actions of this wonderful mystery! What holy and eternal bless-ings are showered upon holy mother Church! She has no desire for the things that perish; all her longing is to find that which may redeem. Even as Mary joyed in holy child-bearing, so the Church exults in the beauty of her children's rebirth. That blessed fount which poured from the side of our Lord has washed away the mass of our sins, and those reborn find at the sacred altars the bread of eternal life.

PASCHAL triumph, Paschal joy,
Only sin can this destroy;
From sin's death do thou set free,
Souls re-born, dear Lord, in thee,
Hymns of glory, songs of praise,
Father, unto thee we raise.
Risen Lord, all praise to thee,
Ever with the Spirit be.

Outside Lent, the Regina Cæli, p. 343, could be sung

HOLY Lord, Light and true salvation of the faithful, illumine our hearts with the brightness of our Lord's resurrection, so that through knowledge of God's trinity and unity we may become worthy to be numbered with the children of light, as mem-bers of Christ and temples of the Holy Spirit.

Quando corpus moriétur	While my body here decays
Fac ut ánimæ donétur	May my soul thy goodness praise
Paradísi glória.	Safe in paradise with thee.
Amen.	Amen.

AT THE HIGH ALTAR AGAIN

A reading from the letter of St Paul to the Romans

IF GOD is for us, who is against us? He who did not spare even his own Son, but delivered him up for us all: has he not also, with him, given us everything? Who shall accuse the elect of God, whom God has justified? Who is it that can condemn? Christ Jesus who died, and who is risen again, who is at the right hand of God and who makes intercession for us?

Who then shall separate us from the love of Christ? Shall tribulation, or distress, or famine, or nakedness, or danger, or persecution, or the sword? In all these things we have overcome because of him who has loved us. For I am sure that neither death, nor life, nor angels, nor principalities, nor powers, nor things present, nor things to come, nor might, nor height, nor depth, nor any other creature shall be able to separate us from the love of God which is in Christ Jesus our Lord.

Romans 8:31-35, 37-39

∾

A reading from the letter of St Paul to the Philippians

CHRIST humbled himself, becoming obedient unto death, even to the death of the cross. For which cause God also has exalted him, and gave him the name which is above all names, that at the name of Jesus every knee should bow, of those who are in heaven, on earth, and under the earth, and that every tongue should confess that the Lord Jesus Christ is in the glory of God the Father.

Philippians 2:8-11

∾

Let us pray.

LOOK down, O Lord, we beg, upon this family of yours, for which our Lord Jesus Christ did not refuse to be delivered into the hands of wicked men and to endure the torments of the cross, and who lives and reigns for ever and ever. Amen.

There is an alternative prayer overleaf

ALMIGHTY God, who by the precious blood of thine only-begotten Son didst sanctify the standard of the cross: grant, we beseech thee, that all those who rejoice in the glory of the same holy cross may at all times and places feel the gladness of thy protection. Through the same Christ our Lord. Amen.

At this point prayers may be offered for the Pope's intentions in order to gain the indulgence attached to the devotion.

AVE verum corpus natum
Ex María Vírgine.
Vere passum, immolátum
In cruce pro hómine.

Cuius latus perforátum
Unda fluxit et sánguine:
Esto nobis prægustátum
Mortis in exámine.

O Iesu dulcis,
O Iesu pie,
O Iesu, Fili Mariæ.

Hail to thee, true body sprung
From the Virgin Mary's womb!
The same that on the cross was hung,
And bore for man the bitter doom!

Thou, whose side was pierced,
 and flowed
Both with water and with blood;
Suffer us to taste of Thee,
In our life's last agony.

Son of Mary, Jesu blest,
Sweetest, gentlest, holiest.

Tr. E. Caswall

THE ROSARY

The Classic Rosary

THE rosary is perhaps the most distinctive form of Catholic lay devotion outside the Mass. In its modern form, it is popularly supposed to have originated with St Dominic in the thirteenth century, and over the years it has gained substantially in popularity. The great sea battle that resulted in victory over the Turks at Lepanto in 1571 and the deliverance of Vienna in 1683 were both credited to the praying of the rosary, and in thanksgiving, October 7th is dedicated as a feast in honour of Our Lady of the Rosary.

As a prayer, the rosary can be prayed on many levels. At its most basic, it is simple vocal prayer, calling on our Lord and praising his Mother in words taken mostly from scripture, and asking for her help. Once one has achieved a certain fluency, however, and can say the prayers fairly automatically, it is recommended that one begin to meditate on the mysteries of our Lord's life while praying the prayers of the rosary, which prayers give the body something to do while the mind occupies itself in contemplating the mystery. Finally, the rosary may be used simply to free the spirit to contemplate our Lord and to enter into the life of the Trinity. In this way, the humble rosary can accompany the Christian through life, from the first beginnings of prayer to the heights of mystical contemplation.

The Prayers of the Rosary

The Apostles' Creed

I BELIEVE in God, the Father Almighty, Creator of heaven and earth; and in Jesus Christ his only Son our Lord; who was conceived by the Holy Spirit, born of the Virgin Mary, suffered under Pontius Pilate, was crucified, dead, and buried; he descended into hell; the third day he rose again from the dead; he ascended into heaven; is seated at the right hand of God the Father Almighty; from thence he shall come to judge the living and the dead. I believe in the Holy Spirit; the Holy Catholic Church; the Communion of Saints; the forgiveness of sins; the resurrection of the body, and life everlasting. Amen.

❧

O UR Father, who art in heaven. Hallowed be thy name; thy kingdom come; thy will be done on earth as it is in heaven; give us this day our daily bread; and forgive us our trespasses, as we forgive those who trespass against us; and lead us not into temptation, but deliver us from evil. Amen.

❧

H AIL Mary, full of grace, the Lord is with thee. Blessed art thou among women, and blessed is the fruit of thy womb, Jesus. Holy Mary, Mother of God, pray for us sinners now and at the hour of our death. Amen.

❧

G LORY be to the Father and to the Son and to the Holy Spirit, as it was in the beginning, is now and ever shall be, world without end. Amen.

❧

The Salve Regina

H AIL, holy Queen, mother of mercy; hail, our life, our sweetness, and our hope! To thee do we cry, poor banished children of Eve, to thee do we send up our sighs, mourning and weeping in this vale of tears. Turn then, most gracious advocate, thine eyes of mercy towards us; and after this our exile, show unto us the blessed fruit of thy womb, Jesus. O clement, O loving, O sweet Virgin Mary.

The Usual Method of Reciting the Rosary

Begin on the tail of the rosary beads:

Holding the Crucifix:	**One Apostles' Creed**
On the first bead:	**One Our Father**
On the three grouped beads:	**One Hail Mary on each bead**
On the next, single bead:	**One Glory be to the Father**

(NB. Many people ignore the tail and begin at this point)

THE FIRST MYSTERY

*Begin on the same bead
the first Mystery with*   **One Our Father.**

Continue on to the loop of beads:

On the first set of ten beads: **Ten Hail Marys,**

meditating on the first mystery.

*On the single bead,
finish the mystery with:*   **One Glory be.**

one decade

THE SECOND TO THE FIFTH MYSTERY

*Begin on the same bead
the second Mystery with*   **One Our Father.**

Repeat the pattern of one Our Father, ten Hail Marys and one Glory Be until you have completed the loop of beads, and have meditated on five mysteries. Then conclude with the following prayers:

One *Salve Regina* (Hail Holy Queen)

℣. Pray for us, Holy Mother of God,
℟. **That we may be made worthy of the promises of Christ.**

Let us pray.

O GOD, whose only-begotten Son by his life, death and resurrection has purchased for us the rewards of eternal life, grant, we beseech thee, that by meditating on the mysteries of the most holy rosary of the Blessed Virgin Mary we may both imitate what they contain and obtain what they promise, through the same Christ our Lord. Amen.

May the Divine assistance remain always with us. Amen.
May the souls of the faithful departed, through the mercy of God, rest in peace. Amen.

THE FIFTEEN MYSTERIES
of the Holy Rosary

∾   ∾   ∾

The Five Joyful Mysteries

customarily prayed on Mondays, Thursdays and Sundays from the first Sunday of Advent to the Feast of the Presentation (2nd February).

∾

1. The Annunciation.

IN THIS mystery we recall how our blessed Lady learnt from the angel Gabriel that she was to be the mother of Jesus, and how she willingly took on this difficult thing which God asked of her. We recall the conception of Jesus: the beginning of his earthly life.

∾

2. The Visitation.

WE RECALL the visit that the expectant Mary paid to her cousin Elizabeth who also was pregnant, bearing John the Baptist within her. As soon as Mary's greeting reached the ears of Elizabeth, we read, the child in Elizabeth's womb leapt for joy. Mary then gave great praise to God in the hymn known as the *Magnificat*.

∾

3. The Nativity.

IN THIS mystery, we remember the miserable and yet glorious birth of our Lord at Bethlehem in a stable, the song of the angels, the visits of the shepherds and the wise men from the east.

∾

4. The Presentation.

WE RECALL how our Lord was presented in the temple as the law of Moses required, offering a young lamb or two turtle doves as a sacrifice to the Lord. We remember how Simeon and Anna recognized who Jesus was, and prophesied coming sorrow for our Lady.

❧

5. The Finding of the Child Jesus in the Temple.

W E RECALL how the child Jesus was lost in Jerusalem for three days, and finally found by St Joseph and our Lady in the temple, discussing with the doctors of the Law. We recall how Jesus gently rebuked his mother and foster-father, saying that surely this was the place where he should be. We remember how Jesus went home with them, and was subject to their authority. And we recall how Mary stored all these things in her heart.

❧   ❧   ❧

The Five Sorrowful Mysteries
customarily prayed on Tuesdays, Fridays and Sundays from the Feast of the Presentation (2nd February) until Easter.

❧

1. The Agony in the Garden.

I N THIS mystery we remember that after the last supper, Jesus and his disciples went into the garden of Gethsemane, where Jesus prayed and his disciples slept. We recall how Jesus' distress was so great that he sweated blood, praying that the cup of suffering be taken away from him, but submitting to the will of God nonetheless.

❧

2. The Scourging at the Pillar.

W E REMEMBER that, in hope that it might satisfy his persecutors, Pilate had Jesus brutally scourged. Truly each of our sins was another blow of the scourges.

❧

3. The Crowning with Thorns.

I N THIS mystery we recall that our Lord's eternal kingship was mocked by this parody of the coronation ceremony. We remember Jesus' saying 'My kingdom is not of this world.'

4. Jesus Bears his Cross to Calvary.

W E RECALL how the heavy cross was laid upon Jesus who was already so weak that he could hardly stand. We remember that Simon of Cyrene helped him to bear it.

5. Jesus Dies on the Cross for our Salvation.

W E RECALL Jesus' hours of agony on the cross, and how he died, promising salvation to the penitent thief, how his side was pierced by a lance, and his body taken down, to be laid in the arms of his blessed Mother.

The Glorious Mysteries

customarily prayed on Wednesdays, Saturdays, and Sundays from Easter until Advent.

1. The Resurrection.

W E RECALL that on the third day in the tomb, Jesus rose from the dead and appeared to Simon Peter, Mary Magdalene and then many others.

2. The Ascension.

W E RECALL that forty days after his resurrection, Jesus went body and soul to heaven, promising the Holy Spirit to his disciples.

3. The Coming of the Holy Spirit at Pentecost.

W E REMEMBER how the Holy Spirit descended in the form of countless tongues of fire, and inspired the disciples to set aside their fear, and preach the Gospel to all nations.

4. The Assumption of our Blessed Lady into Heaven.

WE RECALL in this mystery how the Mother of God was taken up to heaven body and soul when her earthly life was over: a forerunner of the resurrection of the body that awaits us all.

◌

5. The Coronation of our Lady as Queen of Heaven, and the Glory of the Saints.

WE REMEMBER with gratitude the good things that God has promised for those who love him, and the coming glory that awaits those who do his will in this life, and how it will last for ever.

THE MANNER HOW TO RECITE THE ROSARY

from: *Jesus, Maria Joseph, or The Devout Pilgrim of the the Ever Blessed Virgin Mary in his Holy Exercises, Affections, and Elevations. Upon the Sacred Mysteries of Jesus, Maria, Joseph. Published for the benefit of the pious Rosarists, by A.C. and T.V. Religious Monks of the holy Order of S BENNET.* Amsterdam 1657

I N THE *first* place you are to settle yourself reverently in the *divin presence*, and (seriously recollecting your senses) to cast of all evagations of mind and extraversions, (which is the *generall* preparation to all Prayer.)

2ly To the end your *understanding* and *will* (both which concur in all well-order'd Prayer and Meditation) may be profitably employed; you may please to remember these *two Rules…*

The *First Rule* (which concerns the action of your understanding) is, *To represent before the Eyes of your Soul that mysterie, whereon you are to meditate, as even then acted in your presence.*

As for Example, The mysterie whereupon you intend to make your meditation, is, *The Nativity of our Saviour:* Imagin your self standing in a privat corner of the poor *Bethleem* Stable, beholding, hearing, and admiring all that there passed in that sacred night: run over in your mind the condition of the place, and the circumstances of the *Persons,* and think what were their *thoughts,* affections, words, actions: above all consider *who it was,* that appeared to the World in this mean equipage: to wit, the Son of God, the King of Glory, the Monark of the whol Universe: then ponder his love to mankind in generall, and to your self in particular &c.

The *second Rule* (which concerns the action of your will) is, *That you pass speedily from speculative discourses to devout affections, and self-reflections,* as for example, had you been in the Bethleem stable aforesaid, how diligently would you have employ'd your self in the service of little *Jesus*, and his loving *Mother?* How willingly would you have pick'd up sticks, made a fire, ayr'd his swaths, and fetch'd or carry'd whatsoever might have been usefull for their solace and succour, &c.

Such like reflections will rayse enflamed desires, and firm resolutions in your soul of better loving and serving both the Son and Mother for the future, and of suffering for his sake, who suffered so much for yours, &c.

And in some such manner you may conclude each *mysterie* by some particular resolution (drawn from the subject of the *meditation*) either of correcting such an imperfection, or of exercising such a vertu: and assure your self, that if you presently apply your self to the practise of such well made resolutions (humbly imploring the divin assistance therein by the blessed Virgins Intercession:) you shall find it a most speedy and efficacious means to the amendment of your life, the extirpation of vice, the implanting of vertu; and finally much conducing to your generall advancement in all sorts of spirituall Perfections.

3. You may also represent to yourself the sacred Virgin.

Sometimes as sitting or kneeling in her silent and solitary retreat, and attentively listening to the Angell *Gabriels* Salutation and Embassy.

Other times, as infolding gently her Sweet Infant *Jesus* in her sacred arms, imbracing him tenderly in her bosom, suckling him lovingly at her breasts, watching him carefully with her eyes, cherishing him affectionatly with her kisses, contemplating him devoutly with her heart.

Other times as painfully wayting on him from place to place in the time of his *Passion*, sorrowfully standing by him at the foot of his Cross, cheerfully rejoycing with him at his *Resurrection*.

Other times, as gloriously reigning in Heaven, mercifully vouchsafing to hearken to our prayers, and piously presenting them to her Son.

Or otherwise according to the severall mysteries, and sutably to each ones gust and devotion.

4. You are also here to be exhorted to propose to your self the cause (whether common or particular) which moves you now to the recitall of Rosary: as for example, I intend now to prayse my Lord God for the benefit of my Creation, Redemption, Vocation, &c. Or, In the honour of my Saviours sacred Nativity, bitter Passion, glorious Resurrection, admirable Ascension, &c. Or I intend to render thanks to my Creator for such a particular favour

as for mine own, or my friends *[good, or]* any other privat or publick benefit. Or, I intend to implore the divin assistance for the overcoming of such a *Temptation,* extirpating such a *vice* obtaining such a *vertu.* Or, For a good success in such an affair; Or, that I may make a happy progress in my Studies, &c.

Consider therefore briefly at the beginning of your prayers, *what it is* that you chiefly intend: and if it be any temporall or worldly benefit which you desire to obtain, be sure you demand it not *absolutely*, but only *conditionally,* as thus: If it please the divin Majesty, and that it is for my good and his glory: I humbly beg a happy end of such a Law-sute: success in such a journey, prosperity in such an undertaking, &c.

5. Then taking your *Bedes* in hand, or having this your *Book* open before you: begin your *Rosary* with the sign of the *Cross:* saying,
In the name of the Father, and of the Son, and of the Holy Ghost; Amen.

 confine   confine   confine

DEVOTIONS *AD LIBITUM* FOR THE MYSTERIES

THESE prayers and readings should be used entirely according to the devotion of whoever prays them.

In the scripture readings, please note that the small figures do not indicate scriptural verses, but correspond to the ten Hail Marys of each decade: some like to pray the 'Scripture Rosary', reading one small passage of scripture before each Hail Mary.

THE JOYFUL MYSTERIES

The Annunciation:

LET US contemplate in this mystery how the angel Gabriel saluted our Blessed Lady with the title Full of Grace, thus revealing Mary's Immaculate Conception, and how he declared to her the Incarnation of our Lord and Saviour Jesus Christ, to which she willingly assented to be the means.

Suggestions for intercession: *An end to the evils of abortion, resignation to God's will in one's own life, humility, chastity.*

O HOLY Mary, Queen of Virgins, through the most high mystery of the Incarnation of your beloved Son our Lord Jesus Christ, by which our salvation was so happily begun: obtain for us through your intercession, light to be aware of the greatness of the benefit which he has bestowed on us in making himself our Brother, and you, his own beloved Mother, our Mother also. Amen.

[1] In the sixth month, the angel Gabriel was sent from God to a city of Galilee called Nazareth to a virgin espoused to a man whose name was Joseph of the house of David, and the virgin's name was Mary. [2] And the angel, entering, said to her: Hail, full

of grace, the Lord is with you: Blessed are you among women. [3] She, having heard this, was troubled at his words, and considered in herself what manner of greeting this could be. [4] And the angel said to her: Fear not, Mary, for you have found grace with God. [5] Behold, you shall conceive in your womb and bring forth a son, and you shall call his name Jesus. [6] He shall be great, and shall be called the Son of the most High, and the Lord God shall give to him the throne of David his father, and he shall reign in the house of Jacob for ever, and of his kingdom there shall be no end. [7] And Mary said to the angel: How shall this be done, because I am a virgin? [8] And the angel answered her: The Holy Spirit shall come upon you, and the power of the most High shall overshadow you. And therefore also the holy one who shall be born of you will be called the Son of God. [9] And behold, your cousin Elizabeth also has conceived a son in her old age, and this is the sixth month of pregnancy in her who was called barren. Nothing is impossible to God! [10] And Mary said: Behold the handmaid of the Lord: be it done to me according to your word. And the angel departed from her.

Luke 1:26-38

O LORD, who when you came down to redeem our nature chose for yourself the most chaste womb of Mary to be the true Tabernacle of God with men: grant, we beseech you, that by her holy intercession, our souls may be so filled with your grace, that we may be made temples of God, who lives and reigns with you and the Holy Spirit, one God for ever and ever. Amen.

The Visitation:

L ET US contemplate in this mystery how the Blessed Virgin Mary, understanding from the angel that her cousin St Elizabeth had conceived, went with haste into the mountains of Judæa to visit her, and remained with her three months.

Suggestions for intercession: *For those who visit people in need, the St Vincent de Paul Society, stronger devotion to our Lady, gratitude to God, charity to our neighbour.*

O HOLY Virgin, most spotless mirror of humility, by that great love which moved you to visit your holy cousin, St Elizabeth: obtain for us, through your intercession, that our hearts being visited by your most holy Son, and freed from all sin, we may praise and give thanks for ever. Amen.

∾

[1] In those days, Mary rose up and went with haste into the hill country of Judæa. [2] She entered into the house of Zachariah and greeted Elizabeth. [3] And it happened that when Elizabeth heard the salutation of Mary, the infant leapt in her womb. [4] Elizabeth was filled with the Holy Spirit and she cried out with a loud voice, [5] saying: Blessed are you among women, and blessed is the fruit of your womb! [6] And why should this be, that the mother of my Lord should come to me? [7] For behold, as soon as the voice of your greeting sounded in my ears, the infant in my womb leaped for joy. [8] And blessed are you who has believed that those things shall be accomplished that were promised you by the Lord. [9] And Mary said: My soul magnifies the Lord, and my spirit has re-joiced in God my saviour. [10] Mary stayed with her about three months, and then returned to her own house.

Luke 1:39-47, 56

∾

O LORD who, in the visitation of Mary poured forth your heavenly graces on the house of Zachariah and Elizabeth; sanctify us by your sacred and most loving presence, as you sanc-tified your holy servant John, and give us grace so to instruct others in righteousness, and to edify them by our holy life, as to escape from all danger of pride or vain-glory, who live and reign for ever and ever. Amen.

∾   ∾   ∾

The Nativity:

L ET US contemplate in this mystery how the Blessed Virgin Mary, when the time of her delivery was come, brought forth our Redeemer, Jesus Christ and laid him in a manger, because there was no room for them in the inn at Bethlehem.

Suggestions for intercession: *the poor, for the gift of wisdom, for priests, who bring Our Lord into the world on the altars at Mass, for humility.*

∾

O MOST pure Mother of God, through your virginal and most joyful delivery, whereby you gave to the world your only Son our Saviour: we beseech, obtain for us, through your intercession the grace to lead such pure and holy lives in this world, that we may become worthy to sing without ceasing, both day and night, the mercies of your Son, and his benefits to us through you. Amen.

∾

[1] Joseph went up from Galilee, from the city of Nazareth into Judæa, to the city of David called Bethlehem, because he was of the house and family of David, to be enrolled with Mary his espoused wife, who was with child. [2] And it came to pass that when they were there, her time of expectancy ended, that her child could be delivered. [3] And she brought forth her first born son, and wrapped him up in swaddling clothes, and laid him in a manger because there was no room for them in the inn. [4] And there were in the same country shepherds watching and keeping vigil over their sheep. [5] And behold: an angel of the Lord stood by them, and the glory of the Lord shone round about them, and they feared with a great fear. [6] But the angel said to them: Do not fear, for behold, I bring you good tidings of great joy that shall be to all the people. [7] For this day is born to you a Saviour who is Christ the Lord, in the city of David. [8] And this shall be a sign to you: you will find the infant wrapped in swaddling cloths and laid in a manger. [9] And suddenly there was with the angel a multitude of the heavenly army, praising God and saying: Glory to God in the highest, and on earth peace to men of good will. [10] And it came to pass that after the angels had gone back into heaven, the shepherds said to one another: Let us go over to Bethlehem, and see this thing which has come to pass, which the Lord has shown to us. And they went with haste, and they found Mary and Joseph, and the infant lying in the manger.

Luke 2:4-16

∾

W E GIVE you thanks, most loving Jesus, because for our sake you chose to be born in a poor stable and to be wrapped in swaddling cloths, laid in a manger and fed at your Mother's breasts. Grant, dearest Lord, that we may become like little children, humble and poor in spirit. Grant that we may, like the Magi from the East, seek after you with diligence, and find you in the cradle of our hearts, and there adore you, offering up the gold of charity, the incense of devotion, and the myrrh of penance. Amen.

ও   ও   ও

The Presentation:

L ET US contemplate in this mystery how the Blessed Virgin Mary, on the day of her purification, presented the child Jesus in the Temple, where holy Simeon, giving thanks to God with great devotion, received him into his arms.

> Suggestions for intercession: *for generosity, for seeing the Lord even in the strangest situations, for children in need, for our own children, for obedience to the commands of the Lord.*

ও

O HOLY Virgin, most admirable lady, and pattern of obedience, who presented in the Temple the Lord of the Temple, obtain for us from your beloved Son, that with holy Simeon and devout Anna, we may praise and glorify him for ever.

ও

[1] And after eight days were passed, when the child was to be circumcised, they called his name Jesus, which he had been called by the angel before he was conceived in the womb. [2] And after the days of her purification were accomplished according to the law of Moses, they carried him to Jerusalem to present him to the Lord... [3] and to offer a sacrifice, as it is written in the law of the Lord, a pair of turtle doves or two young pigeons. [4] And behold, there was a man in Jerusalem named Simeon, and this man was just and devout, waiting for the consolation of Israel, and the Holy Spirit was in him. [5] He had received an answer from the

Holy Spirit, that he should not see death before he had seen the Anointed of the Lord. [6] And the Spirit inspired him to come into the temple. [7] When his parents brought in the child Jesus, to do for him according to the custom of the law, Simeon took him into his arms [8] and said: Now dismiss your servant, O Lord, according to your word. Because my eyes have seen your salvation which you have prepared before the face of all peoples, a light to the revelation of the Gentiles and the glory of your people Israel. [9] And Simeon blessed them, and said to Mary his mother: Behold, this child is set for the fall and for the resurrection of many in Israel, and for a sign which shall be contradicted. [10] And a sword shall pierce your own soul, that the secret thoughts of many hearts shall be revealed.

Luke 2:21-35

O LORD Jesus Christ, who condescended, together with your holy Mother, for our example to be obedient to the law for sin, grant us grace never to be ashamed of your law, but to labour to fulfil your commandments, to practise penance for our sins, and to approach your holy altar with those ardent desires with which holy Simeon received you into his arms. Amen.

The Finding in the Temple:

L ET US contemplate in this mystery how the Blessed Virgin Mary, after having lost her beloved Son in Jerusalem, sought him for the space of three days, and at length found him the third day in the temple, in the midst of the doctors, discoursing with them, being at the age of twelve years.

Suggestions for intercession: *obedience to legitimate authority, trust in the Lord, knowledge and understanding of the Catholic faith, humility, patience and diligence.*

M OST Blessed Virgin, more than a martyr in your sufferings, and yet the comfort of those who are afflicted: by that deep joy and relief which filled your soul at finding your beloved Son in the Temple, obtain from him that we may so seek him and find him in the holy Catholic Church, as to be never more separated from him. Amen.

∞

[1] The child grew, and waxed strong, full of wisdom, and the grace of God was in him. [2] And his parents went every year to Jerusalem at the solemn day of Passover. And they went up to Jerusalem according to the custom of the feast when he was twelve years old. [3] And having kept the days of the feast, the child Jesus remained in Jerusalem, and his parents did not know it. [4] And thinking that he was in their company, they went a day's journey, and then looked for him among their family and acquaintances. [5] Not finding him, they returned to Jerusalem, seeking him. [6] It came to pass that after three days they found him in the temple, sitting in the midst of the doctors, hearing them and asking them questions. [7] And all that heard him were astonished at his wisdom and his answers. And seeing him, they wondered. [8] And his mother said to him: Son, why have you behaved like this? Your father and I have searched for you in sorrow. [9] But he said to them: How is it that you looked for me? Did you not know that I must be about my Father's business? [10] And he went down with them and came to Nazareth, and was subject to them. And his mother kept all these things in her heart.

Luke 2:40-51

∞

O LORD my God, the only good; you are the sea of sweetness and ocean of all perfection. We are confounded when we think how much our souls are moved at the loss of earthly goods, and yet feel so little trouble when we have lost you by sin. Grant, we beseech, that, despising all earthly things, we may sigh only to enjoy the vision of your glory and beauty in that kingdom, where, together with the Father and the Holy Spirit, you live and reign as God, world without end. Amen.

∞   ∞   ∞

The Sorrowful Mysteries

The Agony in the Garden:

L ET US contemplate in this mystery how our Lord Jesus Christ was so afflicted for us in the Garden of Gethsemane that his body was bathed in a sweat of blood, which ran down in great drops upon the ground.

> Suggestions for intercession: *submission to the will of God, those agonized in mind, awareness of suffering in others, the gift of prayer.*

M OST holy Virgin, more than martyr, by that ardent prayer which your beloved Son poured forth to his Father in the garden, intercede for us, that our passions being reduced to the obedience of reason, we may always, and in all things, conform and subject ourselves to the will of God. Amen.

[1] Jesus went out, according to his custom, to the mount of Olives, and his disciples followed him. [2] And when he came to the place, he said to them: Pray, lest you enter into temptation. [3] And he drew away from them, about a stone's throw, and kneeling down, he prayed, saying: Father, if it be your will, remove this cup from me, but yet not my will but yours be done. [4] And there appeared to him an angel from heaven, strengthening him. [5] And in his agony he prayed the longer. And his sweat became as drops of blood, trickling down upon the ground. [6] And when he rose up from prayer and came to his disciples, he found them sleeping for sorrow. [7] And he said to them: Why are you asleep? Rise, pray, lest you enter into temptation. [8] While he was still speaking, a multitude came, and the one who was called Judas, one of the twelve, went to the front of them and drew near to Jesus in order to kiss him. And Jesus said to him: Judas, are you to betray the Son of man with a kiss?... [9] And Jesus said to the chief priests and magistrates of the temple and the elders that had come out against him: Why have you come out like this, carrying swords

and clubs, as if I were a thief? While I was with you daily in the temple, you did not stretch out your hands against me; but this is your hour, and the hour of darkness. [10] And arresting him, they led him off to the high priest's house.

Luke 22:39-54

☙

O LORD Jesus Christ, who, in the garden of Gethsemane taught us by word and example to overcome temptation by prayer, grant, we pray, that giving ourselves continually to prayer, we may obtain its abundant fruit, who lives and reigns for ever and ever. Amen.

☙   ☙   ☙

The Scourging at the Pillar:

L ET US contemplate in this mystery how our Lord Jesus Christ, being delivered up by Pilate to the fury of the Jews, was most cruelly scourged at a pillar.

Suggestions for intercession: *think of each of my sins as being another stroke of the scourge, those unjustly treated, cruelty and violence, children bullied, the spirit of mortification.*

☙

O MOTHER of God, overflowing fountain of patience, through those blows which your only and most beloved Son suffered for us: obtain from him grace for us, that we may know how to mortify our rebellious senses, and cut off all occasions of sinning with that sword of grief and compassion which pierced your most gentle soul. Amen.

☙

[1] The chief priests accused Jesus of many things. [2] And Pilate interrogated him again, saying: Will you not answer at all? See how many accusations they make against you. But Jesus still said nothing, and Pilate was puzzled. [3] Now on the festival day he was accustomed to release for the Jews whichever of the prisoners they demanded. And there was one called Barabbas, who was in prison with some seditious men, who had committed murder

in the uprising. ⁴ And when the crowd came up, they demanded that he would observe the custom as he had done before. ⁵ And Pilate answered them, saying: Shall I release for you the King of the Jews? For he knew that the chief priests had delivered Jesus up out of envy. ⁶ But the chief priests moved the people to release Barabbas for them. ⁷ And Pilate again said to them: What would you have me do, then, with the king of the Jews? And they again cried out: Crucify him! ⁸ And Pilate said to them: Why? What evil has he done? But they cried out all the more: Crucify him! ⁹ And so Pilate, being willing to satisfy the people, released Barabbas for them, ¹⁰ and delivered up Jesus, when he had scourged him, to be crucified.

Mark 15:3-15

∾

O LORD Jesus Christ who for our sakes took to yourself a human nature and suffered in your flesh for our example: grant that honouring your sacred Passion, we may imitate your blessed life of patience and penance, and attain at last to the glory of your resurrection, who lives and reigns for ever and ever. Amen.

∾   ∾   ∾

The Crowning with Thorns:

L ET US consider in this mystery how those cruel soldiers plaited a crown of sharp thorns and most painfully pressed it on the sacred head of our Lord Jesus Christ.

> Suggestions for intercession: *Earthly kings and rulers, govern-ments, the right use of power, all who suffer, those who suffer mental illness, prayer for intellectual honesty, students and teach-ers, prayer to disregard what others think of us in the quest to do what is right.*

∾

O MOTHER of our eternal Prince and King of Glory, by those sharp thorns with which his most holy head was pierced, we pray that through your intercession, we may be delivered from all motions of pride, and, in the day of judgement, from that con-demnation which our sins deserve. Amen.

[1] So then, Pilate took Jesus and scourged him. And the soldiers plaited a crown of thorns and put it on his head, and clothed him in a purple garment. [2] And they came to him and said: Hail, king of the Jews; and they struck him many blows. Pilate went out and said to the crowd: See, I am bringing him out to you, that you may see that I find you have no case against him. [3] So Jesus came forth, wearing the crown of thorns and the purple garment. [4] And Pilate said to them: Behold the man. [5] So when the chief priests and servants had seen him, they cried out, saying: Crucify him, crucify him! Pilate said to them: Take him yourselves and crucify him, for I find no case against him. [6] The Jews answered: We have a law, and according to the law he ought to die, because he made himself the Son of God. So when Pilate heard this, he feared all the more. [7] And he entered the hall again and said to Jesus: From whence do you come? But Jesus made no answer. So Pilate said to him: Will you not speak to me? Are you unaware that I have power to crucify you, and power to release you? Jesus answered: You would not have any power against me unless it were given to you from above. Therefore, the one who delivered me to you has the greater sin. From that moment Pilate sought to release him. [8] But the Jews cried out, saying: If you release this man, you are not Cæsar's friend. For whoever makes himself a king speaks against Cæsar. [9] Now when Pilate heard these words, he brought Jesus forth and sat down in the judgement seat in the place that is called Lithostratos, and in Hebrew Gabbatha. And it was the preparation day of the Passover, about the sixth hour, when Pilate said to the Jews: Behold your king! But they cried out: Away with him, away with him. Crucify him! [10] Pilate said to them: Shall I crucify your king? The chief priests answered: We have no king but Cæsar. So then he delivered Jesus to them to be crucified.

John 19:1-16

ᘓ

O LORD Jesus Christ, immortal and invisible King: grant we pray, that we who venerate your crown of thorns here upon earth, may receive from you the crown of eternal glory in the life to come, who lives and reigns for ever and ever. Amen.

ᘓ   ᘓ   ᘓ

The Carrying of the Cross:

L ET US consider in this mystery how our Lord Jesus Christ, being sentenced to die, bore, with the greatest patience, the cross which was laid upon him for his greater torment and shame.

Suggestions for intercession: The grace to carry our crosses cheerfully, those who come to the help of the afflicted, those who find life difficult, the spirit of meekness and patience.

ॐ

O HOLY Virgin, example of patience, by the most painful carrying of the cross, in which your Son bore the heavy weight of our sins, obtain for us from him courage and strength to follow his steps and bear our cross after him to the end of our lives. Amen.

ॐ

1 They took Jesus and led him out, and bearing his own cross, he went forth to that place that is called Calvary, but in Hebrew Golgotha. 2 And as they led Jesus away, they laid hold of one Simon of Cyrene, coming in from the country, and they laid the cross on him to carry behind Jesus. 3 And there followed him a great multitude of people, and of women who bewailed and lamented over him. 4 But Jesus turning to them, said: Daughters of Jerusalem, do not weep over me, but weep for yourselves and for your children. 5 For behold, the days shall come when they will say: Blessed are the barren, and the wombs that have not borne, and the breasts which have not given suck. 6 Then they shall begin to say to the mountains: Fall on us, and to the hills: Cover us. For if in the green wood they do these things, what shall be done in the dry? 7 And there were also two other criminals led with him to be put to death. 8 And when they had come to the place which is called Calvary, they crucified him there, 9 and also the robbers, one on the right hand and the other on the left. 10 And Jesus said: Father, forgive them, for they do not know what they are doing.

John 19:16-17 Luke 23:26-34

ॐ

O LORD Jesus Christ, who has said: 'No man can come to me, except he deny himself, and take up his cross and follow me:' grant, we pray, that venerating your blessed patience in the carrying of the cross, we may bear all the crosses and trials of this valley of tears, that being purified by suffering, we may be admitted into your eternal rest, who lives and reigns for ever and ever. Amen.

∾   ∾   ∾

The Crucifixion and Death of our Lord:

L ET US contemplate in this mystery how our Lord Jesus Christ, being come to Mount Calvary, was stripped of his clothes, and his hands and feet were most cruelly nailed to the cross on which he died, in the presence of his most afflicted Mother.

> Suggestions for intercession: *The grace of final repentance, the dying, and those who care for them, gratitude to God for Jesus' sacrifice to save us.*

∾

O HOLY Mary, Mother of God, as the body of your beloved Son was for us stretched on the cross, so may our desires be daily more and more extended in his service, and our hearts wounded with compassion for his most bitter passion; and you, O most Blessed Virgin, grant by your powerful intercession that we may ever follow his example of love unto the end. Amen.

∾

[1] Now there stood by the cross of Jesus, his mother and his mother's sister, Mary of Cleophas, and Mary Magdalene. [2] When Jesus therefore had seen his mother and the disciple whom he loved standing near, he said to his mother: Woman, behold your son. [3] After that, he said to the disciple: Behold your mother. And from that hour the disciple took her as his own. [4] Afterwards, knowing that all things were now accomplished, in order that the scriptures might be fulfilled, he said: I thirst. [5] Now there was a vessel set there full of vinegar. And they, putting a sponge full of vinegar on a hyssop stick, put it up to his mouth. [6] Jesus then, when he had taken the vinegar, said: It is consummated. [7] And bowing his head, he gave up his spirit. [8] Then the Jews, because it

was Passover eve, not wishing the bodies to remain on the cross on the Sabbath—that Sabbath being a great Sabbath day—besought Pilate that their legs might be broken and that they might be taken away. [9] The soldiers came therefore, and they broke the legs of the first, and of the other that was crucified with him. But afterwards they came to Jesus and they saw that he was already dead, so they did not break his legs. [10] Instead one of the soldiers with a lance opened his side, and immediately there came out blood and water.

John 19:25-34

O LORD Jesus Christ, who for your infinite love became, for the sake of sinful man, the scorn of men and the outcast of the people, and died for us on the cross to obtain our relief from eternal shame: grant us, we pray, by the merits of thy most sorrowful crucifixion and by the glorious intercession of your most tender Mother, who stood by you at the cross, the spirit of perfect contrition for our sins, and of a holy death; who lives and reigns for ever and ever. Amen.

THE GLORIOUS MYSTERIES

The Resurrection:

L ET US contemplate in this mystery how our Lord Jesus Christ, triumphing gloriously over death, rose again on the third day, to die no more, to suffer no more.

Suggestions for intercession: *Faith, and confidence when we come to die, those whom we love that have died, the spirit of Christian joy and optimism, the victory of Jesus over our lesser natures.*

O GLORIOUS Virgin Mary, by that great joy which you received in the resurrection of your only Son, we pray you to obtain from him that our hearts may never go astray after the false joys of this world, but may be ever and wholly employed in the pursuit of the only true and solid joys of heaven. Amen.

∾

[1] When the Sabbath was over, Mary Magdalene and Mary the mother of James and Salome bought sweet spices that they might come and anoint Jesus. [2] And very early in the morning, the first day of the week, they came to the sepulchre, the sun being now risen. [3] And they said to one another: Who shall roll back the stone for us from the door of the tomb? [4] And when they looked, they saw that the stone had already been rolled back though the stone was very large. [5] They entered into the sepulchre, and they saw a young man sitting on the right side, clothed with a white robe, and they were astonished. [6] The young man said to them: Do not be afraid; you seek Jesus of Nazareth who was crucified. He is risen; he is not here: see the place where they had laid him. [7] But go, tell Peter and his disciples that he is going before you into Galilee; there you shall see him, as he told you. [8] And going back from the sepulchre, they told all these things to the eleven and to all the rest. [9] And it was Mary Magdalen and Joanna and Mary of James and the other women who were with them who told these things to the apostles. And these words seemed to them like foolish stories, and they did not believe them. [10] But Peter got up and ran to the sepulchre, and stooping down, he saw the linen cloths laid by themselves and went away wondering in himself at that which had come to pass.

Mark 16:1-7 Luke 24:9-12

∾

O LORD Jesus Christ, who sorrowfully descended to the dead and gloriously rose again on the third day: grant to the souls of the faithful departed your eternal light and peace; and to us your servants grace to die each day more and more to ourselves, that we may live wholly unto you; who lives and reigns for ever and ever. Amen.

The Ascension:

LET US contemplate in this mystery how our Lord Jesus Christ, forty days after his resurrection, ascended into heaven, watched by his disciples, to their great wonder.

Suggestions for intercession: *Faith in the unseen God, prayer for the coming of the Holy Spirit, trust in the God whom we cannot see but gives us his grace for every trial, the grace of great desire for heaven.*

૭

O MOTHER of God, comfort of the afflicted, as your beloved Son, when he ascended into heaven, lifted up his hands and blessed his apostles, so, blessed Mother, lift up your hands to him on our behalf, that we also may experience the effects of his blessing. Amen.

૭

[1] The former treatise I wrote, Theophilus, concerned all those things which Jesus began to do and teach until the day when, giving commands by the Holy Spirit to the apostles whom he had chosen, he was taken up. [2] To these he had showed himself alive after his passion by many proofs, for forty days appearing to them and speaking of the kingdom of God. [3] And eating together with them, he commanded them that they should not depart from Jerusalem, but should wait for the promise of the Father, which he had said they had heard about from his own mouth. [4] For John indeed baptized with water, but you shall be baptized with the Holy Spirit not many days from now. [5] So those who were present asked him: Lord, will you now restore the kingdom to Israel? But he said to them: It is not for you to know the times or moments which the Father has kept in his own power. [6] But you shall receive the power of the Holy Spirit coming upon you [7] and you shall be witnesses to me in Jerusalem, and in all Judæa and Samaria, and even to the uttermost parts of the earth. [8] And when he had said these things, while they looked on, he was raised up, and a cloud took him out of their sight. [9] And while they gazed at him going into heaven, behold, two men stood beside them in white garments, who said: Men of Galilee; why do you stand

looking up into heaven? This Jesus who is taken up from you into heaven shall come again in the same way as you have seen him go. [10] Then they returned to Jerusalem from the mount which is called Olivet, which is near Jerusalem, about a Sabbath journey.

Acts 1:1-12

༄

O LORD Jesus Christ, who descended upon earth to be our sacrifice, and ascended into heaven to be our eternal Priest and Advocate: grant us grace that, being detached from all earthly things, we may in heart and mind ascend to where you have already gone before us, who lives and reigns for ever and ever. Amen.

༄   ༄   ༄

The Coming of the Holy Spirit:

L ET US consider in this mystery how our Lord Jesus Christ, being seated at the right hand of God, sent, as he had promised, the Holy Spirit upon his apostles in the form of countless tongues of fire, and how the same apostles were inspired to begin the evangelization of the world.

> Suggestions for intercession: *A renewal of the grace of our own confirmations, courage to share the Gospel with others, people preparing for confirmation, missionaries, for all the gifts of the Holy Spirit: wisdom, understanding, counsel, fortitude, knowledge, piety and the fear of the Lord.*

༄

O SACRED Virgin, spouse of the Holy Spirit, we beseech you to obtain that this same most sweet Comforter whom your beloved Son sent down on you and his apostles, causing such great joy, may teach us in this world the true way to salvation and make us to walk in the paths of virtue and good works. Amen.

༄

[1] And when the days of Pentecost came around, they were all together in one place. [2] And suddenly there came a sound from heaven, as of a mighty wind coming, and it filled the whole house where they were sitting. [3] And there appeared to them parted tongues as it were of fire, and these sat on every one of them. [4] And they were all filled with the Holy Spirit, and they began to speak with various languages, as the Holy Spirit directed them to speak. [5] Now there were Jews dwelling in Jerusalem, devout men out of every nation under heaven. [6] And when the news had spread, the crowd came together, and were astounded because every one heard them speak in his own tongue. [7] But others, mocking, said: These men are full of new wine. [8] But Peter lifted up his voice and spoke to them. [9] And with many words he exhorted them, saying: Save yourselves from this perverse generation. Those, therefore, who received his words were baptized, and there were added about three thousand souls that day. [10] And they persevered in the doctrine of the apostles, in their communion, in the breaking of the bread and the prayers.

Acts 2 passim

❧

O LORD Jesus Christ, to whom is given all power in heaven and on earth: send down upon us the Holy Spirit the Comforter, that he may guide, support and purify the souls of your servants and of your whole Church; who lives and reigns for ever and ever. Amen.

❧   ❧   ❧

The Assumption of our Lady:

L ET US contemplate in this mystery how the glorious Virgin, many years after the resurrection of her Son, herself passed body and soul out of this world to join him whom she had longed for, and for whom she lived.

Suggestions for intercession: *faith in the resurrection of the body on the last day, greater devotion to our Lady, devotion to the angels, the grace never to be satisfied with anything less than perfection in the spiritual life.*

O MOST prudent Virgin, who, entering the heavenly palace filled the holy angels with joy and man with hope, intercede for us, we pray, at the hour of our death, that being delivered from the illusions and temptations of the devil, we may joyfully and securely pass out of this temporal state to enjoy the happiness of eternal life. Amen.

¹ My soul magnifies the Lord: my spirit rejoices in God who is my Saviour, ² who has looked upon the humility of his handmaiden. ³ Behold, all generations from now will acknowledge me blessed. ⁴ For the mighty one has done great things for me: Holy is his name! ⁵ His mercy is from one generation to the next on those who fear him. Mighty is his arm! ⁶ He has scattered the proud in the imagination of their hearts, ⁷ and has put down the powerful from their thrones, exalting those of humble degree. ⁸ The hungry he has filled with good things, ⁹ but the rich he has dismissed with nothing. ¹⁰ Remembering his mercy, he has helped his servant as he promised to our fathers, to Abraham and to his posterity for evermore.

Luke 1:46-55

O LORD Jesus Christ, who, when the work of her perfection was accomplished, called to yourself the soul of your most holy Mother, and did not suffer her body to see corruption: grant us, we beseech you, the desire of perfection, and daily to purify ourselves more and more from all our faults and imperfections, so that at the hour of death we may be found worthy to pass to the blessed vision of your glory, who lives and reigns for ever and ever. Amen.

Our Lady Crowned as Queen of Heaven and the Glory of the Saints:

LET US contemplate in this mystery how the glorious Virgin Mary was, to the great joy and exaltation of the whole court of heaven, crowned by her Son with the brightest diadem of glory,

and how all the saints share with her the reward that awaits the
righteous in heaven.

> Suggestions for intercession: *simply in honour of the saints and
> asking God to make us among their number. The grace to imi-
> tate the virtues of the Blessed Virgin and the saints.*

O GLORIOUS Queen of all the heavenly citizens, we beseech you to accept this rosary, which as a crown of roses
we offer at your feet; and grant, most gracious Lady, that by your
intercession our souls may be inflamed with so ardent a desire of
seeing you so gloriously crowned, that it may never die in us
until we shall be changed from glory into glory, casting down
with you our golden crowns before the throne of divine majesty.
Amen.

[1] Blessed are you, O daughter, by the Lord the most high God,
above all women upon the earth, [2] because he has so magnified
your name this day that your praise shall not depart out of the lips
of men who shall be mindful of the power of the Lord for ever,
[3] because you have not spared your life by reason of the tribulation
of the people, but have prevented our ruin in the presence of our
God. [4] And all the people said: So be it, so be it.

[5] After this I saw a great multitude which no man could count,
of all nations and tribes and peoples and tongues, standing before
the throne and in sight of the Lamb, clothed with white robes and
with palms in their hands. [6] And they cried out with a loud voice,
saying: Salvation to our God, who sits upon the throne, and to
the Lamb. [7] And all the angels stood round about the throne, and
the elders, and the four living creatures, and they fell down before the throne upon their faces, and adored God saying: Amen.
Benediction and glory and wisdom and thanksgiving, honour and
power and strength to our God for ever and ever. Amen. [8] One of
the elders said to me…These are those who have come out of the
great tribulation and have washed their robes white in the blood
of the Lamb. [9] Therefore they stand before the throne of God,
and they serve him day and night in his temple, and he that sits
on the throne shall dwell with them. [10] They shall hunger and
thirst no more, nor shall the sun strike them, nor any heat. For the

Lamb who sits on the throne shall rule them, and shall lead them to the fountains of life, and God shall wipe away all tears from their eyes.

Judith 13:18,19-20 Revelation 7:9-17

O LORD Jesus Christ, who said 'In my Father's house there are many mansions, I go to prepare a place for you;' grant us, we pray, so to copy in our lives the holy virtues of your blessed Mother, that through her glorious intercession, we may attain the place prepared for us in your kingdom from the foundation of the world, who lives and reigns with God the Father and the Holy Spirit, one God, world without end. Amen.

As recommended at Fatima, each decade may conclude with the following prayer, after the Glory be to the Father:

O MY Jesus, forgive us our sins, save us from the fires of hell and lead all souls to heaven, especially those who most need thy mercy.

Another way to pray the Rosary, valuable for those who find their minds wandering, is to interpose a reminder of the current mystery into each Hail Mary:

...and blessed is the fruit of thy womb...

The Annunciation:	...Jesus, incarnate.
The Visitation:	...Jesus, bringer of joy.
The Nativity:	...Jesus, born in poverty.
The Presentation:	...Jesus, light of the nations.
The Finding:	...Jesus, our teacher.
The Agony:	...Jesus, agonised.
The Scourging:	...Jesus, scourged.
The Crowning:	...Jesus, crowned with thorns.
The Carrying:	...Jesus, who bore his cross.
The Crucifixion:	...Jesus, crucified for our sins.
The Resurrection:	...Jesus, risen from the dead.
The Ascension:	...Jesus, ascended into heaven.
Pentecost:	...Jesus, who sends the Holy Spirit.
The Assumption:	...Jesus, receiving thee into heaven.
The Coronation:	...Jesus, crowning thee.

...Holy Mary, Mother of God...

OTHER TYPES
OF
ROSARY

The Divine Mercy Devotion

One Our Father
One Hail Mary
One Apostles' Creed

∞

On each single 'Our Father' bead:

ETERNAL Father, I offer you the Body and Blood, Soul and Divinity of your dearly beloved Son, our Lord Jesus Christ, in atonement for our sins and those of the whole world.

∞

On each 'Hail Mary' bead:

FOR the sake of His sorrowful Passion
have mercy on us and on the whole world.

∞

At the end of each decade is said three times:

HOLY God,
Holy Mighty One,
Holy Immortal One,
have mercy on us and on the whole world.

∞   ∞   ∞

The Rosary of our Lady of Sorrows

This devotion concerning the seven sorrows, or dolours of our Lady is commonly associated with the Servite Order. Traditionally it is recited using a modified form of rosary beads, sometimes called 'dolour beads'. These are, however, not al-

ways easy to obtain. They consist of seven 'decades' of seven beads, and usually have a medal of our Lady attached. Each 'decade' consists of one Our Father, seven Hail Marys and one Glory be, while meditating on the following mysteries, remembering Our Lord's call to the Christian to take up his cross, and the perfect way in which Mary carried this out.

1. Simeon foretells that the sword of sorrow shall pierce the soul of Mary, when Jesus is presented in the temple.
2. Mary and Joseph are forced to flee into Egypt with the infant Jesus, and there live in exile.
3. The child Jesus is lost for three days in Jerusalem, and is eventually found in the temple.
4. Mary meets her Son on the way to execution on Calvary.
5. Mary stands under the cross as her Son dies.
6. Mary receives the body of her dead Son into her arms.
7. Mary sees the body of her Son laid in the tomb.

The Rosary of St Philip Neri

On every bead, simply:

Virgin Mother of God, pray to Jesus for me.

Or even:

Virgin and Mother!

Some like to think of a different person in need at each invocation.

The Jesus Prayer

T*his prayer is a form of rosary used widely among Byzantine Catholics and Orthodox Christians, though the construction of the rosary beads differs. There is no reason why it should not be used on ordinary (western) beads.*

On each bead, simply:

L ORD Jesus Christ, Son of the living God, have mercy on me, a sinner!

THE BLESSING OF A HOME

℣. Peace be to this place.
℟. And to all who dwell here.

It is customary to sprinkle each room with holy water as it is visited.

∾

In the entrance hall

ALMIGHTY God, our most welcome visitor, bless the portals of this home. May those who cross the threshold in peace find within a ready welcome and an open heart. May this door keep out all sin and evil, so that within there may be only goodness and truth, and the presence of your kingdom. Through Christ our Lord. Amen.

∾

In the main room of the house

LORD Jesus Christ, who found a ready welcome in the home of Martha and Mary, grant that in this room may be much laughter and good-nature. May dissension never gain a foothold here, but may joyful companionship become for everyone a fore-taste of heaven, where all the elect will rejoice in the communion of saints, praising God for ever and ever. Amen.

∾

In the kitchen

TEACH us, good Lord, to grow in humility, and in the practical love of our fellow human beings. In this kitchen may we learn that it is truly more blessed to serve than to be served, and that fidelity and affection are most truly learnt in the simplest ways. We ask this through Christ our Lord. Amen.

∾

In the dining room

IN THIS room, O Lord, give us a foretaste of your heavenly banquet, where none goes hungry, where none goes lonely, but all is satisfaction, communion and joy. Grace this table with your blessing, Lord, and accept our thanks for what has been and will be received by those who sit here. We ask this through Christ our Lord. Amen.

On the stairs

O LORD, who never does allow the steps of the just to stumble, keep all who use these stairs safe. May they ascend also in the path of virtue, and thereby come eventually to heaven. We ask this through Christ our Lord. Amen.

In a married bedroom

BLESS this room, O Lord, where we remember the joy of the wedding day. Renew the grace of marriage, and move those who sleep here to the keeping of your commandments in the truest covenant of love. We ask this through Christ our Lord. Amen.

In one bedroom

GUARD our purity, O blessed Lord, and bless our sleep. Make us quick to keep your commandments, that when we finally fall asleep in death we may wake to eternal glory. Through Christ our Lord. Amen.

In the bathroom

WASH us, O Lord, and we will be truly clean. In this room, O Lord Jesus, may we remember the washing of baptism which brought us eternal life, and may we remember your words that inner cleanliness is more important than outer. Let us set aside vanity and self-centredness, and make us fit citizens of your kingdom, where you live and reign for ever and ever. Amen.

In the main room once more

MOST blessed Trinity: we consecrate this home to your honour and glory. May it become for all who dwell here the place wherein they find the means of salvation. Mary, Mother of God, be a mother in this house; angels and saints, protect all who enter or dwell here with your powerful intercession.

ↀ

An image of the Sacred Heart of Jesus may be placed and blessed
at this point, with an act of consecration, such as on p. 322

Our Father

Hail Mary

Let us pray.

VISIT this house, O Lord, we pray, and drive far from it the deadly power of the enemy. May your holy angels dwell here instead, that we may be preserved in peace, with your blessing on us always. Through our Lord Jesus Christ your Son, who lives and reigns with you and the Holy Spirit, one God for ever and ever. Amen.

A priest or deacon may add:

May Almighty God bless this house and all who dwell here, the Father, the ✠ Son, and the Holy Spirit. Amen.

℣. Let us bless the Lord.
℟. Thanks be to God.

ↀ   ↀ   ↀ

ↀ   ↀ

ↀ

THE ITINERARIUM

Before undertaking a journey

Antiphon: In the way of peace and prosperity may the Lord, the Almighty and merciful, direct our steps. And may the angel Raphael accompany us on our way, that we may return to our home in peace, safety and joy.

B LESSED ✠ be the Lord, the God of Israel,
who has visited and redeemed his people,
and has lifted up a horn of salvation for us
in the family of his servant David.
For this he swore through the mouths of holy men:
那those who were prophets, from the beginning:
There would be salvation from our foes,
and from the hand of all those who hate us;
to comfort our fathers,
and to honour his holy covenant,
which oath once he swore to Abraham, our father,
that he would grant us,
that freed from the hand of our enemies,
and without fear, we may serve him,
in holiness and justice in his very presence all our days.
And you, my son, will be named Prophet of the Most High;
for you will go before the presence of the Lord
to prepare his way,
to teach knowledge of salvation to his people
that their sins may be forgiven,
through the merciful heart of our God,
when the Daystar shall visit us from on high
to enlighten those who sit in darkness
and in the shadow of death,
and guide our feet to the way of peace.
Glory be...

Antiphon: In the way of peace and prosperity may the Lord, the Almighty and merciful, direct our steps. And may the angel Raphael accompany us on our way, that we may return to our home in peace, safety and joy.

Lord, have mercy.
Christ, have mercy.
Lord, have mercy.

Our Father…

℣. O Lord, save your servants,
℟. Who trust in you, O God.
℣. Send us help, O Lord, from your holy place,
℟. And defend us out of Sion.
℣. Be unto us, O Lord, a tower of strength,
℟. From the face of the enemy.
℣. Do not let the enemy prevail against us.
℟. Nor let evil-doers approach to hurt us.
℣. Blessed be the Lord from day to day.
℟. God our salvation, make our way prosper before us.
℣. Show us your ways, O Lord,
℟. And teach us your paths.
℣. O, that our footsteps may be directed
℟. To keeping your righteous laws.
℣. The crooked ways shall be made straight,
℟. And the rough places smooth.
℣. God has given his angels charge over you,
℟. To keep you on your way.
℣. O Lord, hear my prayer,
℟. And let my cry come before you.

Let us pray.

O GOD, who made the sons of Israel to walk with dry feet through the midst of the sea, and who opened to the three magi, by the guiding of a star, the way which led to your Son: grant to us, we beg, a prosperous journey and a time of tranquillity, that, attended by your holy angels, we may happily arrive at (N.), and finally at the haven of eternal salvation.

O GOD, who brought Abraham your son out of the land of the Chaldees, and preserved him unhurt through all his journeyings, we beseech you to keep us your servants safe; be to us our support in our setting out, our solace on the way, our shade in the heat, our shelter in the rain and cold, our transport in our weariness, our fortress in trouble, our staff on slippery paths, our harbour on stormy seas, that under your guidance we may safely reach our destination, and at length return home in safety.

L ISTEN, O Lord, we beg, to our prayers, and arrange the way of your servants in the blessedness of your salvation, that amidst all the various changes of this our life and pilgrimage, we may ever be protected by your help.

G RANT to your people, we beg you, almighty God, that they may walk onward in the way of salvation, and by following the exhortations of blessed John the Baptist, the forerunner, that they may come safely to the presence of the One of whom John spoke, Jesus Christ your Son, our Lord, who lives and reigns with you in the unity of the Holy Spirit, one God for ever and ever. Amen.

℣. Let us proceed on our journey in peace.
℟. In the name of the Lord. Amen.

OTHER DEVOTIONS

BEGINNINGS

I N THE name of the Father and ✠ of the Son and of the Holy Spirit. Amen.

∾

Lord, teach us to pray.

Luke 11:1

∾

I F, WHEN we wish to make any request to men in power, we presume not to do except with humility and reverence; how much more ought we with all lowliness and purity of devotion to offer our supplications to the Lord God of all things? And let us remember that not for our much speaking, but for our purity of heart and tears of compunction shall we be heard. Our prayer, therefore, ought to be short and pure, except it be perchance prolonged by the inspiration of Divine Grace.

The rule of St Benedict

∾

M Y LORD and my God, I firmly believe that you are here, that you see me, that you hear me. I adore you with profound reverence; I beg your pardon for my sins and the grace to spend this time of prayer fruitfully. My immaculate Mother, St Joseph my father and lord, my guardian angel, intercede for me.

∾

Actiones nostras

D IRECT, O Lord, our actions by your holy inspirations, and carry them on by your gracious assistance that every prayer and work of ours may begin always with you, and through you be happily ended. Amen.

Roman Ritual

O MY God, I offer to you all the duties that I am about to perform, that they may be to your greater glory, and to the honour of your blessed Mother. Amen.

M Y GOD, I firmly believe that you are here and perfectly see me, and that you observe all my actions, all my thoughts, and the most secret motions of my heart. Though I am a sinner who has often offended you, do not, I pray, turn me away, out of that very goodness and generosity which at this time has called me to you. Give me grace, then, to pray as I ought.

T AKE my life, and let it be
Consecrated, Lord, to thee.
Take my hands, and let them move
At the impulse of thy love.
Take my feet and let them be
'Swift and beautiful' for thee.
Take my voice and let it sing
Always, only for my King.
Take my lips and let them be
Filled with messages from thee.
Take my moments and my days,
Let them flow in ceaseless praise.
Take my intellect, and use
Every power as thou shalt choose.
Take my will, and make it thine,
It shall be no longer mine.
Take my heart—it is thine own,
Let it be thy royal throne.
Take my love—O Lord, O pour
At thy feet its treasure store.
Take myself, and I will be
Ever, only—all for thee.

Frances R. Havergal

Pray as you can, and not as you can't!

Dom John Chapman

TEACH me, dearest Lord, to seek for you, and then show yourself when I search. For I cannot seek unless you show me how, nor find you but when you reveal yourself. Let me long for you with all my heart, and yearn for you as I seek: O fill me utterly with love when I find you!

St Ambrose

THE OUR FATHER

A ND IT came to pass that as Jesus was in a certain place praying, when he ceased, one of his disciples said to him, 'Lord, teach us to pray, as John taught his disciples.' And he said to them, 'When you pray, say: "Father, hallowed be thy name. Thy kingdom come. Give us this day our daily bread; and forgive us our sins, for we also forgive every one that is indebted to us; and lead us not into temptation."'

Luke 11:1-4

∞

The more familiar version from St Matthew's Gospel:

J ESUS said: 'Thus shall you pray: "Our Father who art in heaven, hallowed be thy name. Thy kingdom come. Thy will be done on earth as it is in heaven. Give us this day our daily bread. And forgive us our debts, As we also forgive our debtors. And lead us not into temptation, But deliver us from evil."'

Matthew 6:9-13

∞

Pater noster,
Qui es in cælis.
Sanctificétur nomen tuum.
Advéniat regnum tuum.
Fiat volúntas tua sicut in cælo et in terra.
Panem nostrum quotidiánum da nobis hódie
Et dimítte nobis débita nostra
Sicut et nos dimíttimus debitóribus nostris,
Et ne nos indúcas in tentatiónem
Sed líbera nos a malo.
Amen.

∞

W HICH is the best of all prayers?
The best of all prayers is the 'Our Father' or the Lord's Prayer.
Who made the Lord's prayer?
Jesus Christ himself made the Lord's prayer.

In the Lord's Prayer who is called 'our Father'?
In the Lord's Prayer God is called 'our Father'.

Why is God called 'our Father'?
God is called 'our Father' because he is the Father of all Christians, whom he has made his children by Holy Baptism.

Is God also the Father of all mankind?
God is also the Father of all mankind because he made them all, and loves and preserves them all.

Why do we say 'our' Father, and not 'my' Father?
We say 'our' Father, and not 'my' Father, because, being all brethren, we are to pray not for ourselves only, but also for all others.

When we say 'hallowed be thy name', what do we pray for?
When we say 'hallowed be thy name,' we pray that God may be known, loved, and served by all his creatures .

When we say 'thy kingdom come', what do we pray for?
When we say 'thy kingdom come,' we pray that God may come and reign in the hearts of all by his grace in this world, and bring us all hereafter to his heavenly kingdom.

When we say 'thy will be done on earth as it is in heaven,' what do we pray for?
When we say 'thy will be done on earth as it is in heaven,' we pray that God may enable us by his grace to do his will in all things, as the blessed do in heaven.

When we say 'give us this day our daily bread,' what do we pray for?
When we say 'give us this day our daily bread,' we pray that God may give us daily all that is necessary for soul and body.

When we say 'forgive us our trespasses, as we forgive those who trespass against us,' what do we pray for?
When we say 'forgive us our trespasses, as we forgive those who trespass against us,' we pray that God may forgive us our sins, as we forgive others the injuries they do to us.

When we say 'lead us not into temptation,' what do we pray for?
When we say 'lead us not into temptation,' we pray that God may give us grace not to yield to temptation.

When we say, 'deliver us from evil,' what do we pray for?
When we say, 'deliver us from evil,' we pray that God may free us from all evil, both of soul and body.

A Catechism of Christian Doctrine

☙

I KNEW a nun who could only make vocal prayer, yet, while keeping to this, she enjoyed all the rest as well. Unless she used oral prayer, her thoughts wandered to an unbearable extent—yet I wish we all made such mental prayer as she did! She spent two or three hours in reciting certain *Pater Nosters* and a few other prayers in honour of our Lord's blood-sheddings. One day she came to me in great distress because she did not know how to make mental prayer nor could she contemplate, but was only able to pray orally. I questioned her and found that she enjoyed pure contemplation while saying the *Pater Noster,* and that occasionally God raised her to perfect union with himself. This was evidenced by her conduct, for she lived so holy a life that I thank God for it, and I even envied her such vocal prayer. If this was the fact (as I assure you it was), let not any of you who are the foes of contemplatives feel sure that you run no risk being raised to contemplation yourselves if you say your vocal prayers as well as you ought and keep a good conscience.

St Teresa of Avila

OUR FATHER, which in heaven art,
  Lord, Hallowed be thy Name.
Thy kingdom come, thy will be done
In earth, even as the same
In heaven is. Give us, O Lord,
Our daily bread this day.
As we forgive our debtors,
So forgive our debts, we pray.
Into temptation lead us not,
From evil keep us free:
For kingdom, power and glory is
Thine to eternity.

Sternhold & Hopkins, Metrical Psalms, 1767

OUR SAVIOUR JESUS CHRIST

THE JESUS PSALTER

T his prayer is believed to have been composed in the fifteenth century by one Richard Whytford, who had been first a diocesan priest, and who subsequently joined the highly influential Brigittine double monastery of Syon, Middlesex. The Jesus Psalter is featured in many of the early printed Primers, and was revised by Bishop Challoner (1691-1781).

ฬ   ฬ   ฬ

'There is no other Name under heaven given to men whereby we must be saved' (Acts 4:12)

ฬ

FIRST PART

You must begin by a devout kneeling, or bowing, at the adorable name of JESUS, saying:

A T THE name of Jesus let every knee bow, both in heaven, on earth, and under the earth; and let every tongue acknowledge that the Lord Jesus Christ is in the glory of God the Father.   *(Philippians 2:10)*

The First Petition

J ESUS! *(repeated ten times)* thou God of compassion, have mercy on me, and forgive the many and great offences I have committed in thy sight. Many have been the follies of my life, and great are the miseries I have deserved for my ingratitude. Have mercy on me, dear Jesus, for I am weak; heal me, O Lord, for I am unable to help myself. Deliver me from an inordinate affection for any of thy creatures, which may divert my eyes from incessantly looking up to thee. For the love of thee, grant me henceforth the grace to hate sin, and, out of a just esteem of thee, to despise all worldly vanities.

HAVE mercy on all sinners, I beseech thee, dear Jesus: turn their vices into virtues; and making them sincere lovers of thee, and observers of thy law, conduct them to bliss in everlasting glory. For the sake of thy glorious name, Jesus, and through the merits of thy bitter passion, have mercy also on the souls in purgatory. O blessed Trinity, one eternal God, have mercy on me.

Our Father. Hail Mary.

ᗫ

The Second Petition

JESUS! *(repeated ten times)* help me to overcome all temptations to sin, and the malice of my ghostly enemy. Help me to spend my time in virtuous actions, and in such labours as are acceptable to thee. Enable me to resist and repel every inordinate emotion of sloth, gluttony, and carnality. Render my heart enamoured of virtue, and inflamed with desires of thy glorious presence. Help me to merit and preserve a good name by a peaceable and pious life, to thy honour, O Jesus, to my own comfort, and the edification of others.

Have mercy on all sinners, &c. *as in the first petition.*

Our Father. Hail Mary.

ᗫ

The Third Petition

JESUS! *(repeated ten times)* grant me effectual strength of soul and body, to please thee in the performance of such virtuous actions as may bring me to thy everlasting joy and felicity. Grant me, O merciful Saviour, a firm purpose to amend my life, and to make atonement for the years past; those years, which I have lavished, to thy displeasure, in vain or wicked thoughts, evil words, deeds, and habits. Make my heart obedient to thy will, and ready, for thy love, to perform all the works of mercy. Grant me the gifts of the Holy Ghost, which, through a virtuous life, and devout frequenting of thy most holy sacraments, may at length conduct me to thy heavenly kingdom.

Have mercy on all sinners, &c.

Our Father. Hail Mary.

∾

The Fourth Petition

JESUS! *(repeated ten times)* comfort me, and grant me grace to fix in thee my chief joy and only felicity; inspire me with heavenly meditations, spiritual sweetness, and fervent desires of thy glory; ravish my soul with the contemplation of heaven, where I hope to dwell everlastingly with thee. Bring thy unspeakable goodness to my frequent recollection, and let me always, with gratitude, remember thy gifts; but when thou bringest the multitude of the sins whereby I have so ungratefully offended thee to sad remembrance, comfort me with the assurance of pardon; and by the spirit of true penance, purging away my guilt, prepare me for the possession of thy heavenly kingdom.

Have mercy on all sinners, &c.

Our Father. Hail Mary.

∾

The Fifth Petition

JESUS! *(repeated ten times)* make me constant in faith, hope, and charity. Grant me perseverance in virtue, and a resolution never to offend thee. May the memory of thy passion, and of those bitter pains thou didst suffer for my sake, fortify my patience, and refresh my soul under every tribulation and adversity. Render me a strenuous professor of the Catholic faith, and a diligent frequenter of my religious duties. Let me not be blinded by the delights of a deceitful world, nor my fortitude shaken by internal frauds or carnal temptations. My heart has for ever fixed its repose in thee, and resolved to have contempt for all things in order to gain Thine eternal reward.

Have mercy on all sinners, &c.

Our Father. Hail Mary.

'The Lord Jesus Christ, for our sakes, became obedient unto death, even the death of the cross.' (Philippians 2:8)

HEAR these petitions, O most merciful Saviour, and grant me the grace frequently to repeat and consider them, that they may serve as so many easy steps, whereby my soul may ascend to thy knowledge and love, and to a diligent performance of my duty to thee and my neighbour, through the whole course of my life. Amen.

Our Father. Hail Mary. I believe in God.

ॐ   ॐ   ॐ

SECOND PART

Begin as before, saying,
'At the name of Jesus let every knee bow, both in heaven, on earth and under the earth,' *&c.*
as in the first part.

ॐ

The Sixth Petition

JESUS! *(repeated ten times)* enlighten me with spiritual wisdom, whereby I may arrive at a knowledge of thy goodness, and of everything which is most acceptable to thee. Grant me a perfect apprehension of my only good, and a discretion to regulate my life accordingly. Grant me wisely to proceed from virtue to virtue, till at length I enjoy a clear sight of thy glory. Forbid, dear Lord, that I return to the sins of which I accused myself at the tribunal of confession. Let others be edified by my pious example, and my enemies mollified by my good counsel.

Have mercy upon all sinners, *&c.*

Our Father. Hail Mary.

ॐ

The Seventh Petition

JESUS! *(repeated ten times)* grant me grace inwardly to fear thee, and avoid every occasion whatsoever of offending thee. Let the threats of the torments prepared for sinners, the dread of the loss of thy love, and of thy heavenly inheritance, always keep me in awe. Suffer me not to slumber in sin, but rather rouse me to repentance, lest through thine anger I may be overtaken by the sentence of eternal wrath and endless damnation. Let the powerful intercession of thy blessed Mother and all thy saints, but above all thine own merits and mercy, serve as a rampart between my poor soul and thine avenging justice. Enable me, O my God, to work out my salvation with fear and trembling, and the apprehension of thy sacred judgements. Make me a more humble and diligent suitor to the throne of thy mercy.

Have mercy upon all sinners, *&c.*

Our Father. Hail Mary.

ᴄᴠ

The Eighth Petition

JESUS! *(repeated ten times)* grant me the grace truly to love thee, for thine infinite goodness and those excessive bounties I have received, or shall ever hope to receive from thee. Let the recollection of thy benignity and patience conquer the malice and wretched propensity of my perverse nature. May the consideration of the many deliverances, frequent calls, and continual helps I have received from thee during the course of my life, make me blush at my ingratitude. Ah, what return dost thou require of me for all thy mercies, but that I love thee! And why dost thou require it? Because thou art my only good! thou art my dear Lord! the sole object of my life; and I will diligently keep thy commandments, because I truly love thee.

Have mercy upon all sinners, *&c.*

Our Father. Hail Mary.

ᴄᴠ

The Ninth Petition

JESUS! *(repeated ten times)* grant me the grace always to remember my latter end, and the account I am to give after death; that my soul may be always well disposed, and ready to depart out of this life in thy grace and favour. At that hour, by the powerful intercession of thy blessed Mother, the glorious assistance of St Michael, and my good angel, rescue my poor soul, O Lord, from the snares of the enemy of my salvation. Remember, then, thy mercy, O dear Jesus, and hide not thy face from me on account of my offences. Secure me against the terrors of that awful period, by causing me now to die daily to all earthly things, and to have my conversation continually in heaven. Let the remembrance of thy death teach me to set a just value on life, and the memory of thy resurrection encourage me to descend cheerfully to the grave.

Have mercy upon all sinners, &c.

Our Father. Hail Mary.

The Tenth Petition

JESUS! *(repeated ten times)* send me my purgatory in this life, and thus prevent me from being tormented in the cleansing fire, which awaits those souls who have not been sufficiently purified in this world. Vouchsafe to grant me those merciful crosses and afflictions which thou seest necessary for weaning my affections from things here below. Suffer not my heart to find any repose but in sighing after thee, since no one can see thee who loves anything which is not for thy sake. Too bitter, alas, will be the anguish of the soul that desires to be united to thee, and whose separation is retarded by the heavy chains of sin. Keep me, then, O my Saviour, continually mortified in this world, that being purified thoroughly with the fire of thy love, I may pass from hence to the immediate possession of thee in everlasting glory.

Have mercy upon all sinners, &c.

Our Father. Hail Mary.

'The Lord Jesus Christ, for our sakes, became obedient unto death, even the death of the cross.'   (Philippians 2:8)

HEAR these petitions, O most merciful Saviour, and grant me the grace frequently to repeat and consider them, that they may serve as so many easy steps, whereby my soul may ascend to thy knowledge and love, and to a diligent performance of my duty to thee and my neighbour, through the whole course of my life. Amen.

Our Father. Hail Mary. I believe in God.

ဢ   ဢ   ဢ

THE THIRD PART

Begin as before, saying,
'At the name of Jesus let every knee bow, both in heaven, on earth and under the earth,' &c.
as in the first part.

ဢ

The Eleventh Petition

JESUS! *(repeated ten times)* grant me grace to avoid bad company; or, if I should chance to come in the midst of such, preserve me from being infected with the least temptation to mortal sin, through the merits of thine uncorrupt conversation among sinners. Art thou not always present, O Lord? And wilt thou not take an exact account of all our words and actions, and judge us accordingly? How then dare I converse with liars, slanderers, drunkards, or blasphemers; or with those whose discourse is either vain, quarrelsome, or dissolute. Repress in me, dear Jesus, every inordinate affection to carnal pleasures and to delights of taste; and strengthen me by thy grace to avoid such company as would enkindle the flames of those unruly appetites. May thy power, thy wisdom, and thy fatherly compassion defend, direct and chastise me; and cause me to lead such a life that I may be fit hereafter for the conversation of angels.

Have mercy upon all sinners, &c.

Our Father. Hail Mary.

ᴑᴗ

The Twelfth Petition

JESUS! *(repeated ten times)* grant me the grace to call on thee for help in all my necessities, and frequently to remember thy death and resurrection. Wilt thou be deaf to my cries, Who hast laid down thy life for my ransom? Or canst thou not save me who took it up again for my crown? 'Call on me in the day of trouble, and I will deliver thee.' Whom have I in heaven but thee, O my Jesus, from whose blessed mouth issued such sweet words? Thou art my sure rock of defence against all my enemies, and my gracious assistant in every good work. I will then invoke thee with confidence in all trials and afflictions, and when thou hearest me, O Jesus, thou wilt have mercy on me.

Have mercy upon all sinners, &c.

Our Father. Hail Mary.

ᴑᴗ

The Thirteenth Petition

JESUS! *(repeated ten times)* enable me to persevere in a virtuous life, and never to grow weary in thy service till thou rewardest me in thy kingdom. In pious customs, holy duties, and in all honest and necessary employments, continue, O Lord, to strengthen me both in soul and body. My life is nothing on earth but a pilgrimage towards the heavenly Jerusalem, to which he that sits down or turns out of the way can never arrive. May I always, O Jesus, follow thy blessed example. With how much pain and how little pleasure didst thou press on to a bitter death— the assured way to a glorious resurrection. Let me frequently meditate on those severe words of thine: He only that perseveres to the end shall be saved.

Have mercy upon all sinners, &c.

Our Father. Hail Mary.

The Fourteenth Petition

JESUS! *(repeated ten times)* grant me grace to fix my mind on thee, especially while I converse with thee in time of prayer. Check the wanderings of my fanciful brain, put a stop to the desires of my fickle heart, and suppress the power of my spiritual enemies, who at that time endeavour to withdraw my mind from heavenly thoughts to vain imaginations. Thus shall I joyfully look on thee as my deliverer from all evil, and thank thee as my benefactor, for all the good I have received, or hope to obtain. I shall be convinced that thou art my chief good, and that all other things were ordained by thee only as the means of engaging me to fix my affections on thee alone that by persevering till death in thy love and service, I might be eternally happy. Let all my thoughts, O beloved of my soul, be absorbed in thee, that my eyes being shut to all vain and sinful objects may become worthy to behold thee, face to face, in thy everlasting glory.

Have mercy upon all sinners, *&c.*

Our Father. Hail Mary.

ᚙ

The Fifteenth Petition

JESUS! *(repeated ten times)* grant me the grace to order my life with reference to my eternal welfare, sincerely intending, and wisely referring all the operations of my soul and body towards obtaining the reward of thy infinite bliss and eternal felicity. For what use is this world, but a school for the tutoring of souls, created for eternal happiness in the next? And how are they educated but by an anxious desire of enjoying God, their only end? Break my froward spirit, Jesus, by the reins of humility and obedience. Grant me grace to depart hence with the most sovereign contempt for this world, and with a heart overflowing with joy at the thought of going to thee. Let the memory of thy passion make me cheerfully undergo every temptation or suffering in this state of probation, for love of thee; whilst my soul, in the meantime, languishes after that life of consummate bliss and immortal glory, which thou hast prepared for thy servants in heaven. O Jesus, let me frequently and attentively consider, that whatsoever I may gain, if I lose thee, all is lost; and that whatever I may lose, if I obtain thee, all is gained.

Have mercy upon all sinners, *&c.*

Our Father, Hail Mary

∾

'The Lord Jesus Christ, for our sakes, became obedient unto death, even the death of the cross.'   (Philippians 2:8)

Hear these petitions, O most merciful Saviour, and grant me the grace frequently to repeat and consider them, that they may serve as so many easy steps, whereby my soul may ascend to thy knowledge and love, and to a diligent performance of my duty to thee and my neighbour, through the whole course of my life. Amen.

Our Father. Hail Mary. I believe in God.

OTHER DEVOTIONS TO OUR LORD

B E THOU a light unto my eyes, music to mine ears, sweet-ness to my taste and full contentment to my heart. Be thou my sunshine in the day, my food at table, my repose in the night, my clothing in nakedness, and my succour in all necessities. Lord Jesus, I give thee my body, my soul, my substance, my fame, my friends, my liberty, and my life. Dispose of me and all that is mine as it may seem best to thee and to the glory of thy blessed name.

John Cosin

∾

To Christ the King

O CHRIST Jesus, I acknowledge you to be the King of the universe; all that has been made is created for your rule. Exercise over me all your sovereign rights. I hereby renew the promises of my baptism, renouncing Satan and all his works and empty promises, and I engage myself to lead from now on a truly Christian life. And especially I undertake to bring about the triumph of the Kingdom of God and serve your Church to that end, so far as in me lies. Divine Heart of Jesus, I offer you my poor actions that all may acknowledge your sacred kingly power. In such a way may the kingdom of your peace be firmly established throughout all the earth. Amen.

∾

O MY sweet Saviour Christ, which in thine undeserved love towards mankind, so kindly wouldst suffer the painful death of the cross, suffer not me to be cold nor lukewarm in love again towards thee.

St Thomas More

∾

L ORD Jesus, let me know myself and know thee,
And desire nothing save only thee.
Let me hate myself and love thee.
Let me do everything for the sake of thee.
Let me humble myself and exalt thee.
Let me think nothing except thee.

Let me die to myself and live in thee.
Let me accept whatever happens as from thee.
Let me banish self and follow thee,
And ever desire to follow thee.
Let me fly from myself and take refuge in thee,
That I may deserve to be defended by thee.
Let me fear for myself, let me fear thee,
And let me be among those who are chosen by thee.
Let me distrust myself and put my trust in thee.
Let me be willing to obey for the sake of thee.
Let me cling to nothing save only to thee,
And let me be poor because of thee.
Look upon me, that I may love thee.
Call me that I may see thee,
And for ever enjoy thee. Amen.

St Augustine

MOST sweet Jesus, pierce the interior of my soul with the sweet wound of your love, that my soul may ever languish, and be dissolved with your love, and with the desire of possessing you, and long to quit this life that it may come to be perfectly united with you in a blessed eternity. Grant that my heart may be ever fixed on you, my only hope, my riches, my peace, my refuge, my confidence, my treasure, and my inheritance. Amen.

St Bonaventure

O MY Lord and Saviour, in thy arms I am safe; keep me and I have nothing to fear; give me up and I have nothing to hope for. I know not what will come upon me before I die. I know nothing about the future, but I rely upon thee. I pray thee to give me what is good for me; I pray thee to take from me whatever may imperil my salvation; I pray thee not to make me rich, I pray thee not to make me very poor; but I leave it all to thee, because thou knowest and I do not. If thou bringest pain or sorrow on me, give me grace to bear it well—keep me from fretfulness, and selfishness. If thou givest me health and strength and success in this world, keep me ever on my guard lest these great gifts carry me away from thee.

O thou who didst die on the cross for me, even for me, sinner as I am, give me to know thee, to believe in thee, to love thee, to serve thee; ever to aim at setting forth thy glory; to live for thee; to set a good example to all around me, give me to die just at that time and in that way which is most for thy glory, and best for my salvation.

J.H. Newman

I BELIEVE, O my Saviour, that thou knowest just what is best for me. I believe that thou lovest me better than I do myself, that thou art all-wise in thy providence, and powerful in thy protection. I am as ignorant as Peter as to what is to happen to me in time to come; but I resign myself entirely to my ignorance, and thank thee with all my heart that thou hast taken me out of my own keeping, and, instead of putting such a serious charge upon me, hast bidden me put myself into thy hands. I can ask nothing better than this, to be thy care, not my own.

J.H. Newman

O JESUS! You are my true friend, my only friend. You take part in all my misfortunes; you take them on yourself, you know how to change them into blessings. You listen to me with the greatest kindness when I relate my troubles to you, and you have always balm to pour on my wounds. I find you at all times; I find you everywhere. You never go away; if I have to change my dwelling, I find you there wherever I go. You are never weary of listening to me; you are never tired of doing me good. I am certain of being loved by you, if I love you; my goods are nothing to you, and by bestowing yours on me, you never grow poor. However miserable I may be, no one more noble or clever or even holier can come between you and me, and deprive me of your friendship; and death, which tears us away from all other friends, will unite me forever to you. All the humiliations attached to old age or to the loss of honour will never detach you from me; on the contrary, I shall then enjoy You more fully, and you will never be closer to me than when everything seems to conspire against me, to overwhelm me, and to cast me down. You bear with all my faults with extreme patience, and even my want of fidelity and my ingratitude do not wound you to such a

degree as to make you unwilling to receive me back when I return to you. O Jesus, grant that I may die praising you, that I may
die loving you, that I may die for the love of you. Amen.

St Claude de la Colombière

A prayer on the most sweet name of Jesus

O MOST sweet and most loving Jesus. Jesus is a good name,
a precious name, a name which none may utter except in
the Holy Spirit, O most sweet and most soothing Jesus. O lovable and admirable, O great and healthful name of Jesus. Jesus is
a holy name, a name full of delight, a name of good hope, a name
that gives strength to the sinner. What else is the name of Jesus
but Saviour? Therefore, Jesus, for thine own sake be to me Jesus.
Good Jesus, sweet Jesus, kindly Jesus; for the sake of this thy
name, do to me according to thy name. Thou who didst form me,
lest I perish, be to me Jesus. Good Jesus, best Jesus, Jesus have
mercy on me while yet there is time for mercy: do not condemn
me at the day of judgement. Open the eyes of my mind, that I
may learn to despise with a pure heart everything that is merely
of earth, whether pleasing or displeasing, and may think only of
the things that are of heaven and eternal; and may my soul attain
the strength to be for ever intent upon the contemplation of eternal blessings. Faithful Jesus, kindly Jesus, Jesus full of mercy,
admit me into the number of thy elect; that with them I may deserve to serve and praise and glorify thee now and for ever. Amen.

Fifteenth Century

O Deus Ego Amo Te

O GOD, I love thee mightily,
   Not only for thy saving me,
Nor yet because who love not thee
Must burn throughout eternity.
Thou, thou, my Jesu, once didst me
Embrace upon the bitter tree.
For me the nails, the soldier's spear
With injury and insult, bear—
In pain all pain exceeding,
In sweating and in bleeding,
Yea, very death, and that for me
   A sinner all unheeding!

O Jesu, should I not love thee
Who thus hast dealt so lovingly—
Not hoping some reward to see,
Nor lest I my damnation be;
But, as thyself hast lovèd me
So love I now and always thee,
Because my King alone thou art
Because, O God, mine own thou art!

R.H.Benson

THANKS be to thee, my Lord Jesus Christ,
For all the benefits
which thou hast given me;
For all the pains and insults
which thou hast borne for me;
O most merciful Redeemer,
Friend and Brother,
May I know thee more clearly,
Love thee more dearly,
And follow thee more nearly. Amen.

St Richard of Chichester

THE SACRED HEART
OF JESUS

During the seventeenth and eighteenth centuries, the theological ideas of Cornelius Jansen gained considerable ground on the continent of Europe, and particularly wherever the French exercised influence. Jansenism stressed the power and terrible justice of God, and laid little stress on his mercy and love. At the height of this, our Lord appeared to St Margaret Mary Alacoque (1647-1690), a nun in the town of Paray-le-Monial, showing her his heart, and saying: 'Behold the heart which has loved mankind so much'; in other words, if Jesus has taken the trouble to die for us, surely he must love us. Why should we hold him in such terror? Devotion to the Sacred Heart of Jesus, pierced with a lance out of love for us, spread like wild-fire through those parts of Europe that had formerly been Jansenist.

Devotion to the Sacred Heart of Jesus is older than this, however. Above all, it is a veneration of his humanity, and the love which he bears for us who have done so little in return.

MOST Holy Heart of Jesus, fountain of every blessing, I adore you, I love you, and with a lively sorrow for my sins, I offer you this poor heart of mine. Make me humble, patient, pure and wholly obedient to your will. Grant, good Jesus, that I may live *in* you and *for* you. Protect me in the midst of danger: comfort me in my afflictions: give me health of body, assistance in my temporal needs, your blessing on all that I do, and the grace of a holy death. Amen.

∾

STAY with me, and then I shall begin to shine as you shine, so to shine as to be a light to others. The light, O Jesus, will be all from you. It will be you who shines through me upon others. Give light to them as well as to me; light them with me, through me. Make me preach you without preaching—not by words, but by my example and by the sympathetic influence, of what I do — by my visible resemblance to your saints, and the evident fullness of the love which my heart bears to yours.

J.H. Newman

GRANT, O Sweet Jesus, that in honouring your Sacred Heart, we may learn to practise meekness and humility, obtain the peace you have promised, and find rest for our souls. We beg of you this grace. Amen.

❧

O HEART of Jesus, grant me an increase of faith in you, strong faith to realise you, a loving faith to appreciate you, a trusting faith to turn to you in every want and sorrow. O loving Heart, I commend to you my thoughts, words and works that you may inspire and guide them, my affections, intentions and desires that you may purify and direct them; my dearly-bought soul that you may sanctify and save it; my last sigh that you may receive it united to your own. Amen.

❧

Prayer of Saint Bernard

HOW good and sweet it is, Jesus, to dwell in your heart! All my thoughts and affections will I sink in the Heart of Jesus, my Lord. I have found the Heart of my king, my brother, my friend, the Heart of my beloved Jesus. And now that I have found your Heart, which is also mine, dear Jesus, I will pray to you. Grant that my prayer may reach you, may find entrance to your Heart. Draw me to yourself. O Jesus, who are infinitely above all beauty and every charm, wash me clean from my defilement; wipe out even the smallest trace of sin. If you, who are all-pure, will purify me, I will be able to make my way into your Heart and dwell there all my life long. There I will learn to know your will, and find the grace to fulfil it. Amen.

❧

For the Pope

O MOST Sacred Heart of Jesus, pour down abundantly your blessings upon your Church, upon the supreme Pontiff, Pope N. and upon all the clergy: give perseverance to the just, convert sinners, enlighten unbelievers, bless our parents, friends and benefactors, help the dying, free the souls in Purgatory, and extend over all hearts the sweet empire of your love. Amen.

❧

To the heart of Jesus in the Eucharist

O MOST Sacred, most loving Heart of Jesus, thou art concealed in the Holy Eucharist, and thou beatest for us still. Now as then thou sayest, *Desiderio desideravi*—'With desire I have desired'. I worship thee then with all my best love and awe, with my fervent affection, with my most subdued, most resolved will. O my God, when thou dost condescend to allow me to receive thee, to eat and drink thee, and thou for a while dost take up thy abode within me, O make my heart beat with thy Heart. Purify it of all that is earthly, all that is proud and sensual, all that is hard and cruel, of all perversity, of all disorder, of all deadness. So fill it with thee that neither the events of the day nor the circumstances of the time may have power to ruffle it, but that in thy love and thy fear it may have peace.

J.H. Newman

Act of Consecration to the Sacred Heart of Jesus

I, N. N. , give myself and consecrate to the Sacred Heart of our Lord Jesus Christ, my person and my life, my actions, pains and sufferings, so that I may be unwilling to make use of any part of my being save to honour, love, and glorify the Sacred Heart. This is my unchanging purpose, namely, to be all his, and to do all things for the love of him, at the same time renouncing with all my heart whatever is displeasing to him. I therefore take you, O Sacred Heart, to be the only object of my love, the guardian of my life, my assurance of salvation, the remedy of my weakness and inconstancy, the atonement for all the faults of my life, and my sure refuge at the hour of death. Be then, O Heart of goodness, my justification before God our Father, and turn away from me his justified anger. O Heart of love, I put all my confidence in you, for I fear everything from my own wickedness and frailty, but I hope for all things from your goodness and bounty. Consume in me all that displeases you or resists your holy will; let your pure love imprint itself so deeply on my heart, that I shall never be able to forget or to be separated from you. May I obtain from your loving kindness the grace of having my name written on your heart, for in you I desire to place all my happiness and all my glory, living and dying in your true service.

St Margaret Mary Alacoque

L OVE of the heart of Jesus, inflame my heart.
   Charity of the heart of Jesus, flow into my heart.
Strength of the heart of Jesus, support my heart.
Mercy of the heart of Jesus, pardon my heart.
Patience of the heart of Jesus, grow not weary of my heart.
Kingdom of the heart of Jesus, be in my heart.
Wisdom of the heart of Jesus, teach my heart.
Will of the heart of Jesus, guide my heart.
Zeal of the heart of Jesus, consume my heart.
Immaculate Virgin Mary, pray for me to the heart of Jesus.

Elizabeth Ruth Obbard

THE XV OES

The Devotion of the Fifteen Oes was a great favourite among the prayers in the late mediæval primers: the startling depiction of the sufferings of Jesus is highly typical of the piety of that age, and may well be compared with the depictions of the crucifixion in the Flemish art of the same period. It is given here only slightly modified. The woodcut is from a Sarum primer of 1534 where it is used to accompany this devotion.

I

O JESU, endless sweetness to all that love thee, a joy passing and exceeding all gladness and desire; thou Saviour and Lover of all repentant sinners, that likest to dwell, as thou saidst thyself, with the children of men, for that was the cause why thou wast incarnate and made man in the end of the world. Have mind, blessed Jesu, of all the bitter sorrows that thou suffered in thy manhood, drawing nigh to thy most wholesome passion, the which passion was ordained to be in thy divine heart, by counsel of the holy Trinity, for the ransom of all mankind. Have mind, blessed Jesu, of all the great dreads, anguishes, and sorrows, that thou sufferedst in thy tender flesh, before thy passion on the cross, when thou wast betrayed of thy disciple Judas to the Jews which of singular affection that thou hadst to them should have been thine especial people, after time that thou hadst made thy prayer upon the mount of Olivet, and sweatest there both blood and water. Also have mind of the great anguish that thou wast in, when thou wast taken of the false Jews and by false witness accused. And at Jerusalem in time of Easter, in the flourishing youth of thy body, without trespass receivedst thou thy judgement of death upon the cross unjustly, where also thou wast despoiled of thine own clothes, blindfolded, buffeted, bound to a pillar and scourged, and with thorns crowned and with a reed smitten on the head, and with innumerable pains thy body was all bruised and torn. For mind of this blessed passion, I beseech thee, benign Jesu, grant me afore my death very contrition, true confession and amendment of my life, and of all my sins remission. So be it.

Our Father &c.

❧

II

O BLESSED Jesu, Maker of all the world, that of man may not be measured, which closest in thy hand all the earth, have mind of thy bitter sorrow first when the soldiers fastened thy blessed hands to the cross with blunt nails. And to increase more thy pains, they added sorrow upon sorrow to thy bitter wounds, when they pierced thy tender feet, because thou wouldst not accord to their will. And so cruelly they drew thy blessed body in length and breadth to the measure of the cross, that all the joints of thy limbs were both loosed and broken. For mind of thy blessed passion, I beseech thee, benign Jesu, give me grace to keep with me both thy love and thy dread. So be it.

Our Father &c.

❧

III

O JESU, heavenly Physician, have mind of thy languor, and blueness of thy wounds and sorrow, that thou suffered in the great pain of the cross, when thou wast lift up from the earth, that thou wast all torn in all thy limbs, whereof there was no limb abiding in its right joint, so that no sorrow was like to thine, because that from the soles of thy feet to the top of thy head was no whole place; and yet forgetting in manner all those grievous pains thou prayedst devoutly and charitably to thy Father for thine enemies, saying, Father, forgive it them, for they know not what they do. For thy charitable mercy that thou showedst to thine enemies, and for mind of those bitter pains, grant me that this mind of thy bitter passion be to me plenary remission and forgiveness of all my sins. So be it.

Our Father &c.

❧

IV

O JESU, very freedom of angels, the paradise of all ghostly pleasures, have mind of the dread and hideous fearfulness that thou suffered when all thine enemies, like unto most mad lions, compassed thee about, smiting thee, and spitting on thee, scratching thee, and with many other grievous pains tormenting thee; for mind of all these despiteful words, cruel beatings, and sharp torments, and all the cruel pains which thine enemies put thee to, I beseech thee, blessed Jesu, deliver me from all mine enemies bodily and ghostly, and give me grace to have the defence and protection of health everlasting against them, under the shadow of thy wings. So be it.

Our Father &c.

V

O JESU, mirror of the divine clearness, have mind of that dread and heaviness which thou hadst when thou hangest naked and miserable on the cross and all thy friends and acquaintance stood against thee, and foundest comfort of none but only thy most loving Mother, faithfully standing by thee with great bitterness of heart, whom thou didst betake to thy well-beloved disciple, saying: *Lo, woman, thy son;* and likewise to the disciple: *Lo, thy mother.* I beseech thee, blessed Jesu, by the sword of sorrow that then pierced her heart, to have compassion on me in all my troubles and afflictions bodily and ghostly, and give me comfort in all time of tribulation. So be it.

Our Father &c.

VI

O JESU, King most worthy to be loved, and friend most to be desired, have mind of the sorrow that thou hadst when thou beheldest in the mirror of thy most clear majesty the predestination of all thy chosen souls, that should be saved by the merits of thy passion; for mind of the deepness of thy great mercy which thou hadst upon us, lost and desperate sinners, and namely for the great mercy that thou showedst to the thief that hung on the cross saying this, This day thou shalt be with me in paradise; I pray thee, benign Jesus, to show thy mercy on me in the hour of my death. So be it.

Our Father &c.

❧

VII

O JESU, well of endless pity, that saidst on the cross of thy passion by inward affection of love: *I thirst,* that is to say, for the health of my soul; for mind of this blessed desire I beseech thee, benign Jesu, kindle our desire to every good and perfect work: the thirst of concupiscence, and burning of all unworthy love in us utterly cool and extinguish. So be it.

Our Father &c.

❧

VIII

O JESU, sweetness of hearts and ghostly pleasure of souls, I beseech thee, for the bitterness of the gall that thou tasted and suffered for us at the hour of thy death, grant that we may worthily receive thy most blessed body and blood, the which was betrayed and shed for the remedy of our sins and comfort of our souls. So be it.

Our Father &c.

❧

IX

O JESU, royal strength and ghostly joy, have mind of the anguishes and great sorrows that thou suffered, when thou cried to thy Father with a mighty voice for the bitterness of thy death, and also for the bloody scourging, saying this: *O my God, O my God, why hast thou forsaken me?* By this painful anguish forsake not us in the anguishes of our death. So be it.

Our Father &c.

❧

X

O JESU, beginning and end, way, life, and virtue in every mean, have mind that from the top of thy head unto the soles of thy feet thou sufferedst for us, to be drowned in the water of thy painful passion: for mind of this great pain, and namely for the deepness and wideness of thy wounds, I beseech thee, blessed Jesu, teach me the large precept and commandments of love, who am all drowned in foul sin. So be it.

Our Father &c.

XI

O JESU, deepness of endless mercy, I beseech thee, for the deepness of thy wounds that went through thy tender flesh and thy veins, that thou vouchsafe to draw me from being drowned in deepness of sin. And hide me ever after in thy wounds from the face of thy wrath, unto the time, Lord that thy dreadful fury be passed. So be it.

Our Father &c.

XII

O JESU, mirror of truth, token of unity, and sure bond of charity, have mind of thine innumerable pains and wounds, which from the top of thy head to the sole of thy foot thou wast wounded, and of the wicked people thou wast all so torn and rent, and all thy body made red with thy most holy blood, the which great sorrow, blessed Jesu, in thy clean virgin's body thou sufferedst. What mightest thou do more for us than thou didst? Therefore, benign Jesus, I pray thee heartily to write all thy wounds in my heart with thy most precious blood, that I may both read in them thy dread and thy love, and that I may still continue in praising and thanking thee to my life's end. So be it.

Our Father &c.

XIII

O JESU, most mighty Lion, King immortal, and most victorious, have mind of the sorrow that thou sufferedst when all the powers of thy heart and body failed thee utterly, and then thou inclining thine head, saidst thus: *It is all done.* For mind of that anguish and sorrow, have mercy on me, when my soul in the last consummation and departing of my breath shall be anguished and troubled. So be it.

Our Father &c.

❧

XIV

O JESU, the only begotten Son of Almighty God the Father, the brightness and figure of his godly substance, have mind of that entire commendation, in which thou didst commend thy spirit into the hands of thy Father; and with a torn body and broken heart showing to us for our ransom the bowels of thy mercy, for the redeeming of us didst give up thy breath; for mind of that precious death I beseech thee King of saints, comfort me to withstand the fiend, the world, and my flesh, that I may be dead to the world, and living ghostly toward thee. And in the last hour of my departing from the world, receive my soul, coming to thee, which in this life is an outlaw, and a pilgrim. So be it.

Our Father &c.

❧

XV

O JESU, very true and plenteous vine, have mind of the most exceeding and abundant effusion of blood that thou sheddest most plenteously, as if it had been crushed out of a ripe cluster of grapes, when thou upon the cross didst tread that press alone, gavest us drink both blood and water out of thy side, being pierced with a knight's spear, then at the last like a bundle of myrrh thou wast hanged on the cross on high, where thy tender flesh waxed wan: for mind of this thy most bitter passion, sweet Jesu, wound my heart that the water of repentance, and tears of love, may be my food both night and day. And, good Jesu, turn me whole to thee, that my heart may be ever to thee a dwelling place, and that my living may be ever pleasant and acceptable, and that the end of my life may be so commendable, that I may perpetually praise thee with all thy saints in bliss. So be it.

Our Father. *&c.*

Apostles' Creed p. 214

THE HOLY SPIRIT

VENI, Sancte Spíritus, reple tuórum corda fidélium, et tui amóris in eis ignem accénde.

℣. Emítte spíritum tuum, et creabúntur.
℟. **Et renovábis fáciem terræ.**

Orémus.
DEUS, qui corda fidélium Sancti Spíritus illustratióne docuísti, da nobis in eódem Spíritu recta sápere, et de eius semper consolatióne gaudére. Per Christum Dóminum nostrum. Amen.

COME, Holy Spirit, fill the hearts of thy faithful, and kindle in them the fire of thy love.

℣. Send forth thy Spirit and they shall be created.
℟. **And thou shalt renew the face of the earth.**

Let us pray.
O GOD, who hast taught the hearts of the faithful by the light of the Holy Spirit, grant that by the gift of the same Spirit we may be always truly wise and ever rejoice in his consolation. Through Christ our Lord. Amen.

*An ancient translation of the same prayer
from an English primer of about 1400*

COME, Holy Ghost, fulfil the hearts of thy true servants, and lighten the fire of thy love in them

℣. Send out thy Ghost and they shall be made.
℟. **And thou shalt make new the face of the earth.**

Pray we.
GOD that taughtest the hearts of thy true servants by the lightening of the Holy Ghost: grant us to savour rightfulness in the same Ghost, and to be joyful evermore of his holy comfort. By Christ our Lord. Amen.

IN THE hour of my distress,
When temptations me oppress,
And when I my sins confess,
Sweet Spirit comfort me!

When I lie within my bed,
Sick in heart and sick in head,
And with doubts discomforted,
Sweet Spirit comfort me!

When the house doth sigh and weep,
And the world is drowned in sleep,
Yet mine eyes the watch do keep,
Sweet Spirit comfort me!

When the artless Doctor sees
No one hope but of his fees,
And his skill runs on the lees,
 Sweet Spirit comfort me!

When his potion and his pill,
Has, or none, or little skill,
Meet for nothing but to kill,
Sweet Spirit comfort me!

When the passing-bell doth toll,
And the Furies in a shoal,
Come to fright a parting soul,
Sweet Spirit comfort me!

When the tapers now burn blue,
And the comforters are few,
And that number more than true,
Sweet Spirit comfort me!

When the priest his last hath prayed,
And I nod to what is said,
'Cause my speech is now decayed,
Sweet Spirit comfort me!

When (God knows) I'm tossed about,
Either with despair or doubt,
Yet before the glass be out,
Sweet Spirit comfort me!

When the Tempter me pursu'th
With the sins of all my youth,
And half damns me with untruth,
Sweet Spirit comfort me!

When the flames and hellish cries
Fright mine ears and fright mine eyes,
And all terrors me surprise,
Sweet Spirit comfort me!

When the judgement is revealed,
And that opened which was sealed,
When to thee I have appealed,
Sweet Spirit comfort me!

Robert Herrick

∾

MY GOD, I adore thee, as the third person of the ever-blessed Trinity. Thou art that living love, wherewith the Father and the Son love each other. And thou art the author of supernatural love in our hearts. Increase in me this grace of love, in spite of all my unworthiness. It is more precious than anything else in the world. I accept it in place of all the world can give me. It is my life.

J.H. Newman

∾

COME, Holy Spirit, fill my heart with your holy gifts. Let my weakness be penetrated with your strength this very day, that I may fulfil all the duties of my state conscientiously, that I may do what is right and just.

Let my charity be such as to offend no one, and hurt no one's feelings; so generous as to pardon sincerely any wrong done to me. Assist me, O Holy Spirit, in all my trials of life, enlighten me in my ignorance, advise me in my doubts, strengthen me in my weakness, help me in all my needs, protect me in temptations and console me in afflictions. Graciously hear me, O Holy Spirit, and pour your light into my heart, my soul and my mind.

Assist me to live a holy life and to grow in goodness and grace. Amen.

∾

VENI Creátor Spíritus
Mentes tuórum vísita
Imple supérna grátia
Quæ tu creásti, péctora.

Qui díceris Paráclitus
Altíssimi donum Dei,
Fons vivus, ignis, cáritas
et spiritális únctio.

Tu septifórmis múnere,
Dígitus Patérnæ déxteræ.
Tu rite promíssum Patris,
Sermóne ditans gúttura.

Accénde lumen sénsibus,
Infúnde amórem córdibus.
Infírma nostri córporis
Virtúte firmans pérpeti.

Hostem repéllas lóngius,
Pacémque dones prótinus,
Ductóre sic te prǽvio
Vitémus omne nóxium.

Per te sciámus da Patrem,
Noscámus atque Fílium,
Teque utriúsque spíritum
Credámus omni témpore.

Deo Patris sit glória,
Et Fílio qui a mórtuis
Surréxit, ac Paráclito
In sæculórum sǽcula.
Amen.

COME Holy Ghost, creator, come
From thy bright heavenly throne.
Come take possession of our souls
And make them all thine own.

Thou who art called the Paraclete,
Best gift of God above,
The living spring, the living fire,
Sweet unction, and true love.

Thou who art sevenfold in thy grace,
Finger of God's right hand,
His promise, teaching little ones
To speak and understand.

O guide our minds with thy blest light,
With love our hearts inflame,
And with thy strength which ne'er decays
Confirm our mortal frame.

Far from us drive our deadly foe,
True peace unto us bring,
And through all perils lead us safe
Beneath thy sacred wing.

Through thee may we the Father know,
Through thee the eternal Son.
And thee, the Spirit of them both
Thrice-blessed, three in one.

All glory to the Father be,
With his co-equal Son:
The same to thee, great Paraclete,
While endless ages run

Ascribed to Rabanus Maurus (776-856) Tr. Anon.

ℭℴ

COME Holy Spirit, and make your home within my heart.
Cast out all that is unworthy of your presence, and make it a fit
temple for your holy habitation.

ℭℴ

CREATOR Spirit, by whose aid
    The world's foundations first were laid,
Come visit every pious mind;
Come pour thy joys on humankind;
From sin and sorrow set us free,
And make thy temples worthy thee . . .

Plenteous of grace, descend from high,
Rich in thy sevenfold energy,
Thou strength of his almighty hand,
Whose power does heaven and earth command!
Proceeding Spirit, our defence,
Who dost the gift of tongues dispense,
And crown'st thy gift with eloquence!

Refine and purge our earthy parts;
But, O, inflame and fire our hearts!
Our frailties help, our vice control,
Submit the senses to the soul;
And when rebellious they are grown,
Then lay thy hand and hold them down.

Chase from our minds the infernal foe,
And peace, the fruit of love, bestow;
And lest our feet should step astray,
Protect and guide us in the way.

Make us eternal truths receive,
And practise all that we believe:
Give us thyself that we may see
The Father and the Son, by thee.

Immortal honour, endless fame,
Attend the Almighty Father's Name:
The Saviour Son be glorified,
Who for lost man's redemption died;
And equal adoration be,
Eternal Paraclete, to thee.

John Dryden, 1631-1700 (based on the Veni Creator Spiritus)

Prayer for the Seven Gifts of the Holy Spirit

O LORD Jesus Christ, who, before ascending into heaven did promise to send the Holy Spirit to finish your work in the souls of your apostles and disciples, deign to grant the same Holy Spirit to me, to perfect in my soul the work of your grace and your love.

Grant me the Spirit of *Wisdom*—that I may not be attached to the perishable things of this world, but aspire only after the things that are eternal.

The Spirit of *Understanding*—to enlighten my mind with the light of your divine truth.

The Spirit of *Counsel*—that I may ever choose the surest way of pleasing God and gaining heaven.

The Spirit of *Fortitude*—that I may bear my cross with you, and that I may overcome with courage all the obstacles that oppose my salvation.

The Spirit of *Knowledge*—that I may know God, and know myself, and grow perfect in the science of the Saints.

The Spirit of *Piety*—that I may find the service of God sweet and amiable.

The Spirit of *Fear*—that I may be filled with a loving reverence towards God, and may avoid anything that may displease him.

Mark me, dear Lord, with the sign of your true disciples, and animate me in all things with your Spirit. Amen.

❧

O MY God, I give myself to thee, with all my liberty, all my intellect and heart and will. O Holy Spirit of God, take me as thy disciple, guide me, illuminate me, sanctify me. Bind my hands that I may not do evil, cover my eyes that I may see it with pleasure no more, sanctify my heart that evil may not rest within me. Be thou my God and my Guide. Wheresoever thou leadest me I will go, whatsoever thou forbiddest I will renounce, and whatsoever thou commandest in thy strength I will do. Amen.

❧

DESCEND, O Holy Spirit, and create a new Pentecost among us. Help us to be witnesses to Christ, O heavenly comforter, that his kingdom may stretch to the ends of the earth, and last for ever. Through the same Christ our Lord.

Veni Sancte Spiritus

COME, Holy Ghost, send down those beams
　Which sweetly flow in silent streams
　　　From thy bright throne above;
O come, thou Father of the poor,
O come, thou source of all our store;
　　　Come, fill our hearts with love.

O thou, of comforters the best,
O thou, the soul's delightful guest,
　　　The pilgrim's sweet relief;
Thou art our rest in toil and sweat,
Refreshment in excessive heat,
　　　And solace in our grief.

O Sacred Light! shoot home thy darts,
O pierce the centre of these hearts
　　　Whose faith aspires to thee.
Without thy Godhead, nothing can
Have any price or worth in man,
　　　Nothing can harmless be.

Lord wash our sinful stains away,
Water from Heaven our barren clay,
　　　Our wounds, our bruises, heal;
To thy sweet yoke, our stiff necks bow
Warm with thy fire our hearts of snow
　　　Our wandering feet repeal.

O grant thy faithful, dearest Lord,
Whose only hope is thy sure word,
　　　The seven gifts of thy Spirit;
Grant us in life, to obey thy grace,
Grant us in death, to see thy Face
　　　And endless joys inherit. Amen.

THE HOLY AND UNDIVIDED TRINITY

The Trisagion

HOLY God!
   Holy mighty one!
   Holy, immortal one,
have mercy on us!

❧

GLORY be to the Father, and to the Son and to the Holy Spirit, as it was in the beginning, is now and ever shall be, world without end. Amen.

❧

MOST holy Trinity, Godhead indivisible, Father, Son and Holy Spirit, our first beginning and our last end, you have made us in accord with your own image and likeness. Grant that all the thoughts of our minds, all the words of our tongues, all the affections of our hearts and all the actions of our being may always be conformed to your holy will. Thus, after we have seen you here below in creation, and in a dark manner by means of faith, we may come at last to contemplate you face to face forever in heaven.

❧

St Patrick's Breastplate

I BIND unto myself today
   the strong name of the Trinity
by invocation of the same
the Three in One and One in Three.
of whom all nature hath creation,
eternal Father, Spirit, Word.
Praise to the Lord of my salvation:
Salvation is of Christ the Lord. Amen.

St Patrick (c.373-463) Tr. Cecil Francis Alexander

❧

IT IS right and proper that we worship the Father, and the Son,
and the Holy Spirit, one in essence and undivided Trinity. It is
right and proper to sing to you, to bless you, to honour you, to
thank you and worship you in every place of your rule; for you
are God who is mysterious, incomprehensible, invisible, limitless, together with your only-begotten Son, and the Holy Spirit.
You brought us out of nothing into being, and again raised up the
fallen, overlooking nothing until you brought us to heaven, and
granted us the coming kingdom. For all this we give you thanks,
with your only-begotten Son, and your Holy Spirit, for all the
gifts, seen and unseen, which have been granted us, those which
we know of and those of which we do not. We thank you also for
this worship, which you condescend to accept from our poor
hands, even though thousands of Archangels stand before you,
and hundreds of thousands of Angels, Cherubim and Seraphim,
with six wings and countless eyes, who soar aloft, singing the
triumphant song, calling aloud, lifting their voices and saying:
**HOLY, Holy, Holy is the Lord of Hosts; heaven and earth
are full of his glory. Hosanna in the highest. Blessed is he who
comes in the name of the Lord. Hosanna in the highest.**

Liturgy of St John Chrysostom

I PRAISE you, Father all-powerful!
I praise you, Divine Son, our Lord and Saviour!
I praise you, Spirit of love!

O God, three persons, be near me in the temple of my soul,
You reveal yourself in the depths of my being, Draw me to share
in your life and your love. Your power is beyond all words to
describe, your glory is measureless, your mercy is without limits, your love for mankind is beyond all telling. Look down upon
me and in your kindness grant to me the riches of your compassion and mercy, a share in your divine life. May I come to live
more fully the life I profess and come to the glory of your kingdom.

OUR BLESSED LADY

ONE of these antiphons to our Lady is sung after Compline each evening. They are given here with their traditional seasonal applications, together with the appropriate versicles and collects.

From the First Sunday of Advent until 2nd February:

ALMA Redemptóris Mater, quæ pérvia cæli
Porta manes, et stella maris, succúrre cadénti,
Súrgere qui curat, pópulo: tu quæ genuísti,
Natúra miránte, tuum sanctum Genitórem,
Virgo prius ac postérius, Gabriélis ab ore
Sumens illud Ave, peccatórum miserére.

MOTHER of Christ! hear thou thy people's cry,
Star of the deep, and portal of the sky!
Mother of him who thee from nothing made,
Sinking we strive, and call to thee for aid.
Oh, by that joy which Gabriel brought to thee,
Thou Virgin first and last, let us thy mercy see.

Versicle and Collect from Advent until Christmas Eve:

℣. Angelus Dómini nuntiávit Maríæ.
℟. **Et concépit de Spíritu Sancto.**

℣. The Angel of the Lord declared unto Mary.
℟. **And she conceived by the Holy Spirit.**

Orémus.

GRATIAM tuam, quǽsumus, Dómine, méntibus nostris infúnde: ut qui, Angelo nuntiánte, Christi Filii tui incarnatiónem cognóvimus; per passiónem eius et crucem, ad resurrectiónis glóriam perducámur. Per eundem Christum Dominum nostrum. Amen.

Let us pray.

POUR forth, we beseech thee, O Lord, thy grace into our hearts, that we, to whom the incarnation of Christ, thy Son, was made known by the message of an angel, may, by his passion and cross, be brought to the glory of his resurrection. Through the same Christ our Lord **Amen.**

☙

Versicle and Collect from Christmas Eve until 2nd February

℣. Post partum, Virgo, inviolátata permansísti.

℟. **Dei Génetrix, intercéde pro nobis.**

Orémus.

D EUS, qui salútis ætérne, beátæ Maríæ virginitáte fecúnda, humáno géneri præmia præstitísti: tríbue, quǽsumus; ut ipsám pro nobis intercédere sentiámus, per quam merúimus auctórem vitæ suscípere, Dóminum nostrum Iesum Christum, Fílium tuum. Amen.

℣. After childbirth, thou didst remain a pure virgin.

℟. **O Mother of God, intercede for us.**

Let us pray.

O GOD, who by the fruitful virginity of Blessed Mary hast given to mankind the rewards of eternal salvation, grant, we besech thee, that we may experience her intercession for us, by whom we deserved to receive the Author of life, our Lord Jesus Christ, thy Son. Amen.

From 2nd February until Easter:

A VE, Regína cælórum, Ave, Dómina Angelórum:
Salve, radix, salve, porta,
Ex qua mundo lux est orta:
Gaude, Virgo gloriósa,
Super omnes speciósa,
Vale, o valde decóra,
Et pro nobis Christum exóra

℣. Dignáre me laudáre te, Virgo sacráta.

℟. **Da mihi virtútem contra hostes tuos.**

Orémus.

C ONCEDE, miséricors Deus, fragilitáti nostræ præsídium: ut, qui sanctæ Dei Genetrícis memóriam ágimus; intercessiónis eius auxílio, a

H AIL, O Queen of heaven, Hail, mistress of the angels,
Hail, root of Jesse, heaven's gate,
From whom light dawned on us.
Joy to thee, glorious Virgin,
More beautiful than any other,
Good-night, surpassing beauty!
Pray for us to Christ.

℣. Grant that I may praise thee, O Sacred Virgin.

℟. **Give me strength against thy foes.**

Let us pray.

G RANT to our weakness, O merciful God, the help of thy protection, that we who commemorate the holy Mother of God may, aided by her inter-

nostris iniquitátibus resur-
gámus. Per eúndem Christum
Dóminum nostrum. **Amen.**

cession, arise from all our iniquities. Through the same Christ
our Lord. **Amen.**

Throughout Eastertide:

REGINA cæli, lætáre,
allelúia;
Quia quem meruísti
portáre, allelúia
Resurréxit, sicut dixit, allelúia
Ora pro nobis Deum, allelúia.

REJOICE, O Queen of
heaven, alleluia,
The Son thou wast
found worthy to bear, alleluia,
Has risen as he said, alleluia.
Pray for us to God, alleluia.

℣. Gaude et lætáre, Virgo
Maria, allelúia.
℟. **Quia surréxit Dóminus
vere, allelúia.**

℣. Rejoice, and be glad, O Virgin Mary, alleluia.
℟. **For the Lord hath risen
indeed, alleluia.**

Orémus.
DEUS, qui per resurrec-
tiónem Fílii tui, Dómini
nostri Iesu Christi, mundum
lætificáre dignátus es: præsta,
quǽsumus; ut, per eius
Genetrícem Vírginem Maríam,
perpétuæ capiámus gáudia
vitæ. Per eúndem Christum
Dóminum nostrum. **Amen.**

Let us pray.
GOD who hast brought
gladness to the world
through the resurrection of thy
Son our Lord Jesus Christ, we
beseech thee that through his
virgin mother Mary we may
obtain the joys of everlasting
life. Through the same Christ
our Lord. **Amen.**

From Trinity Sunday until Advent:

SALVE, Regina, mater
misericórdiæ; víta,
dulcédo, et spes nostra,
salve. Ad te clamámus éxsules
fílii Hevæ. Ad te suspirámus
geméntes et flentes in hac
lacrimárum valle. Eia ergo,
advocáta nostra, illos tuos
misericórdes óculos ad nos
convérte. Et Iesum, bene-
díctum fructum ventris tui no-

HAIL, Holy Queen,
Mother of mercy;
hail, our life, our
sweetness and our hope! To
thee do we cry, poor banished
children of Eve. To thee do we
send up our sighs, mourning
and weeping in this vale of
tears. Turn, then, most gracious
advocate, thine eyes of mercy
towards us, and after this exile

bis post hoc exsílium osténde. O clemens, o pia, o dulcis Virgo María.

show unto us the blessed fruit of thy womb, Jesus. O clement, O loving, O sweet Virgin Mary!

℣. Ora pro nobis, sancta Dei Génetrix.
℟. **Ut digni efficiámur promissiónibus Christi.**

℣. Pray for us, holy Mother of God.
℟. **That we may be made worthy of the promises of Christ.**

Orémus.

OMNIPOTENS sempitérne Deus, qui gloriósæ Vírginis Matris Maríæ corpus et ánimam, ut dignum Fílii tui habitáculum éffici mererétur, Spíritu Sancto cooperánte, præparásti: da, ut, cuius commemoratióne lætámur, eius pia intercessióne, ab instántibus malis et a morte perpétua liberémur. Per eúndem Christum Dóminum nostrum. **Amen.**

Let us pray.

ALMIGHTY, everlasting God, who by the co-operation of the Holy Spirit didst prepare the body and soul of the glorious Virgin Mother Mary to become a habitation fit for thy Son, grant that as we rejoice in her commemoration, we may by her loving intercession be delivered from present evils and from eternal death. Through the same Christ our Lord. **Amen.**

OTHER DEVOTIONS TO OUR LADY

The 'Memorare'

REMEMBER, O most loving Virgin Mary, that it is a thing unheard of that any one ever had recourse to thy protection, implored thy help, or sought thy intercession, and was left forsaken. Filled, therefore, with confidence in thy goodness, I fly to thee, O Mother, Virgin of Virgins; to thee I come, before thee I stand, a sorrowful sinner. Despise not my words, O Mother of the Word incarnate, but graciously hear and grant my prayer. Amen.

St Bernard

❧

O BLESSED Virgin Mary, unspotted Mother of my God and Saviour Jesus Christ, be a mother to me, since your adorable Son has been pleased to call us all his brethren, and to recommend us all to thee in the person of his beloved disciple. Take me and mine under your holy protection, and continually represent to the eternal Father, on our behalf, the merits of the death and passion of your Son, our Saviour.

❧

IT IS truly right that we bless you, O *Theotokos,* God-bearer, the ever blessed and most pure Mother of our God: more honoured than the Cherubim, and more glorious beyond compare than the Seraphim, for you, undefiled, gave birth to God the Word: therefore we praise you, O true Mother of God.

Liturgy of St John Chrysostom

❧

Prayer of St Aloysius

TO THEE, O holy Mary, my sovereign Mistress, to thy blessed trust and special charge, and to the bosom of thy mercy, this day and every day, and at the hour of my death I commend myself, my soul and my body: to thee I commit all my hope and all my consolation, my distresses and my miseries, my life and the end thereof; that through thy most holy intercession, and through thy merits, all my works may be directed and disposed, according to thy will and the will of thy Son. Amen.

B LESSED art thou, O Mary, for in thee have been accomplished the mysteries and enigmas of the prophets. Thou
wast prefigured for Moses in the burning bush, and in the cloud;
for Jacob in the heavenly ladder; for David in the ark of the covenant; for Ezekiel in the gate closed and sealed. And now, their
mysterious words are realized. Glory be to the Father, who sent
his only Son to manifest himself through Mary, deliver us from
error and to glorify his memory in heaven and on earth.

Balai the Chorepiscopos (Fifth Century)

~

Verses in Passiontide

L ADY Mary, thy bright crown
        Is no mere crown of majesty;
    For with the reflex of his own
Resplendent thorns Christ circled thee

The red rose of this Passion-tide
        Doth take a deeper hue from thee,
In the five wounds of Jesus dyed,
        And in thy bleeding thoughts, Mary!

The soldier struck a triple stroke,
        That smote thy Jesus on the tree:
He broke the Heart of Hearts, and broke
        The Saint's and Mother's hearts in thee.

Thy Son went up the angels' ways,
        His passion ended; but, ah me!
Thou found'st the road of further days
        A longer way of Calvary:

On the hard cross of hope deferred
        Thou hung'st in loving agony,
Until the mortal-dreaded word
        Which chills *our* mirth, spake mirth to thee.

The angel Death from this cold tomb
        Of life did roll the stone away;
And he thou barest in thy womb
        Caught thee at last into the day,
Before the living throne of whom
        The lights of Heaven burning pray.

Francis Thompson

HAIL Mary, daughter of God the Father! Hail Mary, mother of God the Son! Hail Mary, spouse of the Holy Ghost! Hail Mary, temple of the Most Holy Trinity! Hail Mary, my Mistress, my wealth, my mystic rose, Queen of my heart my Mother, my life, my sweetness and my dearest hope! I am all thine, and all that I have is thine, O Virgin blessed above all things. May thy soul be in me to magnify the Lord; may thy spirit be in me to rejoice in God. Place thyself, O faithful Virgin, as a seal upon my heart, that in thee and through thee I may be found faithful to God. Grant, most gracious Virgin, that I may be numbered among those whom thou art pleased to love, to teach and to guide, to favour and to protect as thy children. Grant that with the help of thy love I may despise all earthly consolation and cling to heavenly things, till through the Holy Spirit, thy faithful spouse, and through thee, his faithful spouse, Jesus Christ thy Son be formed within me for the glory of the Father. Amen.

St Louis Marie Grignon de Montfort

For the assistance of the Blessed Virgin

O ROD of Jesse, holy flower of David, most blessed Virgin Mary: thou hast brought forth for us the long-awaited Emmanuel. Thou art the holy city, founded by God himself, O Virgin worthy of all praise, who never hadst, nor ever wilt have, an equal. Truly art thou 'blessed among women,' who didst bring down from heaven the fruit of life. Thou art, O matchless Virgin, she whom God has laden with all the riches of the universe, the true tree of life, planted in the very midst of Paradise, from whose branches do not hang the fruit of sin, but the food of immortality.

Hail, Queen, clothed with the sun, for whose feet the moon is footstool, whose diadem is set with the stars of heaven! Hail, Mother, than all other mothers more fortunate, in that thou becamest for fallen man the gate of paradise! Hail, glory of heaven, splendour of the kingdom of God, ark of the eternal alliance, first fruit of our regeneration, fairest creature of the hand of God!

More beautiful than the rose art thou, purer than the lily's purity, more spotless than the fallen snow: thou dost shine with greater glory than the radiant sun. Thou art above all angels and all saints. Thou art the child of grace and blessing who hast given the children of Eve eternal life, in giving them thy Son.

O sweet, O loving Mother: to God, thy Son, do thou commend us, for by him thy every prayer is honourable. Obtain for us that while on earth we praise thee, we may by the innocence of our lives please thee, and thus merit to reach heaven, where, for all eternity, in thy glorification, we shall rejoice. Amen.

St Venantius

໙

An ancient hymn to Mary Immaculate

TOTA pulchra es, Maria
Et mácula originális non
  est in te.
Tu glória Jerúsalem
Tu lætítia Israel.
Tu honorificéntia pópuli
  nostri.
Tu advocáta peccatórum
  O María
  O María
Virgo prudentíssima
Mater clementíssima
  Ora pro nobis
Intercéde pro nobis ad
  Dóminum Iesum Christum.

THOU art all-lovely, O
Mary, and the stain of sin
  is not found in thee.
You are the glory of Jerusalem,
You are the joy of Israel,
You are, the greatest honour of
  our people.
You are the advocate of sinners.
  O Mary,
  O Mary,
Virgin most prudent,
Mother most merciful,
  Pray for us,
Intercede for us with our Lord
  Jesus Christ.

໙

O MARY, you are the 'good ground' on which the seed fell
You have brought forth fruit a hundredfold. Draw us close
to your loving heart and keep us there in gentle lowliness and
perfect trust. Teach us to receive the Spirit as you did to open our
hearts to the Sacred Word, to ponder it in silence and yield a rich
harvest. Teach us to be apostles of love.

Ruth Burrows

໙

*Ane Ballat of our Lady**

H ALE, STERNE superne! Hale, in etern,
In Godis sicht to schyne!
Lucerne in derne for to discerne
    Be glory and grace devyne;
Hodiern, modern, sempitern,
    Angelicall regyne!
Our tern inferne for to dispern
    Helpe, rialest rosyne.
        Ave Maria, gracia plena!
    Haile, fresche floure femynyne!
Yerne us, guberne, virgin matern,
    Of reuth baith rute and ryne.

Haile, yhyng, benyng, fresche flurising!
    Haile, Alphais habitakle!
thy dyng of spring maid us to syng
    Befor his tabernakle;
All thing maling we doune thring,
    Be sicht of his signakle;
Quhilk king us bring unto his ryng,
    Fro dethis dirk umbrakle.
        Ave Maria, gracia plena!
    Haile, moder and maide but makle!
Bricht syng, gladyng our languissing,
    Be micht of thi mirakle.

Haile, bricht be sicht in hevyn on hicht!
    Haile, day sterne orientale!
Our licht most richt, in clud of nycht,
    Our dirknes for to scale:
Hale, wicht in ficht, puttar to flicht
    Of fendis in battale!
Haile, plicht but sicht! Hale, mekle of mycht!
    Haile, glorius Virgin, haile!
        Ave Maria, gracia plena!
    Haile, gentill nychttingale!
Way stricht, cler dicht, to wilsome wicht,
    That irke bene in travale.

---

* *In this glorious sixteenth-century Scottish poem, Dunbar would seem
to be inventing many of the words, many deriving directly from Latin.
So I haven't provided a glossary. Try reading it aloud, if you have any
difficulty understanding!*

Hale, qwene serene! Hale, most amene!
  Haile, hevinlie hie emprys!
Haile, schene unseyne with carnale eyne!
  Haile, ros of paradys!
Haile, clene, bedene, ay till conteyne!
  Haile, fair fresche flour delyce!
Haile, grene daseyne! Haile, fro the splene,
  Of Jhesu genetrice!
    Ave Maria, gracia plena!
  Thow baire-the prince of prys;
Our teyne to meyne, and ga betweyne
  As humile oratrice.

Haile, more decore than of before,
  And swetar be sic sevyne,
Our glore forlore for to restore,
  Sen thow art qwene of hevyn!
Memore of sore, stern in Aurore,
  Lovit with angellis stevyne;
Implore, adore, thow indeflore,
  To mak our oddis evyne.
    Ave Maria, gracia plena!
  With lovingis lowde ellevyn.
Quhill store and hore my youth devore,
  thy name I sall ay nevyne.

Empryce of prys, imperatrice,
  Brycht polist precious stane;
Victrice of vyce, hie genetrice
  Of Jhesu, lord soverayne:
Our wys pavys fra enemys,
  Agane the feyndis trayne;
Oratrice, mediatrice, salvatrice,
  To God gret suffragane!
    Ave Maria, gracia plena!
  Haile, sterne meridiane!
Spyce, flour delice of paradys,
  That baire the gloryus grayne.

Imperiall wall, place palestrall,
    Of peirles pulcritud;
Tryumphale hall, hie trone regall
    Of Godis celsitud;
Hospitall riall, the lord of all
    thy closet did include;
Bricht ball cristall, ros virginall,
    Fulfillit of angell fude.
        Ave Maria, gracia plena!
    thy birth has with his blude
Fra fall mortall, originall,
    Us raunsound on the rude.

William Dunbar

O VIRGIN full of all goodness, Mother of Mercy, I recommend to thee my body and my soul, my thoughts, my
actions, my life and my death. Obtain for me the grace of loving
thy Son my saviour Jesus Christ with a true and perfect love, ad
after him of loving thee with my whole heart.

St Thomas Aquinas

ண   ண   ண

ANGELS

O SWEET angel, to me so dear,
that night and day standeth me near
full lovingly with mild mood,
Thanking, loving, love and praising
Offer for me to Jesu our King,
For his gifts great and good,
As thou goeth betwixt him and me
And knoweth my life in every degree,
Saying it in his presence.
Ask me grace to love him truly,
To serve my lord with heart duly,
With my daily diligence.
Keep me from vice and all perils,
Whilst thou with me daily travels
In this world of wickedness.
Set me my petitions granted,
By thy prayer daily haunted,
If it please thy holiness.

℣.O sweet Angel that keepeth me,
℟. **Bring me to bliss, I pray thee.**

O MY Lord Jesu Christ, as it hath pleased thee to assign an
Angel to wait on me daily and nightly with great attendance
and diligence, so I beseech thee through his going betwixt us,
that thou cleanse me from vices, clothe me with virtues, grant me
love and grace to come, see, and have without end thy bliss before thy fair face that liveth and reigneth after thy glorious passion with the Father of heaven, and with the Holy Ghost one God
and persons three, without end in bliss. Amen.

The Fifteenth-Century Processional of the Nuns of Chester

A ngel of God, my guardian dear
To whom God's love commits me here,
Ever this day be at my side
To light and guard, to rule and guide. Amen.

To the Archangel Michael

HOLY Michael Archangel, defend us in the day of battle. Be our safeguard against the wickedness and snares of the devil. May God rebuke him, we humbly pray, and do thou, prince of the heavenly host, by the power of God, thrust down to hell Satan and all wicked spirits who wander through the world for the ruin of souls. Amen.

CREATION

Canticle of the Sun

MOST High!
Most Mighty!
Most Just Lord!
To you be all praise, glory, worship and blessing.
Yours they are, and unworthy is our praise.

Be praised, my Lord, in all that you have made!

Be praised for Brother Sun who lights our day.
His beauty, his radiance, his splendour
Surely are but reflections of yours.

Be praised, my Lord, for Sister Moon
and for the stars which shine clearly
decking the heavens with loveliness.

Be praised, my Lord for our Sister, Water
who humbly serves our many needs
yet is so precious and so pure.

Be praised, my Lord, for our Brother, Fire
who lightens our darkness, who brightens and cheers,
who is strength and power.

Be praised, my Lord, for our Mother the Earth
who feeds and tends us,
who sends forth fruit, many-hued flowers, and grasses.

Be praised, my Lord, in those who forgive for your sake,
and in those who bear troubles and sickness.
O blessed are those who peacefully persevere
To gain a crown from you, Most High Lord.

Be praised, my Lord, for our Sister Death,
Death of the body that none may escape.
Pity those that die in sin.
Blessed are those found walking in virtue.

Praise the Lord! Bless the Lord! Give thanks to the Lord!
Serve him with great humility!

St Francis of Assisi

There is an Irish tradition that each Easter Sunday morning the sun dances as it rises, in joy at the Lord's resurrection. The compiler knows people who claim to have seen this. This is one account, from The Sun Dances.

THE glorious gold-bright sun was after rising on the crests of the great hills, and it was changing colour—green, purple, red, blood-red, white, intense-white, and gold-white, like the glory of the God of the elements to the children of men. It was dancing up and down in exultation at the joyous resurrection of the beloved Saviour of victory.

To be thus privileged, a person must ascend to the top of the highest hill before sunrise, and believe that the God who makes the small blade of grass to grow is the same God who makes the large, massive sun to move.

Barbara Macphie

Hildegard of Bingen

A RAY of shining light,
Of pure creative energy
Poured through the open window
Of God's grace,
Stirring the spirit of Hildegard
And filling her mind with warmth,
Insight and fullness

Her spirit awoke,
Her mind expanded,
Her heart refreshed with the dew
Of her baptism
Rejoiced in the beauty of creation,
Her soul experienced the wonder
Of Christ's risen life.

She found freedom in faith,
Freedom like the freedom of a feather
Blown about by the breath of God,
While the soft springs of the Spirit
Moistened her wilting heart.
Germinating the divine seed within her,
Making what had withered green.

A mirror of dazzling light,
A 'symphonia' of divine harmony,
   A spring of living water,
A source of joy and healing
A living symbol of a loving heart,
   A green branch for all time -
Became this 'Sybil of the Rhine'

T.J.Rhidian Jones

FOR RAIN IN DUE SEASON

Psalm 146

PRAISE the Lord for praising him is good;
to our God be joyful and comely praise!

The Lord builds up Jerusalem
he will gather together the dispersal of Israel.
It is he who heals the broken-hearted,
he binds up all their bruises.
He can tell the number of the stars,
and calls each one by its name.

Great is our Lord, and great is his power;
the acts of his wisdom are numberless.
The Lord lifts up the meek;
and brings the wicked down to the dust.
Sing to the Lord with praise:
sing to our God upon the harp.

It is he who covers the heavens with clouds;
and prepares rain for the earth,
making grass to grow on the mountains
and with herbs for the service of men.

He gives the beasts their food
and feeds the young ravens that call upon him.
His delight is not in the power of the horse,
nor his pleasure in the strength of a man's legs.
But the Lord takes pleasure in those who fear him,
and in those who hope in his mercy.

Glory be...

℣, O Lord, cover the heavens with clouds
℟. **And prepare rain for the earth.**
℣. May it make grass to grow upon the mountains,
℟. **And herbs for the service of men.**
℣. Water the hills from above,
℟. **And the earth shall be filled with the fruit of your works.**
℣. O Lord hear my prayer.
℟. **And let my cry come to you**

Let us pray

O GOD, in whom we live, move and have our being, grant us seasonable rain, that when our temporal needs are sufficiently supplied, we may seek with more confidence after things eternal.

A LMIGHTY God, we beseech that we, who in our trouble put our trust in thy mercy, may be strengthened by your defence against all adversity.

G RANT us wholesome rain, O Lord, we beseech, and graciously pour forth showers from Heaven on the parched face of the earth. Through our Lord Jesus Christ who lives and reigns with you in the unity of the Holy Spirit, one God, world without end. Amen.

FOR FINE WEATHER

Psalm 66

GOD be merciful unto us, and bless us:
  may he cause the light of his countenance
  to shine upon us, and have mercy on us.
That we may know your way upon earth:
  your salvation in all the nations.

Let the people praise you, O God:
  let all the people praise you.

Let the nations be glad and rejoice:
  for you judge the people with justice,
  and govern the nations upon earth

Let the people praise you, O God:
  let all the people praise you:
  the earth has yielded her fruit.

May God, our own God bless us, may God bless us:
  and may all the ends of the earth fear him.

Glory be to the Father…

℣. You brought, O Lord, your wind upon the earth
℟. And the rain from heaven was restrained.
℣. When I shall cover the sky with clouds
℟. My rainbow shall appear and I will remember my covenant.
℣. May your face shine upon your servants, O Lord,
℟. And bless those who hope in you.
℣. O Lord, hear my prayer.
℟. And let my cry come to you.

Let us pray.

GRACIOUSLY hear us, O Lord, who cry to you, and grant
fair weather to your suppliants, that we who are justly
afflicted for our sins may experience your mercy and clemency.

WE BESEECH your clemency, Almighty God, that you
would restrain the inundation of waters and vouchsafe to
show us the brightness of your countenance. Through our Lord
Jesus Christ, who lives and reigns with you in the unity of the
Holy Spirit, one God, world without end. Amen.

PRAYER FOR FAMILIES

Parents' prayer to the Holy Family

JESUS, Son of the Eternal Father, we most fervently implore you to take our children under your special care and enclose them in the love of your sacred Heart. Rule and guide them that they may live according to our holy faith, that they may not waver in their confidence in you, and may ever remain faithful in your love.

O Mary, blessed Mother of Jesus, grant to our children a place in your pure maternal heart. Spread over them your protecting mantle when danger threatens their innocence; keep them firm when they are tempted to stray from the path of virtue; and should they have the misfortune to fall, raise them up again and reconcile them with your divine Son.

Holy foster father, St Joseph, watch over our children. Protect them from the assaults of the wicked enemy, and deliver them from all dangers of soul and body.

Mary and Joseph, dear parents of the holy Child Jesus, intercede for us that we may be a good example and bring up our children in the love and fear of God, and one day attain with them the beatific vision in Heaven. Amen.

∾

Prayer of engaged couples

FATHER, in my heart, love has come alive for a person you made, and whom you too know and love. It was you who brought me to meet her/him and come to know her/him as once, in Paradise, you brought Eve and Adam together so that man should not remain alone. I want to thank you for this gift. It fills me with profound joy. It makes me like you who are love itself, and brings me to understand the value of life you have given me. Help me not to squander the riches you have stored in my heart. Teach me that love is a gift that must not be suffocated by selfishness; that love is pure and strong and must not be soiled or corrupted; that love is fruitful and should, beginning even now, open up a new life for myself and for the person who has chosen me. Loving Father, I pray for the person who is thinking of me and waiting for me, and who has placed in me complete trust for the future. I pray for this person who will walk along the path of life with me; help us to be worthy of one another and to be an encouragement and example to one another. Help us to prepare for marriage, for its grandeur and for its responsibilities, so that the love which fills us body and spirit may rule our lives for evermore.

ᘯ

F ATHER, we bless you for this our family. Keep us strong and united in your love. May all our quarrels be little ones, and our forgiveness great. Unite us one day with the Holy Family in your kingdom forever. Amen.

ᘯ

For parents, at the birth of a child

B LESSED be God the Father of our Lord Jesus Christ! Almighty God we praise and thank you for once more repeating your miracle of creation. May this beloved child grow strong and healthy, wise and happy, and above all, holy. Mother Mary, watch over this child. And we greet our child's Guardian Angel: welcome to our family! We place our child in your care, to keep him/her from sin all his/her life. And we pray for ourselves: may our joy in our child never grow less: may we be good parents: friends as well as adults. May we never fail to set good example, so that we all, parents and child may come to your heavenly kingdom.

ᘯ

A child's prayer*

L ITTLE Jesus, meek and mild,
   Look on me, a little child.
Pity mine, and pity me,
Suffer me to come to thee.
Heart of Jesus, I adore thee;
Heart of Mary, I implore thee;
Heart of Joseph, pure and just:
In these three hearts I put my trust.

---

* This prayer has been taught to children in the compiler's family for many generations.

Prayer to St Monica for our lapsed children

St Monica's wayward son became one of the church's greatest theologians.

BLESSED Monica, mother of St. Augustine, we give thanks to our Father in heaven who looked with mercy upon your tears over your wayward son. His conversion and heroic sanctification were the fruit of your prayers. Dear St Monica we now ask you to pray with us for all those sons and daughters that have wandered away from God and to add your prayers to those of all mothers who are worried over their children. Pray also for us that, following your example, we may, in the company of our children, one day enjoy the eternal vision of our Father in heaven. Amen.

Terence, Cardinal Cooke

IN TRIBULATION

MAY the most just, most high and most amiable will of God be done, praised, and eternally exalted in all things. Amen.

∞

Act of self-abandonment

O MY GOD, I believe in your infinite goodness; not only that goodness which embraces the world, but also in that particular and personal goodness which extends to me, poor creature that I am, and which disposes everything for my greatest good. For this reason, Lord, even when I cannot see, perceive or understand, I believe that what and where I am and everything that happens to me is the work of your love. With all my will, I prefer this to all other situations which would be more pleasant for me, but which do not come from you. I commend myself into your hands: do with me what you please, leaving me no other consolation than that of obeying you. Amen.

∞

On a disastrous issue

O JESUS, I am come to seek consolation from you, my most tender and most faithful friend. You can see how dejected I am, from what has happened. Grant me strength, I beseech you, that I may be able to bear my affliction with fortitude, and receive it in your spirit. I adore your divine justice, which has overtaken me; I receive with respect and submission all its chastisements; I return thanks for them as I would for so many signs and testimonies of the love of God. I accept them in the spirit of homage, and with the view of honouring your own labours and sufferings. I offer them through your hand, and in union with your sufferings to my heavenly Father as a penance for my sins, sincerely acknowledging that I have deserved much worse. I praise his goodness for having treated me with so much gentleness, and readily submit to whatever else he may please to inflict on me in the future. I only beg of him strength to bear them in the manner I ought, and the undeserved favour of not being punished during eternity. Amen.

For those who do us harm

L ORD God, it is your will that we should love even those
 who speak or act against us. Help us to observe the commandments of the new law, returning good for evil and learning
to forgive as your Son forgave those who persecuted him. Through
the same Christ our Lord. Amen.

ॐ

A LMIGHTY God, hear your people who cry to you in their
 affliction, but for the glory of your name turn again to us,
and help us in our tribulation through Christ our Lord. Amen.

ॐ

M Y MOST loving God, I offer you this trial and commend it
 to you with that same intention with which you brought it
down to me from the Heart of Jesus, beseeching you to record it
for me on high, together with my deepest thankfulness. Amen.

St Mechtilde

ॐ

A LMIGHTY God, have mercy on all that bear me evil will,
 and would me harm, and their faults and mine together by
such easy, tender, merciful means, as thine infinite wisdom best
can devise, vouchsafe to amend and redress and make us saved
souls in heaven together, where we may ever live and love together with thee and thy blessed saints, O glorious Trinity, for
the bitter passion of our sweet Saviour Christ. Lord, give me patience in tribulation and grace in everything to conform my will
to thine, that I may truly say, 'thy will be done on earth as it is in
heaven.' The things, good Lord, that I pray for, give me grace to
labour for. Amen.

St Thomas More

ॐ

On Distractions and Coldness in Prayer

D O NOT be troubled or uneasy in consequence of your coldness and tepidity; all these trials which you feel in prayer,
when accepted with patience, glorify God. Remember the beautiful
psalm in which the prophet calls on the ice, snow and tempests to
praise the Lord! Our Lord is so tender and loving; he knows so well
what we are made of, and he thinks of such little things.

Olivaint

*A prayer of Saint Thomas More, written in the margin of his
book of hours after his troubles had begun, and he had resigned
his dignities at court.*

G IVE me thy grace, Good God, to set the world at nought, to
set my mind fast upon thee and not to hang upon the words
of men's mouths, to be content to be solitary, not to long for
worldly company, little by little utterly to cast off the world, and
rid my mind of all besides thee, not to long to hear any worldly
things, but that the hearing of worldly fantasies may be to me
displeasing, gladly to be thinking of God, piteously to call for his
help, to lean unto the comfort of God, busily to labour to love
him, to know my own vileness and wretchedness, to humble and
abase myself under the mighty hand of God, to bewail my past
sins, for the purging of them patiently to suffer adversity, gladly
to bear my purgatory here, to be joyful in tribulations, to walk
the narrow way that leadeth to life, to bear the cross with Christ,
to have the last things in remembrance, to have ever before mine
eye my death that is ever at hand, to make death no stranger to
me, to foresee and consider the everlasting fire of hell, to pray for
pardon before the Judge do come, to have continually in mind
the passion Christ suffered for me, for his benefits incessantly to
give him thanks, to buy the time again that I have lost, to abstain
from vain conversations, to eschew light foolish mirth and gladness, recreations not necessary to cut off, to set the loss of worldly
substance, friends, liberty, life and all at right nought for the win-
ning of Christ, to think my worst enemies my best friends, for the
brethren of Joseph could never have done him so much good
with their love and favour as they did him with their malice and
hatred.

These wishes are more to be desired by every man than all the
treasure of all the princes and kings, Christian and heathen, were
it gathered and laid together all upon one heap.

IN SICKNESS

O LORD Jesus Christ, I receive this sickness which you are pleased to grant me, as coming from your fatherly hand. It is your will, and therefore I submit;—'not my will, but yours be done.' May it be to the honour of your holy name, and for the good of my soul. I here offer myself with an entire submission to all that you will; to suffer whatever you please, as long as you please, and in what manner you please; for I am your child, O Lord, who has often and most ungratefully offended you, and whom you might justly have visited with your severest punishments. Oh, let your justice be tempered with mercy and let your heavenly grace come to my assistance to support me under this affliction! Fortify my soul with strength from above, that I may bear with true Christian patience all the uneasiness, pains, nuisances and troubles which I endure; preserve me from all temptations and murmuring thoughts, that in this time of affliction I may in no way offend you, and grant that this and all other earthly trials may be the means of preparing my soul for its passage into eternity, that being purified from all my sins, I may believe in you, hope in you, love you above all things, and finally, through your infinite merits, be admitted into the company of the blessed in heaven, there to praise you for ever and ever. Amen.

∾

L ORD God, I do not know why you have given me this sickness: I just ask your grace to bear it with fortitude, and to give as little trouble as possible to those who care for me. I offer to you such pains as I may suffer today together with the pains that Jesus offered on the cross for the salvation of the world. May my pain be, as it were, an ease and a comfort to him.

∾

H EAVENLY Father, accept my pains this day as a prayer for this intention of mine *(name the intention close to your heart)*. Accept it, dearest Lord, and grant my prayer for the merits of our beloved Saviour Jesus Christ, who willingly offered his pains for my salvation. Amen.

LORD, thy will be done, I take this for my sins. I offer up to thee my sufferings, together with all that my Saviour has suffered for me; and I beg of thee, through his sufferings, to have mercy on me. Free me from this illness and pain if thou wilt, and if it be for my good. Thou lovest me too much to let me suffer unless it be for my good. Therefore, O Lord, I trust myself to thee; do with me as thou pleasest. In sickness, and in health, I wish to love thee always.

Footsteps

ONE NIGHT, a man had a dream. He dreamed that he was walking along the beach with the Lord. Across the sky flashed scenes from his life. For each scene he noticed two sets of footprints in the sand. He noticed that many times along the path of his life there was only one set of footprints. He also noticed that this happened at the very lowest and saddest times in his life. This really bothered him, and he questioned the Lord about it: 'Lord, you said that once I'd decided to follow you, you'd walk with me all the way. But I have noticed that during the most troublesome times of my life there is only one set of footprints. I don't understand why when I needed you most you would leave me.' The Lord replied: 'My son, my precious child; I love you and I would never leave you. During your times of trial and suffering, when you see only one set of footprints, it was then that I carried you.

LOOK down O Lord on me, poor man.
In thee I live and move and am.
O clear my soul and conscience,
That I in thee my peace may find.
Rest to my heart, joy to my mind,
Freed from my sins and mine offence!

William Byrd

IN TROUBLE

L ORD, make me an instrument of your peace: where there is hatred, let me sow love; where there is injury, let me sow pardon; where there is doubt, let me sow faith; where there is despair, let me give hope; where there is darkness, let me give light; where there is sadness, let me give joy.

O Divine Master, grant that I may try not to be comforted, but to comfort; not to be understood, but to understand; not to be loved, but to love. Because it is in giving that we receive, it is in forgiving that we are forgiven, and it is in dying that we are born to eternal life.

Attrib: St Francis of Assisi

O BLESSED Jesus, make me understand and remember that whatsoever we gain, if we lose you, all is lost, and whatsoever we lose, if we gain you, all is gained.

St Thomas Cottam

L ORD, give me patience in tribulation.
Let the memory of your Passion,
and of those bitter pains you suffered for me,
strengthen my patience
and support me
in this tribulation and adversity.

St John Forrest

A 'black sonnet'

N O WORST, there is none. Pitched past pitch of grief,
More pangs will, schooled at forepangs, wilder wring.
Comforter, where, where is your comforting?
Mary, mother of us, where is your relief?
My cries heave, herds-long; huddle in a main, a chief
Woe, world-sorrow; on an age-old anvil wince and sing-
Then lull, then leave off. Fury had shrieked 'No ling-
ering! Let me be fell: force I must be brief '.

O the mind, mind has mountains; cliffs of fall
Frightful, sheer, no-man-fathomed. Hold them cheap
May who ne'er hung there. Nor does long our small
Durance deal with that steep or deep. Here! creep,
Wretch, under a comfort serves in a whirlwind: all
Life death does end and each day dies with sleep.

Gerard Manley Hopkins SJ

IN ALL things may the most holy, the most just, and the most lovable will of God be done, praised, and exalted above all for ever. Thy will be done, O Lord, thy will be done. The Lord has given, the Lord has taken away; blessed be the name of the Lord.

FOR THE DYING
AND THE DEAD

MY LORD God, resignedly and willingly, I accept at thy hand with all its anxieties, pains and sufferings, whatever kind of death it shall please thee to be mine. Amen.

∞

JESUS, Mary and Joseph, I give you my heart and my soul.
Jesus, Mary and Joseph, assist me in my last agony.
Jesus, Mary and Joseph, may I breathe forth my soul in peace with you. Amen.

∞

Prayer for a happy death

O MY Lord and Saviour, support me in that hour in the strong arms of thy sacraments, and by the fresh fragrance of thy consolations. Let the absolving words be said over me, and the holy oil sign and seal me, and thy own body be my food, and thy blood my sprinkling; and let my sweet Mother, Mary, breathe on me, and my Angel whisper peace to me, and my glorious saints... smile upon me; that in them all, and through I them all, I may receive the gift of perseverance, and die, as I desire to live, in thy faith, in thy Church, in thy service, and in thy love. Amen.

J.H. Newman

∞

Hymn to God My God, in My Sickness

S INCE I am coming to that holy room,
Where, with thy quire of saints for evermore,
I shall be made thy music; as I come
    I tune the instrument here at the door,
    And what I must do then, think here before.

Whilst my physicians by their love are grown
    Cosmographers, and I their map, who lie
Flat on this bed, that by them may be shown
    That this is my South-west discovery
    Per fretum febris, by these straits to die,

I joy, that in these straits, I see my West;
 For, though their currents yield return to none,
What shall my West hurt me? As West and East
 In all flat maps (and I am one) are one,
 So death doth touch the resurrection.

Is the Pacific Sea my home? Or are
 The Eastern riches? Is Jerusalem?
Anyan, and Magellan, and Gibraltar,
 All straits, and none but straits, are ways to them,
 Whether where Japhet dwelt, or Cham, or Sem.

We think that Paradise and Calvary,
 Christ's cross and Adam's tree, stood in one place;
Look, Lord, and find both Adams met in me;
 As the first Adam's sweat surrounds my face,
 May the last Adam's blood my soul embrace.

So, in his purple wrapp'd receive me, Lord,
 By these his thorns give me his other crown
And as to other's soul I preach'd thy word.
 Be this my text, my sermon to mine own,
 Therefore that he may raise the Lord throws down.

John Donne

ॐ

A Litany for the Dying

KYRIE eléison, Christe eléison, Kýrie eléison.
Holy Mary, pray for him.
All holy Angels, pray for him.
Holy Abraham, pray for him.
St. John Baptist, St. Joseph, pray for him.
St. Peter, St. Paul, St. Andrew, St. John,
All Apostles, all Evangelists, pray for him.
All holy Disciples of the Lord, pray for him.
All holy Innocents, pray for him.
All holy Martyrs, all holy Confessors,
All holy Hermits, all holy Virgins,
All ye saints of God, pray for him.
Be merciful, be gracious; spare him, Lord.

Be merciful, be gracious; Lord, deliver him
From the sins that are past;
From thy frown and Thine ire;
From the perils of dying;
From any complying
With sin, or denying
His God, or relying
On self, at the last;
From the nethermost fire;
From all that is evil;
From power of the devil;
thy servant deliver,
For once and for ever.
By thy birth, and by thy Cross,
Rescue him from endless loss;
By thy death and burial,
Save him from a final fall;
By thy rising from the tomb,
By thy mounting up above,
By the Spirit's gracious love,
Save him in the day of doom.

Rescue him, O Lord, in this his evil hour,
As of old so many by thy gracious power:—Amen.
Enoch and Elias from the common doom; Amen.
Noe from the waters in a saving home; Amen.
Abraham from th'abounding guilt of Heathenesse; Amen.
Job from all his multiform and fell distress; Amen.
Isaac, when his father's knife was raised to slay; Amen.
Lot from burning Sodom on its judgement-day; Amen.
Moses from the land of bondage and despair; Amen.
Daniel from the hungry lions in their lair; Amen.
And the children Three amid the furnace-flame; Amen.
Chaste Susanna from the slander and the shame; Amen.
David from Golia and the wrath of Saul; Amen.
And the two Apostles from their prison-thrall; Amen.
Thecla from her torments; Amen.
—so, to show thy power,
Rescue this thy servant in his evil hour.

The Roman Ritual, Tr. Newman in The Dream of Gerontius

After Death

PROFISCISCERE, *ánima Christiána, de hoc mundo*
　　Go forth upon thy journey, Christian soul!
Go from this world! Go, in the name of God
The omnipotent Father, who created thee!
Go, in the name of Jesus Christ, our Lord,
Son of the living God, who bled for thee!
Go, in the Name of the Holy Spirit, who
Hath been poured out on thee! Go, in the name
Of Angels and Archangels; in the name
Of Thrones and Dominations; in the name
Of Princedoms and of Powers; and in the name
Of Cherubim and Seraphim, go forth!
Go, in the name of Patriarchs and Prophets;
And of Apostles and Evangelists,
Of Martyrs and Confessors; in the name
Of holy Monks and Hermits; in the name
Of holy Virgins; and all Saints of God,
Both men and women, go! Go on thy course;
And may thy place to-day be found in peace,
And may thy dwelling be the Holy Mount
Of Sion—through the Same, through Christ, our Lord.

Roman Ritual: Tr. Newman in The Dream of Gerontius

ALL-POWERFUL and merciful Father, in the death of Christ
　　you have opened a gateway to eternal life. Look kindly upon
our brother/sister who is suffering his/her last agony. United to
the passion and death of your Son, and saved by the blood he
shed, may he/she come before you with confidence. Through the
same Christ our Lord. Amen.

For the dead

GOD OF all spirits and of all flesh, who trampled upon death, and overthrew the devil, giving life to the world: O Lord, grant rest to the soul of your departed servant [N.], in a place of light, in a place of pasture, in a place of rest, from whence pain, sadness and tears have all fled; and forgive him/her all sins, whether committed in thought, word or deed, O good God that loves humanity: for there is no one living who is sinless: you alone are without sin; your justice is eternal justice, and your word is truth. For you yourself are the resurrection, and the life, and the rest of your departed servant [N.], O Christ our God, and to you we offer glory, together with your eternal Father, and your most holy, good, and life-giving Spirit, now, and always, and for ages unending. Amen.

Byzantine

❧

O DIVINE Lord, whose adorable heart ardently sighs for the happiness of your children, we humbly pray that you remember the souls of your servants for whom we pray; command that your holy angels receive them and convey them to a place of rest and peace. Amen.

❧

MAY the bright company of angels bear your soul to paradise. May the glorious band of apostles greet you at the gates. May the white-robed army of martyrs welcome you as you come. May the cheerful throngs of saints lighten your heart for ever. May those you have loved and lost be glad of your coming. May Mary enfold you in her tender arms, and lead you to Jesus your love for ever, and for whom you have longed all this while. May your home be in the heavenly Jerusalem this day and forever. Rest in peace, N. God keep you in his care. Amen.

❧

MAY the souls of the faithful departed, through the mercy of God, rest in peace. Amen.

❧

Psalm 129: De Profundis

O UT OF the depths I have cried unto thee O Lord:
Lord, hear my voice.
Let thine ears be attentive:
to the voice of my supplication.
If thou, O Lord, shalt observe iniquities
Lord, who shall endure it?
For with thee there is merciful forgiveness:
and by reason of thy law I have waited for thee, O Lord.
My soul hath waited on his word:
my soul hath hoped in the Lord.
From the morning watch even unto night
let Israel hope in the Lord.
For with the Lord there is mercy:
and with him is plentiful redemption.
And he shall redeem Israel:
from all his iniquities.

℣. Eternal rest give unto them, O Lord.
℟. And let perpetual light shine upon them.
℣. May they rest in peace.
℟. Amen.
℣. O Lord, hear my prayer.
℟. And let my cry come unto thee.

Let us pray.

O GOD, the Creator and Redeemer of all the faithful; grant to
the souls of thy servants departed the remission of all their
sins, that through pious supplications they my obtain the pardon
which they have always desired. Who livest and reignest world
without end. Amen.

A prayer upon the day of a person's decease or burial

O GOD, whose nature is always to have mercy and to spare,
we humbly pray to you for the soul of your servant [N.]
whom you have this day called out of the world, that you would
not deliver him/her up into the hands of the enemy, nor forget
him/her eternally, but command him/her to be received by your
holy angels, and to be carried to Paradise, his/her true country;
that as in you [N.] had faith and hope he/she may not suffer the
pains of loss, but may take possession of everlasting joys. Through
Christ our Lord. Amen.

On the anniversary of decease

O LORD, the God of mercy and pardon, grant to the soul of your servant the happiness of rest and the brightness of light. Through Christ our Lord. Amen.

For one recently deceased

G RANT your forgiveness, Lord, to the soul of your servant [N.] that, being dead to this world, he/she may live now to you alone, and whatever sins he/she committed through human frailty, do you, in your mercy, absolve. Through Christ our Lord. Amen.

For a Bishop or a Priest

O GOD, who amongst your apostolic priests raised up your servant [N.] to the dignity of a Bishop, [or a Priest,] grant, we pray, that he may also be admitted in heaven to their everlasting fellowship. Through Christ our Lord. Amen.

For Father and Mother

O GOD, who commanded us to honour our Father and Mother, have mercy on the souls of my Father and Mother; and grant that I may see them in the glory of eternity. Through Christ our Lord. Amen.

For Friends, Relations, and Benefactors

O GOD, the giver of pardon and lover of the salvation of mankind, we ask your clemency on behalf of our friends relations, and benefactors who have departed this life; that the blessed Virgin Mary and all the saints interceding for them, they may come to the fellowship of eternal happiness. Through Christ our Lord. Amen.

FOR JUSTICE AND PEACE

The Beatitudes

SEEING the multitude, Jesus went up onto a mountain, and when he sat down, his disciples came to him. And opening his mouth he taught them, saying:

Blessed are the poor in spirit, for theirs is the kingdom of heaven.

Blessed are the meek, for they shall possess the land.

Blessed are those who mourn, for they shall be comforted.

Blessed are those who hunger and thirst for justice, for they shall have their fill.

Blessed are the merciful, for they shall obtain mercy.

Blessed are the clean of heart, for they shall see God.

Blessed are the peacemakers, for they shall be called the children of God.

Blessed are those who suffer persecution for justice' sake, for theirs is the kingdom of heaven.

Blessed are you when men shall revile you and persecute you, and speak all that is evil against you falsely for my sake.

Be glad and rejoice, for your reward is very great in heaven, for so men persecuted the prophets who were before you.

Matthew 5:1-12

FATHER, those who work for peace are called your sons. May we never tire in working for that justice which alone guarantees true and lasting peace. Through Christ our Lord. Amen.

FATHER, you have called men and women through their daily work, to share in your work of creation. May we recognize every person as our brother or sister, and, by the power of your Spirit, strive with them for a more just world where men and women will find work in accordance with the dignity of their vocation, and will contribute to the progress of all humanity. Through Christ our Lord. Amen.

ALMIGHTY and eternal God, may your grace enkindle in everyone a love for the many unfortunate people whom poverty and misery reduce to a condition of life unworthy of human beings. Arouse in the hearts of those who call you Father a hunger and thirst for social justice, and for fraternal love in deed and in truth. Grant, O Lord, peace in our days, peace to souls, peace to families, peace to our country, and peace among nations. Amen.

Pope Pius XII

∾

Prayer for Peace attributed to Saint Francis of Assisi

LORD, make me an instrument of your peace! Where there is hatred, let me sow love; where there is injury, let me sow pardon; where there is doubt, faith; where there is despair, hope; where there is darkness, light; where there is sadness, joy. Amen.

∾

O GOD, our Father, you have set us over all the works of your hands. You have shared with us your creative power to build a world of peace and justice—a world in which everyone can live as brothers and sisters endowed with human dignity as members of your human family.

O God, our Father, bestow on us who live in this age of space a share in your vision. Grant that we, who have seen battlefields where we have sought to destroy one another and ghettos where many of us live without dignity or hope, may now look to the stars and see our world, as the astronauts did, as 'small and blue and beautiful in the eternal silence in which it floats.' Grant that we, who witness millions of homeless, hungry children in a world of unparalleled scientific achievements, may enjoy the prophetic vision which sees all the members of your human family as 'riders on the earth together,' brothers and sisters on 'that bright loveliness in the eternal cold.'

O God, our Father, inspire us with faith to believe that this vision of our earth can be fulfilled. Grant us the grace to believe firmly that you have given us sufficient resources for this purpose. Show us how to use them generously to provide food, decent shelter, education, and meaningful employment for all in your family.

O God, our Father, strengthen us with humility and wisdom. Teach us to be thankful for the precious mystery of life that you have made ours. Bless our efforts to promote the total development of each and every human being that all might reach the fullness of their potential and dignity as your sons and daughters. Amen.

Terence, Cardinal Cooke

FOR THE CHURCH

O GOD, our refuge and strength, look down on thy people who cry to thee, and by the intercession of the glorious and blessed ever-virgin Mary, of St Joseph her spouse, of thy holy apostles Peter and Paul and of all the saints, in mercy and goodness hear our prayers for the conversion of sinners and for the liberty and exaltation of our holy mother the Church. Amen.

ॐ

For the Pope

O GOD, the pastor and governor of all the faithful, mercifully look down upon your servant *John Paul* whom you have been pleased to confirm as the chief pastor of your flock on earth, grant we pray, that both by word and example he may edify those over whom he is set, and together with the flock committed to his care, may attain everlasting life, through Christ our Lord. Amen.

ॐ

For the Bishop

A LMIGHTY and everlasting God, who alone works great marvels, send down upon your servants the Bishops of your Church, and especially upon N. the Bishop of this diocese the spirit of your sanctifying grace, and so that they may truly please you, pour on them the refreshing dew of your blessing, through Christ our Lord. Amen.

ॐ

Another prayer for the Bishop

D EAREST Lord, we thank you for the prayer and ministry of our Bishop N. Be a tower of strength to him, that he may be the same to us. Make him a fearless defender of the faith committed to his charge, and a holy and humble father in God to us his spiritual children. Make him a worthy successor of the apostles, to the end of his own salvation and ours.

ॐ

For priests

O JESUS, great King, good shepherd, eternal priest, living bread, my wisdom, my hope, my reward; with Mary my Mother I adore your wounded heart, I thank you for your seven holy sacraments, and I pray for all priests who minister them. In charity remember those whose charity has aided me: some have guided, warned, instructed, absolved me, some have remembered me in their supplications, tears and sacrifices; some have commended their life, their agony, their judgement, their purgatory to my prayers. Preserve them for the glory of your name for they have proclaimed your praise. Look upon them with mercy, for they have shown mercy, gladden them in their troubles, for they have brought joy to the sorrowful; keep unstained their anointed hands, for they have blessed; keep unearthly their hearts sealed with the sublime marks of your priesthood. Bless their labours, the souls they love, the souls they seek, the souls they pray for. May those to whom they have ministered be here their joy and consolation, and in heaven their beautiful crown. Amen.

For religious sisters

O UR FATHER, we offer this prayer in thanksgiving for Sisters, whose unique role of consecrated dedication to the Church is so in keeping with their fulfilment as christian witnesses and christian women. We rejoice in their courage and vision, manifested by their efforts to express religious community as an answer to the special needs of your Church today. We pray that they will have the clarity of vision and the courage of conviction to be open to the working of the Holy Spirit, so that their lives will express a spirit of living prayer and the power of true christian witness. We ask that by their leadership they will be looked on as symbols of hope in a world which is uncertain and troubled. Finally, we pray that they will be heartened by the living presence of Christ, in whom 'we live and move and have our being,' so that their lives will be a unique testimony to the value of religious community in the pilgrim Church. Amen.

Terence, Cardinal Cooke

For vocations to the priesthood and the religious life

LORD Jesus Christ, Saviour of the world! We humbly beg you to manifest in your Church the Spirit whom you so abundantly bestowed upon your apostles. Call, we pray you, very many to your priesthood and to the religious life. And may zeal for your glory and the salvation of souls inflame these whom you have chosen. By your Spirit strengthen them, that they may be saints in your likeness. Amen.

Stir up in your Church, O Lord, the devotion and fortitude needed to make worthy ministers for your altar and powerful preachers of your word. In your kindness be attentive to our prayers and offerings that the stewards of your mysteries may increase in number and persevere to the end in loving you. Grant that those whom you have chosen as ministers of the redemption may, with pure minds, be worthy servants of your boundless love. Amen.

Terence, Cardinal Cooke

∾

For Christian Unity

O GOD, the Father of our Saviour, Jesus Christ, give us the grace seriously to take to heart the great dangers we are in by our unhappy divisions. Remove from us all hatred and prejudice and whatever else may keep us from union and concord. As there is but one Body and one Spirit, one hope of our calling, one Lord, one faith, one baptism, one God and Father of us all, so may we all be of one heart and of one soul, united in one holy bond of truth and peace, of faith and charity. May we together glorify you through Christ our Lord. Amen.

Terence, Cardinal Cooke

∾

For catechumens

O LORD our God, who dwells on high and yet looks down on the lowly, who sent salvation to the human race in the person of your only-begotten Son, our Lord and our God, Jesus Christ: look upon your servants, the catechumens, who bow their heads before you; make them worthy, in due time, of the washing of baptismal regeneration, of forgiveness of sins, and of the white garment of innocence; unite them with your Holy, Catholic and Apostolic Church and number them with your chosen flock, that they, too, together with us, may glorify your most honourable and majestic name, Father, Son, and Holy Spirit, now, and always, and for ages unending. Amen.

Liturgy of St John Chrysostom

MEETINGS

Before

C OME, Holy Spirit, fill the hearts of your faithful, and kindle in them the fire of your love.

℣. Send forth your Spirit and they shall be created
℟. **And you will renew the face of the earth.**

Lord have mercy, Christ have mercy, Lord have mercy
Our Father...

℣. Remember your people, O Lord,
℟. **Who have been yours from of old.**
℣. O Lord, hear my prayer,
℟. **And let my cry come to you.**

Let us pray.

I LLUMINE our minds, we beseech you, Lord, with the light of your glory, that we may be enabled to see what needs to be done, and be empowered to see it soon and fruitfully effected. Through Christ our Lord. Amen.

ℜ

After

Lord have mercy, Christ have mercy, Lord have mercy
Our Father...

℣. Strengthen, O God what has been done among us
℟. **And give us help from your holy temple.**
℣. O Lord, hear my prayer,
℟. **And let my cry come to you.**

Let us pray.

G RANT us, O Lord, the help of your grace, that since we have deliberated by the help of your inspiration, we may continue to acknowledge you, the author of all good, and thus see our good resolutions put into effect. Through Christ our Lord. Amen.

ℜ ℜ ℜ

Adsumus: Before meetings

WE HAVE come, O Lord, Holy Spirit, we have come before you hampered indeed by our many and grievous sins, but for a special purpose gathered together in your name. Come to us and be with us and enter our hearts.

Teach us what we are to do and where we ought to tend; show us what we must accomplish, in order that, with your help, we may be able to please you in all things.

May you alone be the author and the finisher of our judgements, who alone with God the Father and his Son possess a glorious name.

Do not allow us to disturb the order of justice, you who love equity above all things. Let not ignorance draw us into devious paths. Let not partiality sway our minds or respect of riches or persons pervert our judgement.

But unite us to you effectually by the gift of your grace alone, that we may be one in you and never forsake the truth; inasmuch as we are gathered together in your name, so may we in all things hold fast to justice tempered by mercy, so that in this life our judgement may in no wise be at variance with you and in the life to come we may attain to everlasting rewards for deeds well done. Amen.

Roman Pontifical

❧

Before Parish Meetings

HEAVENLY Father, be present with us now. Let all our deliberations tend to your glory and the furtherance of the Gospel. Let our discussions be charitable and our conclusions fruitful. May the breeze of your Holy Spirit breathe among us instead of long-windedness, let there be no fighting of corners or sacrificing long term trust for short term popularity. In short, dear Father, may this meeting end on time, with your kingdom furthered. Through the one who used few words but to great effect, Jesus Christ our Lord. Amen.

FOR OUR COUNTRY

LORD God, you guide the universe with wisdom and love. Hear the prayer we make to you for our country: Through the honesty of our citizens and the wisdom of those who govern may concord and justice flourish and lasting peace be achieved.

❧

Prayer for England

O BLESSED Virgin Mary, Mother of God and our most gentle Queen and Mother, look down in mercy upon England, thy 'Dowry', and upon us all who greatly hope and trust in thee. By thee it was that Jesus, our Saviour, was given unto the world, and he has given thee to us that we might hope still more. Plead for us, thy children, whom thou did receive and accept at the foot of the cross, O sorrowful Mother. Intercede for our separated brethren, that with us in the one, true fold they may be united to the Chief Shepherd, the Vicar of thy flock. Pray for us all, dear Mother, that by faith fruitful in good works we may all deserve to see and praise God together with thee in our heavenly home. Amen.

Traditional

❧

Hail Mary, &c.

O MERCIFUL God, let the glorious intercession of thy saints assist us; above all the most blessed Virgin Mary, Mother of thy only-begotten Son, and thy holy Apostles, Peter and Paul, to whose patronage we humbly recommend this our land. Be mindful of our fathers, Eleutherius, Celestine and Gregory, bishops of the holy city; of Augustine, Columba, and Aidan, who delivered to us inviolate the faith of the holy Roman Church. Remember our holy martyrs, who shed their blood for Christ; especially our first martyr, Saint Alban, and thy most glorious bishop, Saint Thomas of Canterbury. Remember all those holy confessors, bishops and kings, all those holy monks and hermits, all those holy virgins and widows, who made this once an island of saints, illustrious by their glorious merits and virtues. Let not their memory perish from before thee, O Lord, but let their supplication enter daily into thy sight; and do thou, who didst so often spare thy sinful people for the sake of Abraham, Isaac and Jacob, now also, moved by the prayers of our fathers reigning with thee, have mercy upon us, save thy people, and bless thy inheritance; and suffer not those souls to perish, which thy Son hath redeemed with his most precious blood. Who liveth and reigneth with thee, world without end. ℟. Amen.

Let us pray.

LOVING Lord Jesus, who, when thou wert hanging on the Cross, didst commend us all, in the person of thy disciple John, to thy most sweet Mother, that we might find in her our refuge, our solace and our hope; look graciously upon our beloved land, and on those who are bereaved of so powerful a patronage; that, acknowledging once more the dignity of this holy Virgin, they may honour and venerate her with all affection of devotion, and own her as Queen and Mother. May her sweet name be lisped by little ones, and linger on the lips of the aged and the dying; and may it be invoked by the afflicted, and hymned by the joyful; that this Star of the Sea being their protection and guide, all may come to the harbour of eternal salvation. Who livest and reignest, world without end. Amen.

A prayer for the sovereign

O ALMIGHTY God, by whom kings reign and from whom they derive their power, we humbly beseech thee to look down upon *Elizabeth our Queen* and *all the royal family,* leading them to a knowledge of thy truth, and giving *her* a right judgement of *her* mighty office, with courage, mercy and prudence in the execution thereof, that the sword of justice in *her* hand may protect us, to our free progress in virtue and to the obtaining of *her* own eternal salvation. Amen.

℣. Dómine, salvum fac regínam nostram Elísabeth
℟. **Et exáudi nos in die qua invocavérimus te.**
Orémus.

QUAESUMUS, omnípotens Deus, ut fámula

℣. O Lord, save Elizabeth our Queen
℟. **And hear us on the day when we call upon you.**
Let us pray.

ALMIGHTY God, we pray for your servant Elizabeth

tua Elísabeth, regína nostra, quæ tua miseratióne suscépit regni gubernácula, virtútum etiam ómnium percípiat increméntum: quibus decénter ornáta, et vitiórum monstra devitáre (hostes superáre), et ad te qui via, véritas et vita es, cum consórte et prole regia, gratiósa váleat perveníre. Per Christum Dóminum nostrum. Amen.

our Queen, who now according to your mercy has taken authority over us. May she experience a growth in all virtues, as is only fitting, and remove from her way all that is evil, so that with her husband and all the royal family, she may at last happily come to you, the way the truth and the life. Through Christ our Lord. Amen.

☙

Prayer for Scotland

LORD, win over the minds of our countrymen so that all may acknowledge you as the way, the truth and the life. Having seen and believed that you are the Son of God, may they see your Spirit, Truth and Life in the one true Church which you have founded. Amen.

Hail Mary &c.

Our Lady, help of Christians,	*pray for us.*
St Andrew	*pray for us*
St Margaret	*pray for us*
St John Ogilvie,	*pray for us*
All you saints of Scotland,	*pray for us.*

☙

Prayer for Wales

O ALMIGHTY God, who in thy infinite goodness hast sent thy only-begotten Son into this world to open once more the gates of heaven, and to teach us how to know, love and serve thee, have mercy on thy people who dwell in Wales. Grant to them the precious gift of faith, and unite them in the one true Church founded by thy

Gweddi dros Gymru

O HOLLALLUOG Dduw a ddanfonodd, o'th anfeidrol ddaioni, dy uniganedig Fab i ailagor porth y nefoedd, ac i ddysgu inni dy adnabod, dy garu a'th wasanaethu, trugarha wrth dy bobl sy'n byw yng Nghymru. Dyro iddynt y werthfawr ddawn Ffydd, ac una hwy yn yr un wir Eglwys a sylfaenwyd gan dy divine Son; that, acknowledging her authority and obeying her voice, they may serve thee, love thee, and worship thee as thou desirest in this world, and obtain for themselves everlasting happiness in the world to come. Through the same Christ our Lord. Amen.

Our Lady, Help of Christians, *pray for Wales.*

Saint David, *pray for Wales.*

Saint Winifride, *pray for Wales.*

Holy Martyrs of Wales, *pray for Wales.*

ddwyfol Fab, fel, gan arddel ei hawdurdod a chan ufuddhau i'w llais y'th wasanaethont i, a'th garu a'th addoli yn ôl dy ewyllys yn y byd hwn, ac felly dderbyn ohonynt ddedwyddwch yn y byd a ddaw. Trwy'r un Iesu Grist ein Harglwydd. Amen.

Ein Harglwyddes, Gymorth Cristnogion, *gweddïa dros Gymru.*

Dewi Sant, *gweddïa dros Gymru.*

Santes Wenfrewi, *gweddïa dros Gymru.*

Holl Ferthyron Cymru, *gweddïwch dros Gymru.*

❧

Prayer to St David for Wales

O GOD, who raised Blessed David to be an apostle and patron for thy people in Wales; grant, we implore, that through his prayers these people may be restored to the truth which he taught, and to attain from him everlasting life. Through Jesus Christ our Lord. Amen.

Gweddi ar Ddewi Sant

O DDUW a gyfododd y bendigedig Ddewi yn apostol ac yn noddwr i'th bobl yng Nghymru, caniatâ, atolygwn arnat, trwy ei eiriolaeth edfryd y bobl hyn i'r gwirionedd a ddysgwyd ganddo ef, a chael ohonynt fywyd tragwyddol. Trwy Iesu Grist ein Harglwydd. Amen.

Tr. Iestyn Evans

❧

Prayer for Ireland

ALMIGHTY God, who has made this land a land of saints, raise up in your Irish children the spirit of St Patrick, St Brigid, St Oliver and all those who intercede for us now in heaven at your throne of glory. Keep this country strong in the true faith, and in practice of all the virtues, that with our holy forefathers we may at last come to heaven where we may praise your holy name for ever.

Our Lady of Knock *Pray for us.*
All saints of Ireland, *Pray for us.*

 confidence

Prayer for America

HEAVENLY Father, who hast made us citizens of this wonderful land, bless our President, N. and strengthen him/her
with all holy virtues, that he/she and the legislature may govern
wisely this land of the free. Bless, too, our State of N. and its
Governor, N. and make them wise, that they may seek the ways
of justice and truth, and your ways above all. And may the Ameri-
can people so shine before the world in virtue and in fidelity to
thy holy Gospel that the whole world may be converted to Christ
and his true Church. Mother Mary, help us with your prayers.

confidence

Another Prayer for America

WE PRAY thee, O Almighty and Eternal God, who through
Jesus Christ hast revealed thy glory to all nations, to preserve the works of thy glory to all nations, to preserve the works
of thy mercy; that thy Church, being spread through the whole
world, may continue, with unchanging faith, in the confession of
thy name. We pray thee, who alone art good and holy, to endow
with heavenly knowledge, sincere zeal, and sanctity of life our
chief bishop, N., the vicar of our Lord Jesus Christ in the government of His Church: our own bishop, N., all other bishops, prel-
ates, and pastors of the Church; and especially those who are
appointed to exercise among us the functions of the holy ministry, and conduct thy people into the ways of salvation. We pray
thee, O God of might, wisdom, and justice, through whom authority is rightly administered, laws are enacted, and judgements
decreed, assist, with thy Holy Spirit of counsel and fortitude, the
President of these United States, that his administration may be
conducted in righteousness, and be eminently useful to thy people, over whom he presides, by encouraging due respect for virtue and religion; by a faithful execution of the laws in justice and
mercy; and by restraining vice and immorality. Let the light of
thy divine wisdom direct the deliberations of Congress, and shine
forth in all the proceedings and laws framed for our rule and government; so that they may tend to the preservation of peace, the

promotion of national happiness, the increase of industry, sobriety, and useful knowledge, and may perpetuate to us the blessings of equal liberty. We pray for his Excellency the Governor of this State, for the members of the Assembly, for all judges, magistrates, and other officers who are appointed to guard our political welfare; that they may be enabled, by thy powerful protection, to discharge the duties of their respective stations with honesty and ability. We recommend likewise to thy unbounded mercy all our brethren and fellow-citizens, throughout the United States, that they may be blessed in the knowledge, and sanctified in the observance of thy most holy law; that they may be preserved in union, and in that peace which the world cannot give; and, after enjoying the blessings of this life, be admitted to those which are eternal. Finally, we pray thee, O Lord of mercy, to remember the souls of thy servants departed who are gone before us with the sign of faith, and repose in the sleep of peace: the souls of our parents, relations, and friends; of those who, when living, were members of this congregation; and particularly of such as are lately deceased; of all benefactors who, by their donations or legacies to this Church, witnessed their zeal for the decency of divine worship, and proved their claim to our grateful and charitable remembrance. To these, O Lord, and to all that rest in Christ, grant, we beseech thee, a place of refreshment, light, and everlasting peace, through the same Jesus Christ, our Lord and Saviour. Amen.

Archbishop John Carroll (1735-1815)

Before an election

COME, Holy Spirit, and inspire all those standing for office in this land. May they have you and your holy laws as their most important principle, and may they be ready to listen to the promptings of your holy inspiration. Be with us, too, as we prepare to exercise our duties as citizens of this country. May we place our vote inspired, not with short-term personal greed, but with due regard for justice and the welfare of all citizens, and, above all, the glory of your holy name.

After an Election

HEAR our prayers, Almighty God, whose kingdom is not of this world. May our new government model their earthly kingdom on your heavenly one, that justice may be done, and that your holy name may be glorified here on earth as in heaven. Bless our new *premier,* N. Fill *him* with your spiritual gifts, especially prudence, wisdom, courage and faith. May *he* lead this land in peace, that we all may come at last from this mere reflection to the true kingdom of heaven, where you live and reign for ever and ever.

THROUGH THE DAY

I T IS the saying of holy men that, if we wish to be perfect, we have nothing more to do than to perform the ordinary duties of the day well. A short road to perfection—short, not because easy, but because pertinent and intelligible. There are no short ways to perfection, but there are sure ones.

I think this is an instruction which may be of great practical use to persons like ourselves. It is easy to have vague ideas what perfection is, which serve well enough to talk about, when we do not intend to aim at it; but as soon as a person really desires and sets about seeking it himself, he is dissatisfied with anything but what is tangible and clear, and constitutes some sort of direction towards the practice of it.

We must bear in mind what is meant by perfection. It does not mean any extraordinary service, anything out of the way, or especially heroic—not all have the opportunity of heroic acts, of sufferings—but it means what the word perfection ordinarily means. By perfect we mean that which has no flaw in it, that which is complete, that which is consistent, that which is sound— we mean the opposite to imperfect. As we know well what *im*-perfection in religious service means, we know by the contrast what is meant by perfection.

He, then, is perfect who does the work of the day perfectly, and we need not go beyond this to seek for perfection. You need not go out of the *round* of the day

I insist on this because I think it will simplify our views and fix our exertions on a definite aim. If you ask me what you are to do in order to be perfect, I say, first— Do not lie in bed beyond the due time of rising; give your first thoughts to God; make a good visit to the Blessed Sacrament; say the Angelus devoutly; eat and drink to God's glory; say the Rosary well; be recollected; put out bad thoughts; make your evening meditation well; examine yourself daily; go to bed in good time, and you are already perfect.

J.H. Newman

MORNING

THESE things I will think over in my heart, and therefore I will hope: the mercies of the Lord never come to an end, his compassions never fail; they are new every morning; great is your faithfulness. 'The Lord is my portion,' said my soul, 'therefore I will wait for him.'

Lamentations 3:21-24

❧

O MY God, through the most pure heart of Mary, I offer thee all the prayers, works and sufferings of this day for the intentions of thy divine heart in the holy Mass.

Traditional

❧

MOST holy and adorable Trinity, one God in three persons, I praise you and give you thanks for all the favours you have bestowed on me. Your goodness has preserved me until now. I offer you my whole being, and in particular all my thoughts, words, and deeds, together with all the trials I may undergo this day. Give them your blessing. May your divine love animate them and may they serve your greater glory.

I make this morning offering in union with the divine intentions of Jesus Christ who offers himself daily in the holy sacrifice of the Mass, and in union with Mary, his virgin Mother and our Mother, who was always the faithful handmaid of the Lord. Amen.

❧

Morning offering of St Leonard of Port Maurice

O MY eternal God, behold me prostrate before your immense majesty in humblest adoration. I offer you all my thoughts, words and actions of this day; and I intend to do all for your love, for your glory, to fulfil your divine will, to serve you, to praise you and to bless you; to be enlightened in the mysteries of the holy faith, to secure my salvation, and to hope in your mercy; to satisfy your divine justice for my sins, so many and so grievous; to give help to the holy souls in Purgatory, and to obtain the grace of a true conversion for all sinners: in short, I intend to do this day every thing in union with those most pure intentions which

Jesus and Mary had in life, and all the saints who are in heaven, and all the just who are upon earth; and I should wish to be able to subscribe with my own blood this my intention, and to repeat it as many times every moment as there will be moments in eternity. Accept, O my beloved God, this my good desire; give me your holy blessing, with powerful grace not to commit mortal sin throughout the whole course of my life, but particularly on this day, on which I desire, and intend to gain all the indulgences which I can, and to assist spiritually at all the Masses which shall be celebrated today throughout the whole world, applying them all as help to the holy souls in Purgatory that they may be freed from those pains. Amen.

∾

I OFFER to thee, O my God, the life and death of thine only Son, and with them these, mine affections and resolutions, my thoughts, words, deeds and sufferings of this day and of all my life, in honour of thine adorable majesty, in thanksgiving for all thy benefits, in satisfaction for my sins, and to obtain the assistance of thy grace; that, persevering to the end in doing thy holy will, I may love and enjoy thee for ever in thy glory.

∾

O MY God, I offer you my thoughts, words, actions, and sufferings; and I beseech you to give me your grace that I may not offend you this day, but may faithfully serve you and do your holy will in all things. Amen.

∾

G RANT, O Lord, that none may love you less this day because of me; that never word or act of mine may turn one soul from thee; and, ever daring, yet one more grace would I implore that many souls this day, because of me, may love thee more. Amen.

∾

F ATHER, unless you help me I shall no good today whatever, but great evil.

St Philip Neri

GIVE us, Lord, a humble, quiet, peaceable patient, tender and charitable mind, and in all our thoughts, words and deeds a taste of the Holy Spirit. Give us, Lord, a lively faith, a firm hope, a fervent charity, a love of you. Take from us all lukewarmness in meditation, dullness in prayer. Give us fervour and delight in thinking of you and your grace, your tender compassion towards us. The things that we pray for, good Lord, give us grace to labour for. Through Jesus Christ our Lord.

St Thomas More

❧

GOD be in my head,
  And in my understanding;
God be in mine eyes,
  And in my looking;
God be in my mouth
  And in my speaking;
God be in my heart,
  And in my thinking;
God be at my end and at my departing.

Sarum Primer: Sixteenth Century

❧

GOD, our Father we are very feeble and not inclined to any virtuous or gallant undertaking. Fortify our weakness, we beg, that we may be valiant in this spiritual war; help us against our own neglect and timorousness, and protect us from the treachery of our unfaithful hearts, for the love of Jesus Christ our Lord. Amen.

Thomas Kempis

❧

Actiones nostras

DIRECT, we beseech you, Lord, our actions by your holy inspiration and further them with your gracious assistance, that our every word and work may always begin with you, and through you be happily ended. Amen.

Roman Breviary

❧

L ORD, I give you my feet to go your way
  my body to do whatever you want me to do,
my tongue to say whatever you want me to say.
Now take away from me whatever I do not need.

L ORD, God Almighty, since you have brought us safely to the
  beginning of this day, defend us as this day proceeds by
your mighty power, so that we do not fall into any sin, but that all
our words, our thoughts and actions may be so governed, as to be
ever righteous in your sight. Through Christ our Lord. Amen.

Roman Breviary

A NGEL of God, my guardian dear
  To whom God's love commits me here,
Ever this day be at my side
To light and guard, to rule and guide.
Amen.

Traditional

U SE ME, my Saviour, for whatever purpose and in whatever
  way thou mayest require. Here is my poor heart, an empty
vessel; fill it with thy grace. Here is my sinful, troubled soul;
quicken it and refresh it with thy love. Take my heart for thine
abode; my mouth to spread abroad the glory of thy name; my
love and all my powers for the advancement of thy believing
people and never suffer the steadfastness and confidence of my
faith to abate.

Dwight Moody

THE ANGELUS

recited at morning, noon and in the evening

Other than during Eastertide:

℣. The Angel of the Lord declared unto Mary,
℟. And she conceived of the Holy Spirit.

Hail Mary.

℣. Behold the handmaid of the Lord,
℟. Be it done unto me according to your word.

Hail Mary.

℣. And the Word was made flesh,
℟. And dwelt among us.

Hail Mary.

℣. Pray for us, O holy Mother of God,
℟. That we may be made worthy of the promises of Christ.

Let us pray.

POUR forth, we beg you, O Lord, your grace into our hearts: that we, to whom the Incarnation of Christ your Son was made known by the message of an Angel, may by his passion and cross be brought to the glory of his Resurrection. Through the same Christ our Lord. Amen.

During the Easter Season: *Regina Cœli*

QUEEN of Heaven, rejoice, alleluia:
For he whom you merited to bear, alleluia,
Has risen, as he said, alleluia.
Pray for us to God, alleluia.

℣. Rejoice and be glad, O Virgin Mary, alleluia.
℟. Because the Lord is truly risen, alleluia.

Let us pray.

O GOD, who by the resurrection of your Son, our Lord Jesus Christ, granted joy to the whole world: grant, we beg you, that through the intercession of the Virgin Mary, his mother, we may lay hold of the joys of eternal life. Through the same Christ our Lord. Amen.

BEFORE WORK

L ORD, thou knowest how busy I must be this day. If I forget
   thee, do not thou forget me.

Jacob Astley at the battle of Edgehill, 1642.

∾

A LMIGHTY God, the giver of all good things, without whose
   help all labour is ineffectual, and without whose grace all
wisdom folly, grant, we beseech thee, that in all our undertakings, thy Holy Spirit may not be withheld from us: but that we
may promote thy glory, and the salvation both of ourselves and
others. Grant this, O Lord, for the sake of Jesus Christ our Lord.

Samuel Johnson

∾

I KNOW not, O my God, what may befall me today, but I am
   well convinced that nothing will happen which thou hast not
foreseen and ordained from eternity. I adore thy eternal and im-
penetrable designs, I submit to them for thy love, I sacrifice myself in union with the sacrifice of Jesus Christ my divine Saviour.
I ask in his holy name for patience and resignation in my
sufferings, and perfect conformity of my will to thine in all things,
past, present and to come.

My God, I have nothing worthy of thy acceptance to offer
thee, I know nothing, I can do nothing. I have but my heart to
give thee; I may be deprived of health, reputation and even life,
but my heart is my own. I consecrate it to thee, hoping never to
resume it and desiring not to live if not for thee. Amen.

Madame Elizabeth of France, sister to Louis XVI

∾

Prayer of St Thomas Aquinas before work

O THOU Creator, of whom my tongue is powerless to tell,
   thou who from the infinite depths of thy wisdom hast fash-
ioned the choirs of angels, and arranged them marvellously above
the highest heavens, each in its proper rank; thou who hast set all
things most perfectly and beautifully in place; thou, I pray, who
art acclaimed as the true fount of light and wisdom, from whom

all things take their origin, pour out thy clear radiance upon the obscurity of my mind. Take away the double darkness in which I was born, of sin, that is, and of ignorance. Thou, who makest the lips of babes to utter praise, give eloquence to my lips and pour out the grace of thy blessing upon my speech. Grant me intelligence to learn, memory to retain, method and ease to understand, facility to explain, and abundant fluency to speak. Give me knowledge as I begin, guide me in the progress of my work, and bring me out with my task well done, O thou who art true God and true man. Amen.

Tr. Jerome Bertram

∾

Another prayer of St Thomas Aquinas before beginning study

O INCOMPREHENSIBLE Creator, the true fountain of light and only author of all knowledge, enlighten, we pray, our understanding, and remove from us all darkness of ignorance. Give us a diligent and obedient spirit, quickness to grasp subtleties, capacity to remember and the powerful assistance of thy holy grace, that what we learn we may apply to the honour of our own souls, through Jesus Christ our Lord. Amen.

∾

O MY GOD, I offer to thee the duties I am going to perform, to thy greater honour and glory. I desire to praise and glorify thy holy name and that of thy holy Mother now and for ever. Amen.

∾

A prayer before reading the scriptures:

L ORD, may your sacred scriptures be my delight; turn to me, my God. You are fullness of day to those that can see; you are light to the blind; you are power to the strong, strength to the weak: turn to me. Listen to my cry from the depths. There are so many mysteries in the Scriptures, and yet it was not without purpose that you wished them to be written. Let me praise you for all the truths I discover in these sacred books. Help me to listen to the voice of prayer; refresh me as I meditate on the wonders of your law; from the beginning of time when you created the heavens and the earth to the moment when shall reign with you in your holy city for ever.

St Augustine

ENKINDLE in our hearts, Master and lover of mankind, the pure light of thy divine knowledge, and open the eyes of our understanding, that we may comprehend the teachings of thy gospel: instill in us a fear of thy blessed commandments that, trampling all desires of the flesh, we might live a spiritual life, thinking and doing all those things which are pleasing to thy holy will. For thou art the light of our souls and of our bodies, O Christ our God, and to thee do we offer glory, together with thy eternal Father, and to thy most holy, good and life-giving Spirit, now, and always, and forever and ever. Amen.

Liturgy of St John Chrysostom

GRACE BEFORE AND AFTER MEALS

Formal Grace Before Meals

℣. Bless the Lord!
℟. Bless the Lord!

At midday meal:

THE EYES of all look to you, O Lord, **And you grant them food when it is needed. You open wide your hand and fill all your creatures with blessings.**

At evening meal:

THE POOR shall eat and have their fill, **And shall praise the Lord who has blessed them, for they shall live for ever and ever.**

Lord have mercy,
Christ have mercy,
Lord have mercy.

Our Father.

Let us pray.

BLESS us, O ✠ Lord, and these your gifts which we are about to receive from your bounty. Through Christ our Lord. Amen.

The cook, or another person says:

Lord, give us your blessing!

Whoever presides replies:

MAY the King of eternal glory make us partakers one day of his heavenly banquet.
℟. Amen.

MAY the King of eternal glory draw us to share in the banquet of everlasting life.
℟. Amen.

Formal Grace After Meals

After midday meal:

ALL YOUR works, O Lord, proclaim your goodness.

After evening meal:

THE GOOD and merciful Lord has caused us to remember his goodness:

| And all your holy people rejoice in you. | He has given food to those who love him. |

WE GIVE you thanks, O Lord, for all your benefits, who lives and reigns for ever and ever. Amen.

Psalm 116

PRAISE the Lord, all you nations,
Praise him, all you peoples.
For his mercy has been shown forth towards us,
And the Lord keeps his word for ever.
Glory be…

Lord have mercy,
Christ have mercy,
Lord have mercy.

Our Father.

℣. The Lord gives freely to the poor.
℟. **And his justice shall last for ever.**
℣. I will bless the Lord at all times.
℟. **His praise shall be always on my lips.**
℣. My soul will ever praise the Lord.
℟. **The redeemed shall hear it and be glad.**
℣. Bless the Lord with me.
℟. **Let us praise his name together.**
℣. May the name of the Lord be blessed.
℟. **Now and for evermore.**

REWARD, O Lord, with eternal life all those who have been good to us, for the sake of your holy name. Amen.

℣. Let us bless the Lord.
℟. **Thanks be to God.**

May the souls of the faithful departed, through the mercy of God, rest in peace. ℟. **Amen.**

☙

Simple Grace before meals

BLESS us, O Lord, and these thy gifts which we are about to receive from thy bounty, through Christ our Lord. Amen.

Simple Grace after meals

WE GIVE thee thanks, almighty God for these and all thy
benefits, who livest and reignest world without end. Amen.
May the souls of the faithful departed, through the mercy of God
rest in peace. Amen.

∞

A Celtic Grace

BE with me, O God at breaking of bread,
Be with me, O God at close of our meal,
Let no whit adown my body
That may hurt my sorrowing soul.

∞

Before...

BLESS us, gracious Lord,
Bless this food, set before us,
Bless those who have prepared it
And give bread to those who have none.

∞

and After...

WE GIVE you thanks, generous Lord,
for the food which we have shared.
Make us open-handed to those in need,
and ever grateful for the good things you give us.
Through Christ our Lord. Amen.

∞

TO GOD who gives our daily bread
A thankful song we raise,
And pray that he who sends us food
May fill our hearts with praise.

Thomas Tallis

∞   ∞   ∞

∞   ∞

∞

EJACULATORY PRAYERS

THESE are prayers which we fire up to heaven whenever it occurs to us during the day. They help us to keep the presence of God before us at all times. 'Pray constantly,' says St Paul: these prayers may help us to do just that.

Some people like to attach these little prayers to particular actions: one to say when opening a door, another when switching on a light. Some like to use them when tempted to do wrong: following them up by thanking the devil for giving us an reminder to praise God!

WE adore you, O Christ, and we bless you; because by your holy Cross you have redeemed the world.

(Roman Breviary)

May the Holy Trinity be blessed.   *(Roman Missal)*

Christ conquers! Christ reigns! Christ commands!

O Heart of Jesus, burning with love for us, inflame our hearts with love for you.

O Heart of Jesus, I place my trust in you.

O Heart of Jesus, all for you.

Most Sacred Heart of Jesus, have mercy on us.

My God and my all.

O God, have mercy on me, a sinner.   *(Lk 18:13)*

Grant that I may praise you, O sacred Virgin; give me strength against your enemies.   *(Roman Breviary)*

Teach me to do your will, because you are my God.   *(Ps 142:10)*

O Lord, increase our faith.   *(Lk 17:5)*

O Lord, may we be of one mind in truth and of one heart in charity.

O Lord, save us, lest we perish.   *(Mt 8:25)*

My Lord and my God.   *(Jn 20:28)*

Sweet Heart of Jesus, be my salvation.

Glory be to the Father, and to the Son, and to the Holy Spirit.

Jesus, Mary, Joseph, I give you my heart and my soul.

Jesus, Mary, Joseph, assist me in my last agony.

Jesus, Mary, Joseph, may I breathe forth my soul in peace with you.

(Roman Ritual)

Jesus, meek and humble of heart, make my heart like your heart.

(Roman Ritual)

May the Most Blessed Sacrament be praised and adored forever.

Stay with us, O Lord.   *(Lk 24:29)*

Mother of Sorrows, pray for us.

My Mother, my Hope.

Send, O Lord, labourers into your harvest.   *(see Mt 9:38)*

May the Virgin Mary together with her loving Child bless us.

(Roman Breviary)

Hail, O Cross, our only hope!   *(Roman Breviary)*

Pray for us, O Holy Mother of God, that we may be made worthy of the promises of Christ.   *(Roman Ritual)*

Father, into your hands I commend my spirit *(Lk 23:46; see Ps 30:6).*

Merciful Lord Jesus, grant them everlasting rest.   *(Roman Missal)*

Queen conceived without original sin, pray for us. *(Roman Ritual)*

Holy Mother of God, Mary ever Virgin, intercede for us.

(Roman Breviary)

Holy Mary, pray for us.   *(Roman Ritual)*

You are the Christ, the Son of the living God.   *(Mt 16:16)*

The 'Golden Arrow': for use when one has heard a blasphemy:

MAY the most holy, most sacred, most adorable, most mysterious and unutterable name of God be praised, blest, loved, adored, glorified in heaven, on earth and in hell, by all God's creatures, and by the Sacred Heart of our Lord and Saviour Jesus Christ in the most holy sacrament of the altar. Amen.

EVENING

I F YOU are really fighting, you need to make an examination of conscience. Take care of the daily examination: find out if you feel the sorrow of love, for not getting to know our Lord as you should.

Bd José Maria de Balaguer

❧

The Apologist's Evening Prayer

F ROM all my lame defeats and oh! much more
From all the victories that I seemed to score;
From cleverness shot forth on thy behalf
At which, while angels weep, the audience laugh;
From all my proofs of thy divinity,
Thou, who wouldst give no sign, deliver me.

Thoughts are but coins. Let me not trust, instead
Of thee, their thin-worn image of thy head.
From all my thoughts, even from my thoughts of thee,
O thou fair silence, fall, and set me free.
Lord of the narrow gate and the needle's eye,
Take from me all my trumpery lest I die.

C.S.Lewis

❧

B LESSED Jesus, still my soul in you. Reign in me, O mighty calm. Rule in me, O gentle King, O peaceful King. Give me self-control, strong self-control over what I say, what I think, what I do. Deliver me, beloved Lord, from fractiousness, irritability, lack of gentleness and by your own profound patience, give the same to me, with a soul that loves to be still in you. Make me again in your likeness, in this as in everything. Amen. O rest in the Lord forever, my soul, for he is the eternal repose of the saints.

St John of the Cross

❧

B LESSED Jesus, make me love you entirely. Let me deeply consider the greatness of your love towards me. Sweet Jesus, possess my heart, hold and keep it only to you. O Blessed Lord, you have overcome me; you have utterly bound me by your grace and manifold benefits to be your servant. From now on, I will never leave you. Amen.

St John Fisher

❧

THOU being of marvels,
 Shield me with might,
Thou being of statutes
And of stars.

Compass me this night,
Both soul and body,
Compass me this night
And on every night.

Compass me aright
Between earth and sky,
Between the mystery of thy laws
And mine eye of blindness;

Both that which mine eye sees
And that which it reads not;
Both that which is clear
And is not clear to my devotion.

Celtic

❧

The Pillar of the Cloud

LEAD, Kindly Light, amid the encircling gloom
 Lead thou me on!
The night is dark, and I am far from home—
 Lead thou me on!
Keep thou my feet; I do not ask to see
The distant scene—one step enough for me.

I was not ever thus, nor pray'd that thou
        Shouldst lead me on.
I loved to choose and see my path, but now
        Lead thou me on!
I loved the garish day, and, spite of fears,
Pride ruled my will: remember not past years.

So long thy power hath blest me, sure it still
        Will lead me on,
O'er moor and fen, o'er crag and torrent, till
        The night is gone;
And with the morn those angel faces smile
Which I have loved long since, and lost awhile.

J.H. Newman

THROUGH THE YEAR

ADVENT

The season of Advent begins the liturgical year of the church, and has two phases. The first phase, lasting until the seventeenth of December, puts before the Christian the prospect of the return of the Lord at the end of time. Though the anticipation of this event is a rather nervous one—the images tend to be apocalyptic, and the Lord, after all, will be returning as our judge—nevertheless it is an event waited for and prayed for eagerly, as it marks the beginning of the reign of God, and the righting of all wrongs. Maranatha, Come, Lord! is one of the oldest of Christian prayers.

STIR up your power, we beseech you O Lord, and come, that we may be protected from the dangers to which our sins expose us, and thus we may be saved.

❧

GRANT the will, we beseech you, almighty God, to your faithful people, that, running to meet the coming of your Anointed with the gift of good works, we may be found worthy to be gathered at his right hand and thus possess the heavenly kingdom.

❧

ALMIGHTY God, give us grace that we may cast away the works of darkness, and put upon us the armour of light, now in the time of this mortal life, in which thy Son Jesus Christ came to visit us in great humility; that in the last day, when he shall come again in his glorious Majesty to judge both the quick and the dead, we may rise to life immortal.

❧

LO! HE comes with clouds descending,
Once for favoured sinners slain;
Thousand thousand Saints attending
Swell the triumph of his train:
Alleluya!
God appears, on earth to reign.

Every eye shall now behold him
  Robed in dreadful majesty;
Those who set at nought and sold him
  Pierced and nailed him to the tree;
        Deeply wailing
Shall the true Messiah see.

Those dear tokens of his passion
  Still his dazzling body bears,
Cause of endless exultation
  To his ransomed worshippers:
        With what rapture
Gaze we on those glorious scars!

Yea, amen! let all adore thee,
  High on thine eternal throne;
Saviour, take the power and glory:
  Claim the kingdom for thine own
        O come quickly!
Alleluya! Come, Lord, come!

C.Wesley & J.Cennick

LORD Jesus Christ, the world's true sun, always rising, never setting, whose life-giving warmth engenders, preserves, nourishes and gladdens all things in heaven and on earth, shine into my soul, I pray: scatter the night of sin and the clouds of error; blaze within me, so that I may go on my way without stumbling, taking no part in shameful deeds done in the dark, but ever walking as one born to the light. Amen.

Erasmus

THE second phase of Advent changes to the preparation for the coming of Christ at Christmas. The best known of the liturgical devotions for this time are given here. They are called the 'O Antiphons', sung to a haunting melody before and after the Magnificat at Vespers during the days immediately leading up to Christmas. In the revised English lectionary they are also used, though without the distinctive 'O' and in a different order, before the Gospel at Mass.

17th December

O SAPIENTIA, quæ ex ore Altíssimi prodísti, attíngens a fine usque ad finem, fórtiter suáviter disponénsque ómnia: veni ad docéndum nos viam prudéntiæ.

O WISDOM, who came forth from the mouth of the Most High, and reaching from beginning to end, strongly and sweetly orders all things: come and teach us the way of prudence.

18th December

O Adonai, et Dux domus Israel, qui Moysi in igne flámmæ rubi apparuísti, et ei in Sina legem dedísti: veni ad rediméndum nos in bráchio exténto.

O Lord, and leader of the house of Israel, who appeared to Moses in the burning bush, and gave him the law on Mount Sinai, come and save us with outstretched arm.

19th December

O radix Iesse, qui stas in signum populórum, super quem continébunt reges os suum, quem gentes deprecabúntur: veni ad liberándum nos, iam noli tardáre.

O root of Jesse, raised as a sign to the people, to put kings to silence and to whom all nations shall have recourse: come without delay and save us.

20th December

O clavis David, et sceptrum domus Israel: qui áperis et nemo claudit, claudis et nemo áperit, et educ vinctum de domo cárceris, sedéntem in ténebris et umbra mortis.

O key of David, and sceptre of the house of Israel, who opens that none may close, closes that none may open: come and lead the captive from prison, who sits in darkness and the shadow of death.

21st December

O Oriens, splendor lucis ætérnæ, et sol iustítiæ: veni et illúmina sedéntes in ténebris et umbra mortis.

O Daystar, radiance of the eternal light, and sun of justice, come and shine on those who sit in darkness and the shadow of death.

22nd December

O Rex géntium, et desiderátus eárum, lapísque anguláris, qui facis útraque unum: veni et salva hóminem, quem de limo formásti.

O King of the people, and their desire, O corner stone binding each together, come and save mankind whom you formed from the dust.

23rd December

O Emmánuel, Rex et légifer noster, exspectátio géntium, et Salvátor eárum: veni ad salvándum nos Dómine Deus noster.

O God-with-us, our King and lawgiver, the expected of nations and their Saviour: come and save us, O Lord our God.

☙

R orate cæli désuper, et nubes pluant justum

D rop down dew, you heavens: clouds, rain the just one.

℣. Ne irascáris Dómine, ne ultra memíneris iniquitátis: ecce cívitas Sancti facta est desérta: Sion desérta facta est: Jerúsalem desoláta est: domus sanctificatiónis tuæ et glóriæ tuæ, ubi laudavérunt te patres nostri.

℣. Be not angry, O Lord, remember our sin no more: behold your holy city is abandoned: Sion is deserted: Jerusalem stands lonely, that house of your holiness and of your glory where our forefathers praised you.

℣. Peccávimus, et facti sumus tamquam immúndus nos, et cecídimus quasi fólium univérsi: et iniquitátes nostræ quasi véntus abstulérunt nos: abscondísti fáciem tuam a nobis, et allisísti nos in manu iniquitátis nostræ.

℣. We have sinned, and as bad as those who afflicted us; so we have fallen like the leaves of any tree, blown away because of our sins: you have hidden your face from us, and made us bear the consequence of our sins.

℣. Vide Dómine afflictiónem pópuli tui, et mitte quem missúrus es: emítte Agnum dominatórem terræ, de petra desérti ad montem fíliæ Sion: ut áuferat ipse iugum captivitátis nostræ.

℣. See the sadness of your people, O Lord, and send us the one promised: send us a Lamb to rule the earth, from the rocky desert to the mount of the daughter of Sion, that he may remove the yoke of our captivity.

℣. Consolámini, consolámini, pópule meus: cito véniet salus tua: quare mœróre consúmeris, quia innovávit te dolor? Salvábo te, noli timére, ego enim sum Dóminus Deus tuus, Sanctus Israel, redémptor tuus.

℣. Comfort ye; be comforted my people: your salvation quickly comes: Why are you eaten up with weeping: why renew your sorrow? I will save you, do not be afraid, for I am the Lord your God, the Holy one of Israel, your redeemer.

CHRISTMAS

A Prayer Before the Crib

D EVOUTLY we approach your cradle, Lord, to find the one of whom the prophets spoke, and here behold the mighty God of thunders lying helpless on the straw. O grant us some of this humility that we may conquer mightily the reign of sin within us. And grant us, too, the protection of your gentle mother, whose tender eye and loving heart attend your every wish.

ॐ

H AIL and blessed be the hour and moment in which the Son of God was born of the most pure Virgin Mary at midnight in Bethlehem, in piercing cold. In that hour vouchsafe, O my God, to hear my prayer and grant my desires, through the merits of our Saviour, Jesus Christ and of his blessed Mother.

ॐ

The Nativity of Christ

B EHOLD the father is his daughter's son,
　　The bird that built the nest is hatch'd therein,
The old of years an hour hath not outrun,
　　Eternal life to live doth now begin,
The word is dumb, the mirth of heaven doth weep,
Might feeble is, and force doth faintly creep.

O dying souls! behold your living spring!
　　O dazzled eyes! behold your son of grace!
Dull ears attend what word this word doth bring!
　　Up, heavy hearts, with joy your joy embrace!
From death, from dark, from deafness, from despairs,
This life, this light, this word, this joy repairs.

Gift better than himself God doth not know,
　　Gift better that his God no man can see;
This gift doth here the giver given bestow,
　　Gift to this gift let each receiver be:
God is my gift, himself he freely gave me,
God's gift am I, and none but God shall have me.

Man alter'd was by sin from man to beast;
    Beast's food is hay, hay is all mortal flesh;
Now God is flesh, and lives in manger press'd,
    As hay the brutest sinner to refresh:
Oh happy field wherein this fodder grew,
Whose taste doth us from beasts to men renew!

St Robert Southwell

O GLORIOUS Mother of God and Queen of heaven, my especial patroness, I greet you through the most tender and affectionate heart of your beloved Son Jesus, and I commend myself this day to your maternal love. In every danger and difficulty, in every trial and temptation, help me, O merciful, O loving, O gentle Virgin Mary. Through your sacred virginity and Immaculate Conception obtain for us purity both of soul and body.

H OLY the womb that bare him,
Holy the breasts that fed,
But holier still the royal heart
That in his passion bled.

J.H. Newman

Holy Family
First Sunday after Christmas

J ESUS, Mary and Joseph, guide our families here on earth. Jesus, Mary and Joseph, make our lives and our homes like yours. Jesus, Mary and Joseph, make our home life a foretaste of heaven here on earth.

ALMIGHTY God, whose only-begotten Son was born of a virgin and submitted himself to the authority and vocation of a carpenter, grant us a share in his humility so that we may be raised to share the joyful company of that same Virgin and Carpenter in your heavenly kingdom. Through the same Christ our Lord. Amen.

ꙮ ꙮ ꙮ

Epiphany, 6 January

ALL-POWERFUL God, who manifested your only be-gotten Son to the gentiles by the light of a star, grant in your mercy that we who know you now only by faith may when we die see your glorious Godhead in its fullness. Through the same Christ our Lord. Amen.

Roman Liturgy

ꙮ

YOUR birth, O Christ our God, arose upon the world as the light of knowledge, for those that worshipped the stars, learned from a star to adore you, the Sun of righteousness, and to recognize in you the Daystar from on high. Glory to you O Lord.

The Virgin today gives birth to the one who is above nature, and earth offers a lowly home to the transcendent. The angels and the shepherds sing glory, and the Magi follow the star: for to us is born a Son, God himself who is before all time.

Byzantine Menaion

ꙮ ꙮ ꙮ

Purification, 2 February

NOW, dismiss your servant O Lord,
    according to your word, in peace:
    because my eyes have seen your salvation
which you have prepared before the face of all peoples,
a light for the revelation to the Gentiles
    and the glory of your people Israel.

Luke 2:29-32

THE Angel-lights of Christmas morn
Which shot across the sky,
Away they pass at Candlemas,
They sparkle and they die.

Comfort of earth is brief at best,
Although it be divine;
Like funeral lights for Christmas gone
Old Simeon's tapers shine.

And then for eight long weeks and more
We wait in twilight grey,
Till the high candle sheds a beam
On Holy Saturday.

We wait along the penance-tide
Of solemn fast and prayer;
While song is hush'd and lights grow dim
In the sin-laden air.

And while the sword in Mary's soul
Is driven home, we hide
In our own hearts, and count the wounds
Of passion and of pride.

And still, though Candlemas be spent
And Alleluias o'er,
Mary is music in our need,
And Jesus light in store.

J.H. Newman 1849

Lent

A prayer before beginning Lent with a good confession

HEAVENLY Father; sackcloth and ashes are a little old-fashioned these days: help me instead to tear my sins instead of my clothes, and put on good works of prayer, fasting, and almsgiving instead of ashes. From this moment I intend to be all yours, living like Jesus and never sinning again.

ATTENDE Dómine et miserére, quia peccávimus tibi.

PAY heed, O Lord, and have mercy, for we have sinned against you.

℣. Ad te Rex summe, ómnium Redémptor, óculos nostros sublevámus flentes: exáudi, Christe, supplicántum preces.

℣. To you, O highest King, redeemer of all, we lift our weeping eyes: hear, O Christ, the pleading of your people.

℣. Déxtera Patris, lapis anguláris, via salútis, ianua cæléstis, ablue nostri máculas delícti.

℣. O right hand of the Father, O cornerstone, O way of salvation, O gate of heaven, wash away the stain of our sin.

℣. Rogámus, Deus, tuam maiestátem: áuribus sacris gémitus exáudi: crímina nostra plácidus indúlge.

℣. We pray your majesty, O God, to hear our weeping cries: for our sins, be gracious and forgiving.

℣. Tibi fatémur crímina admíssa: contríto corde pándimus occúlta: tua Redémptor, píetas ignóscat.

℣. To you we acknowledge our sins, with contrite hearts we open our hearts: be gentle, O our Redeemer!

℣. Innocens captus, nec repúgnans ductus, téstibus falsis pro ímpiis damnátus: quos redemísti, tu consérva Christe.

℣. O innocent captive, not refusing to be taken, and condemned for the guilty by false witnesses, preserve, O Christ, those whom you have redeemed.

Easter

SEEING that Christ has risen, let us worship the holy Lord Jesus, the sinless one. We adore your cross, O Christ, and we praise and glorify your holy resurrection. For you are our God, and we know no other but you, we call upon your name. Come, all faithful people, and let us worship Christ's holy resurrection; for through the cross joy has come into the world. Always blessing the Lord, let us praise his rising; for having undergone crucifixion for us, through death itself he destroyed death.

Although you descended into the tomb, Immortal One, yet you have destroyed the power of hell; and you have risen as a conqueror, Christ our God, proclaiming to the women who went to anoint your body: rejoice! and leaving peace on your Apostles: you who bring the dead to life.

Byzantine Pentecostal

ॐ

℟. Allelúia! Allelúia! Allelúia!

O FILII et fíliæ
Rex cæléstis, Rex glóriæ
Morte surréxit hódie.
Alleluia!

O SONS and daughters of the king,
Whom heav'nly hosts in glory sing,
Today the grave hath lost its sting.
Alleluia.

Et máne príma sábbati,
Ad óstium monuménti
Accessérunt discípuli.
Alleluia!

On that first morning of the week,
Before the day began to break,
Disciples went their Lord to seek.
Alleluia.

Et María Magdaléne,
Et Jácobi, et Salóme
Venérunt córpus úngere
Alleluia!

There Mary went, called Magdalene
Mary of James, and Salome
For to anoint him and array,
Alleluia.

In álbis sédens Angelus
Praedíxit muliéribus:
In Galilǽa est Dóminus.
Alleluia!

An angel white bade sorrow flee,
For thus he spake unto the three:
'Your Lord is gone to Galilee.'
Alleluia.

Et Joánnes Apóstolus
Cucúrrit Pétro cítius
Monuménto vénit prius
Alleluia!

So John th'Apostle fleeting fled
And slower Peter thither led
He reached the tomb a while ahead
Alleluia.

Discipulis adstántibus, In médio stétit Chrístus Dícens: Pax vóbis ómnibus. Alleluia!	That night th'Apostles met in fear, Amidst them came the Lord so dear And said: 'Peace be unto you here' Alleluia.
Ut intelléxit Dídymus Quia surréxerat Jésus, Remánsit fere dúbius. Alleluia!	When Thomas afterwards had heard That Jesus had fulfilled his word, He doubted if it were the Lord. Alleluia.
Víde, Thóma, víde látus, Víde pédes, víde mánus, Noli esse incrédulus. Alleluia!	'Thomas, behold my side,' said he, 'My hands, my feet, my body see, 'And doubt not, but believe in me' Alleluia.
Quando Thómas Chrísti latus, Pédes vídit atque manus, Díxit: Tu es Déus méus. Alleluia!	No longer Thomas then denied He saw the feet, the hands, the side; 'Thou art my Lord & God,' he cried. Alleluia.
Beati qui non vidérunt Et fírmiter credidérunt Vítam ætérnam habébunt. Alleluia!	Blesséd are they that have not seen And yet whose faith has constant been, In life eternal they shall reign. Alleluia.
In hoc fésto sanctíssimo Sit laus et jubilátio, Benedicámus Dómino. Alleluia!	On this most holy day of days, To God your heart and voices raise In laud and jubilee and praise Alleluia.
Ex quíbus nos humíllimas Devótas atque débitas Deo dicámus grátias. Alleluia!	And we with holy Church unite As evermore is just and right, In glory to the King of Light. Alleluia.

Trans. J.M.Neale alt.

Collect for Easter Sunday

O GOD, who this day through the victory of your only-be-gotten Son over death opened a passage for us to eternity, grant that our prayers, inspired by your protecting grace, may by your grace become effective. Through Christ our Lord. Amen.

A LMIGHTY God, who, in the death and glorious resurrection of Christ your Son has opened for us the way to salvation, grant that we may also die to our sins and so rise with him to
everlasting life. Through the same Christ our Lord.

❧

An Prayer for Altar-Servers on Easter Sunday

E XHAUSTED, Lord, on your sanctuary, we offer our tired-
out liturgical efforts to your greater glory, and while the dried
candle wax gets well trodden into the carpet, and the vestments
lie in untidy piles at the bottom of cupboards, we beg you to
accept what we have done in your honour. Overlook our tan-
trums, our skimping this or overdoing that, and raise up our humble fumblings in your sight as being, perhaps, a faint shadow of
the worship of heaven, for thus it was intended. On this your
rising day, O Lord, accept our praise. Amen. Alleluia!

❧ ❧ ❧

Pentecost

Whitsuntide

H OLY Spirit from above
Sweet Comforter most dear
Inspire us with your love;
To restless souls draw near

Holy Spirit from above
Your sevenfold gifts impart
Inspire us with your love
Seek out the pure in heart

Holy Spirit from above
Tongue of eternal fire
Inspire us with your love
Become our souls' desire

Holy Spirit from above
Grant us to know your peace
Life-giving Holy Dove
Bid all our striving cease

T.J.Rhidian Jones

See also Prayers to the Holy Spirit, p. 331

GENERAL

Two prayers of St Ignatius Loyola

TEACH us, good Lord, to serve you as you deserve; to give and not to count the cost, to fight and not to heed the wounds, to toil and not to seek for rest, to labour and not ask for any reward, save that of knowing that we do your will.

∽

RECEIVE, O Lord, my memory, my will, my understanding, and entire liberty. You have given me all I have, and I surrender all to your divine will, that you may dispose of me as it shall please you. Give me only your love and thy grace, and I shall be happy, and shall have no more to ask.

∽

The Universal Prayer, ascribed to Pope Clement XI:

LORD, I believe, but I would believe more firmly;
I hope, but I would hope more surely;
I love, but I would love more ardently;
I repent, but I would repent more passionately.

I adore you as my first beginning;
I long for you as my final end;
I honour you as my constant benefactor;
I call on you as my prompt defender.

Direct me according to your wisdom,
Correct me according to your justice,
Comfort me according to your mercy,
Protect me according to your power.

I offer you my thinking, Lord, that it be fixed on you.
I offer you my speaking, Lord that it have you for its theme;
I offer you my actions, Lord, that they may be yours alone;
I offer you my crosses, Lord, that I may bear them for your sake.

I desire to do whatever you ask of me,
Simply because you ask it,
In the way you ask it to be done,
And for as long as you wish it.

I pray you Lord, to enlighten my understanding,
to impassion my will,
to purify my heart,
and sanctify my soul.

May I repent the evil that is past,
and shun temptations to come;
correct my evil tendencies
and grow in all virtues.

Grant me, gracious Lord, to love what is yours,
and detach myself from what is mine,
Give me zeal towards my neighbour,
and contempt for worldliness.

Grant me obedience to those over me,
and graciousness to those under me.
Make me true to my friends,
and merciful to my enemies.

May I conquer self-indulgence with self-control,
Selfishness with generosity,
Anger with gentleness,
and coldness with warmth.

Make me prudent in advice,
Constant in dangers,
Patient in adversity
and unassuming in prosperity.

Make me attentive when I pray,
Moderate when celebrating
Generous in giving,
and true to my commitments.

May I keep my innocence within,
and my modesty without;
May my conversation be pure
and my life well-ordered.

May I keep my appetites in check,
Let me treasure your grace,
Let me keep your law,
that I may come to your salvation.

Teach me how fleeting is this world,
how wonderful the next;
how insignificant are the things of time,
how lasting those of eternity.

Grant me to well prepare for death
with a proper fear of judgement
that I may fly from the fires of hell
and come to the joys of paradise.

Through Christ our Lord. Amen.

∽

The Adorable Presence

WITH peeping pace and silent step
    They pass the sleepy nest of books
Imprisoned under lock and key
Beneath the ever-watchful gaze
    Of two-faced time.

Soon touched with holy awe they cross
Themselves and see with wakened eyes
Christ himself gazing lovingly
Surrounded by his Mother blest
    And the heavenly company

They yearn to utter the splendour
Of heaven's everlasting joy
They yearn to quench their thirsty souls
Upon the tears of Christ divine.
    Such yearning is also mine.

T.J.Rhidian Jones

∽

For grace to do God's will

GRANT me grace, O merciful God, to desire ardently all that
is pleasing to you, to examine it prudently, to acknowledge
it truthfully, and to accomplish it perfectly for the praise and glory
of your name. Amen.

St Thomas Aquinas

Prayer Before a Crucifix

O MOST kind and sweet Jesus: behold, I cast myself on my knees in your sight, and with all the fervour that is in me, I beg you to plant deeply in my heart the virtues of faith, hope and charity, together with a true sorrow for my sins and a firm purpose of amendment, as I have before my eyes and I contemplate with the utmost sorrow of soul the image of your five wounds, and I remember the words of the prophet David: They have pierced my hands and feet: they have even counted my bones. *(Ps.21:17)*

Prayer for Vocations

JESUS, High Priest and Redeemer forever, we beg you to call young men and women to your service as priests and religious. May they be inspired by the lives of dedicated priests, brothers, and sisters. Give to parents the grace of generosity and trust toward you and their children so that their sons and daughters may be helped to choose their vocations in life with wisdom and freedom.

Lord, you told us that 'the harvest indeed is great but the labourers are few. Pray, therefore, the Lord of the harvest, to send labourers into his harvest.' We ask that we may know and follow the vocation to which you have called us. We pray particularly for those called to serve as priests, brothers, and sisters; those whom you have called, those you are calling now, and those you will call in the future. May they be open and responsive to the call of serving your people. We ask this through Christ, our Lord. Amen.

Another prayer for vocations

LORD Jesus Christ, Saviour of the world, through thy gentle Heart we humbly beseech thee, the Eternal Shepherd, not to desert thy flock in its afflictions, but to enliven it with that spirit which thou didst pour out in such abundance on thine apostles. Call, we pray thee, more and more souls to enter the priestly and religious orders, and may those whom thou callest be fired with zeal for the salvation of souls, by virtue be sanctified, and by thy spirit be strengthened against every obstacle.

Prayer in honour of St Thérèse of Lisieux

ETERNAL Father, whose infinite love watches in wisdom over each day of my life; grant me the light to see in sorrow as in joy in trial as in peace, in uncertainty as in confidence, the way your divine providence has marked for me. Give me that faith and trust in your care for me which was so pleasing to you in St Thérèse of the Child Jesus, and I will walk in darkness as in light, holding your hand and finding in all the blessings I receive from your loving bounty that everything is a grace. Amen.

Elizabeth Ruth Obbard

Prayer of Saint Thomas More for a Happy Death

GOOD Lord, give me the grace so to spend my life, that when the day of my death shall come, though I feel pain in my body, I may feel comfort in soul; and with faithful hope of thy mercy, with due love toward thee, and charity toward the world, I may, through thy grace, depart into thy glory.

Prayer on a Birthday

GOD of all creation, you are the life of the faithful, the guardian and saviour of those who fear you, and who has brought N. your servant through another year, enlarge your favour toward him/her; protect his/her life in your safekeeping; give him/her length of days; and by your grace lead him/her through a happy old age to the joys of your heavenly kingdom. Amen.

A prayer when feeling tepid

MERCIFUL God, almighty Father, so generous with your benefits to me, forgive the ingratitude with which I have repaid your goodness. Here I am before you with a dead, unfeeling heart, cold despite the warmth of your gentle and patient goodness. Turn again, merciful Father! Try once more! Make me hunger for you as the bread of life with all my longing. Make me desire to serve you only, make me long to do only what you desire me to do. Grant my prayer, beloved Lord, lest I die of this wretched chill.

from St Anselm

Prayer When Making an Important Decision

L ORD Jesus Christ, open the eyes and ears of my heart, so
that I may hear and understand your word and do your will,
for in this world, Lord, I am a stranger and an exile. Hide not
your commandments from me. Draw the veil from my eyes, and
let me ponder the wonderful workings of your law. Make known
to me the obscure and hidden ways of your wisdom and of my
own heart. For in you, God, is my hope; enlighten my thoughts
and my understanding. Amen.

G IVE me, O my Lord, that purity of conscience which alone
can receive, which alone can improve thy inspirations. My
ears are dull, so that I cannot hear thy voice. My eyes are dim, so
that I cannot see thy tokens. Thou alone canst quicken my hearing, and purge my sight, and cleanse and renew my heart. Teach
me, like Mary, to sit at thy feet, and to hear thy word. Give me
that true wisdom which seeks thy will by prayer and meditation,
by direct intercourse with thee, more than by reading and reason-
ing. Give me the discernment to know thy voice from the voice
of strangers, and to rest upon it and to seek it in the first place as
something external to myself; and answer me through my own
mind, if I worship and rely on thee as above and beyond it.

J.H. Newman

Prayer for a young person when choosing a state of life

O ALMIGHTY God, whose wise and kind providence watches
over every human event, be my light and my counsel in all
my undertakings, particularly in the choice of a state of life. I
know that on this important step my sanctification and salvation
may in a great measure depend. I know that I am incapable of
discerning what is truly best for me; and so I throw myself into
your arms, beseeching you, my God, who sent me into this world
only to love and serve you, to direct with your grace every moment and action of my life to the glorious purpose of my creation. I renounce most sincerely every other wish than to fulfil
your will for my soul, whatever it may be; and I beseech you to
give me the necessary grace, in the true spirit of a Christian, to
qualify myself for any vocation your kindly providence may as-

sign me. O my God, whenever it may become my duty to make a choice, be my light and my counsel, and mercifully *make the way known to me wherein I should walk, for I have lifted up my soul to you.* Preserve me from listening to the suggestions of my own self-love, or wordly prudence in preference to your holy and wiser inspirations. *Let your good Spirit lead me into the right way,* and your kind providence place me, not necessarily where I may be happiest according to the world, but in the state in which I shall love and serve you best, and meet with most abundant means for working out my salvation. This is all that I ask, and all that I desire; for what would it avail me to gain the whole world if, in the end, I were to lose my soul, and be so unfortunate as to prefer temporal advantages and worldly honours to the enjoyment of your divine presence in a happy eternity?

Most holy Virgin, take me under thy protection.

My Angel Guardian and Patron Saints pray for me.

ᐁ

Another prayer for the same purpose

MY HEAVENLY Father, I sincerely wish to dedicate my whole life to you, to please you in everything I do, and to guide my life by your will. I realize, Father, that you wish me to use the freedom you have given me. I am deeply concerned about my free choice of the state of life in which I can live most happily and serve you best. Guide me in my choice, O Lord, and help me to decide wisely. Give me also the strength to persevere in following my decision. I ask this grace through Jesus Christ your Son, who perfectly knew and fulfilled your will for him.

Terence, Cardinal Cooke

ᐁ

A prayer to implore the divine light before any particular undertaking

O ADORABLE Jesus, I come to thee before I commence this undertaking to implore thy Divine assistance, and to consecrate it, through thee, to the greater honour and glory of God: thou knowest that of myself I can do nothing, assist me therefore, I beseech thee, to accomplish the will of God—that divine will which was so dear to thee, as to be thy food whilst thou wert upon earth. Direct me particularly in the affair I am about to undertake, and teach me to act in a manner pleasing to thy divine Majesty—or rather, do thou thyself deign to act in and by me; govern me by thy wisdom; support me by thy power and by thy infinite goodness direct all my exertions on this and on every other occasion, to thy greater honour and glory, and my own eternal salvation. Amen.

∾

For dear friends

ALMIGHTY God, who has poured the gift of love into the hearts of your faithful people, grant to (N. *or* those) whom I love health of mind and body, that (they) may come to love you with all (their) strength, and accomplish all that is pleasing to you. Through Christ our Lord. Amen.

∾

To repel bitter thoughts

O GOD, almighty and yet most meek, hear my prayers and free my heart from bitter thoughts, and from all harmful wanderings of the imagination, that your Holy Spirit may find this his temple a more worthy home. Through Christ our Lord. Amen.

∾

For the gift of charity

O GOD, who smooths the path for those that love you, grant to our hearts the gift of charity, that those things which have been undertaken through your inspiration may not be diverted through the interference of our selfishness. Through Christ our Lord. Amen.

∾

For the gift of patience

O GOD, whose only-begotten Son conquered the pride of his enemies through his singular patience, grant, we beseech, that inspired by his example as we recall his sufferings, we may face our adversities with equanimity. Through the same Christ our Lord. Amen.

∾

For continence

PURIFY our hearts and minds, O Lord, with the gift of your Holy Spirit, that we may serve you with a pure body and a clean soul. Through Christ our Lord. Amen.

In thanksgiving

O GOD, whose mercies are numberless and whose treasury of goodness is limitless, we give you grateful thanks for your countless blessings, and we pray that our wise use of your gifts may fit us for the joys of heaven. Through Christ our Lord. Amen.

ॐ

In honour of St Peter

GLORIOUS Saint Peter, in reward for your generous faith, your sincere humility and burning love, you were honoured by Jesus Christ with the leadership of the other apostles and the primacy of the whole Church, of which you were made the foundation stone. Obtain for us the grace of lively faith that shall not fear to profess itself openly, fully, and in all its manifestations, even to the giving of blood and life should occasion demand it. May we sacrifice life itself rather than deny our faith. Obtain for us also a sincere attachment to our Holy Mother the Church.

Grant that we may ever keep sincerely and closely united to the Holy Father who is the heir of your authority, and the true, visible head of the Catholic Church. Grant that we may follow the teaching and counsels of the Church. May we be obedient to all her precepts so as to enjoy peace here on earth, and to attain one day eternal happiness in heaven.

Terence, Cardinal Cooke

ॐ

In honour of St Paul

GLORIOUS St. Paul, from being a persecutor of the Christian name, you became its most zealous apostle. To make Jesus, our Divine Saviour, known to the uttermost parts of the earth, you suffered prison, scourging, stoning, shipwreck, and all manner of persecution, and shed the last drop of your blood. Obtain for us the grace to accept the infirmities, sufferings, and misfortunes of this life as favours of the divine mercy. So may we never grow weary of the trials of our exile, but rather show ourselves ever more faithful and fervent. Amen.

Terence, Cardinal Cooke

Prayer in honour of St Joseph

SAINT Joseph, I humbly invoke you and commend myself and all who are dear to me to your intercession. By the love you have for Jesus and Mary do not abandon me during life and assist me at the hour of my death. Loving St Joseph, faithful follower of Jesus Christ, I raise my heart to you to implore your powerful intercession in obtaining from the heart of Jesus all the graces necessary for my spiritual and temporal welfare, particularly the grace of a happy death. Be my guide, my father and my model through life, that I may merit to die as you did in the arms of Jesus and Mary. Amen.

Elizabeth Ruth Obbard

GOD's will would I do,
My own will bridle.

God's due would I give,
My own due yield.

God's path would I ponder,
My own death remember;

Christ's agony would I meditate,
My love to God make warmer;

Christ's cross would I carry,
My own cross forget;

Repentance of sin would I make,
Early repentance choose;

A bridle to my tongue would I put,
A bridle on my thoughts I would keep;

God's judgement would I judge,
My own judgement guard;

Christ's redemption would I seize,
My own ransom work;

The love of Christ would I feel,
My own love know.

Celtic

ACTS OF FAITH, HOPE AND CHARITY

Preparation

O ALMIGHTY and eternal God, grant to us the increase of faith, hope and charity; and that we may deserve to obtain what you promise, make us love whatever you command, through Christ our Lord. Amen.

Acts of Faith

O MY GOD, I firmly believe that you are one God in three divine Persons, Father, Son, and Holy Spirit; I believe that your divine Son became man and died for our sins, and that he will come to judge the living and the dead. I believe these and all the truths which the holy Catholic Church teaches, because you revealed them, who can neither deceive nor be deceived. Amen.

I FIRMLY believe there is one God; and that in this one God there are three persons, the Father, the Son and the Holy Spirit; that the Son took to himself the nature of man from the womb of the Virgin Mary, by the operation of the power of the Holy Spirit, and that in this our human nature he was crucified and died for us, that afterwards he rose again and ascended into heaven, from whence he shall come to repay the just with everlasting glory and the wicked with everlasting punishment. Moreover, I believe whatsoever the Catholic Church proposes to be believed, and this because God, who is the sovereign truth that can never deceive or be deceived, has revealed all these things to this his Church.

O MY GOD I believe in you and in all that your Church teaches, because you have said it, and your word is true.

Acts of Hope

O MY GOD, relying on your infinite goodness and promises, I hope to obtain pardon of my sins, the help of your grace, and life everlasting, through the merits of Jesus Christ, my Lord and Redeemer. Amen.

❧

O MY GOD, relying on your almighty power and your infinite mercy and goodness, and because you are faithful to your promises, I trust in you that you will grant me the forgiveness of my sins through the merits of Jesus Christ your Son; and that you will give me the assistance of your grace, with which I will labour to continue to the end in the diligent exercise of all good works, and may deserve to obtain in heaven the glory which you have promised.

❧

O MY GOD, I hope in you, for grace and for glory, because of your promises, your mercy and your power.

❧ ❧ ❧

Acts of Charity

O MY GOD, I love you above all things, with my whole heart and soul, because you are all good and worthy of all my love. I love my neighbour as myself for the love of you. I forgive all who have injured me and I ask pardon of all whom I have injured. Amen.

❧

O LORD my God, I love you with my whole heart, and above all things, because you, O God, are the Sovereign good and for your own infinite perfections are most worthy of all love. For your sake, I also love my neighbour as myself.

❧

O MY GOD, because you are so good, I love you with all my heart, and for your sake I love my neighbour as myself.

Possible Scheme for Biblical Reading

The Redeemer	*Strong in the Faith*	*Wisdom*
Genesis	Joshua	Wisdom
Isaiah	Judges	Proverbs
Luke	1&2 Maccabees	John again
Romans	Acts of the Apostles	Colossians
		Ecclesiastes *Qoheleth*
Joel	Psalms	Ecclesiasticus *Sirach*
Obadiah	Lamentations	
Galatians		*The Church*
	Apocalypse	Leviticus
The Law	Ezekiel	Matthew again
Exodus	Mark, again	1&2Timothy
Matthew	Daniel	Titus
Hebrews	1&2 Thessalonians	
Deuteronomy	Revelation	1&2 Chronicles
		Habbakuk
Defeating Evil	*Holy Women*	Zephaniah
1&2 Samuel	Judith	Philemon
Hosea	Luke, again	Haggai
Mark	Esther	Zechariah
Jonah	Ephesians	Malachi
	Ruth	Jude
Micah		
Nahum	Ezra	❧
Baruch	Nehemiah	
Love of Neighbour	*Seeking for the Lord*	
Amos	Tobit	
James	Job	
Song of Songs		
1, 2 & 3 John	Numbers	
	Philippians	
Prophetic Signs		
Jeremiah	*God's Kingdom*	
John	1&2 Kings	
1&2 Corinthians	Matthew again	
	1&2 Peter	

Some Suggested Spiritual Reading

Writings of the great Fathers of the Church (Ss Augustine, Ambrose, Gregory &c)
Biographies of Saints

The Cloud of Unknowing *	Anon
Crossing the Threshold of Hope	Pope John Paul II
Dialogue of Comfort in Tribulation *	St Thomas More
Eucharistic Meditations	St John Vianney
Holy Wisdom *	Fr Augustine Baker
How to Pray	Fr Jean-Nicolas Grou
Imitation of Christ	Thomas á Kempis
In conversation with God	Francis Fernandez
Introduction to the Devout Life	St Francis de Sales
The Interior Castle	St Teresa of Avila
Letters to Persons in the World	St Francis de Sales
The Life of Christ	Fulton Sheen
Meditations for Layfolk	Bede Jarrett
Mirror of Charity	St Ælred of Rivaulx
Opening to God (& sequels)	Thomas Green
Revelations of Divine Love *	Julian of Norwich
The Sacrament of the Present Moment	Jean de Caussade
The Scale of Perfection *	Walter Hilton
Spiritual Friendship	St Ælred of Rivaulx
Spiritual Letters	Dom John Chapman
Union with God	Abbot Marmion

Also, the writings of C.S. Lewis, Thomas Merton and many others, especially saints.

* Take a look inside the cover before you buy: you may find the language too archaic for your taste. In my opinion it's usually worth persevering, though in most cases you will find modernized versions available.

ACKNOWLEDGEMENTS

other than those noted in the text

THE compiler and publishers are most grateful to all those who have permitted their material to appear in this book. While all efforts have been made to trace the owners of copyright works, apologies are offered to any whose material may possibly have been inadvertently used. Amendments will, of course, be made in future editions. In the references below, the arabic numerals refer to the page, and the roman numerals to the position on the page.

From *St Benedict's Prayer Book,* by permission of Ampleforth Abbey Trustees: 401iii, 401iv, 402i.

From assorted publications of *Scepter Publishers:* 189i 190i 195ii, iii, 297iii, 413i.

From the *Essential Catholic Handbook* published by Liguori Publications, Liguori Missouri USA: 321iii, 400iv, 434ii, 435ii, 435iii, 436i, 443ii, 444i, 444iv.

From the *Gold Book of Prayers:* copyright 1989 The Riehle Foundation; All world rights reserved; Printed with permission; Imprimatur: Most Rev. James H. Garland, Auxiliary Bishop of the Archdiocese of Cincinnati, February 24 1989: 333iii, 336i, 363i, 365i.

Prayers from *St Paul's Prayer Book* reproduced with kind permission of St Paul's Publishers (UK): 315i, 373i, 373ii, 373iii, 391i, 403iv, 431i.

Prayers from *Prayers for Today* by Terence, Cardinal Cooke Booke, published by Alba House. Permission from Society of St Paul (USA): 384ii, 386ii, 387i, 387ii, 437i, 439iii, 439iv.

From the *St Vincent Prayer Book,* published by John S. Burns & Sons, Glasgow: all prayers by Dom Hubert Van Zeller in the Stations of the Cross, also 320i, 321i, 321ii, 321iv, 393i.

201 New Prayers by Canon Francis Ripley, Print Origination (1989) 211iii.

The Pope's Prayer Book published by E.J. Dwyer (Australia) Pty Ltd. 406iv, 363ii, 367ii, 368i, 378ii, 383ii, 383iii.

The following are reproduced with permission from the *Enchiridion of Indulgences:* Copyright © 1969 Catholic Book Co. New York, N.Y. All rights reserved. 390i, 411ff.

The following are reproduced with permission from *Catholic Book of Prayers* Copyright © 1990, 1982, Catholic Book Co. New York, N.Y. All rights reserved. 189ii 212ii, 339iii.

The following is reproduced with permission from *Treasury of Novenas* Copyright © 1986 Catholic Book Co. New York, N.Y. All rights reserved. 340ii.

This was reproduced from *Poems* by C.S. Lewis, published in 1994, and reproduced by kind permission of HarperCollins Publishers Ltd.: 413ii.

A Walsingham Prayer Book by Elizabeth Ruth Obbard published by Canterbury Press Norwich and used with permission. 323i, 348ii, 435i, 440i.

From *Hymns Ancient and Modern* published by Canterbury Press Norwich, and used with permission. 232iii.

From *The New English Hymnal,* published by Canterbury Press Norwich, and used with permission. 250ii, 298iii, 339iv, 317iv, 426ii.

These are the sources of material believed to be in the public domain

Traditional: 182, 184, 199all, 206ii, 207ii, all on pp 254-5, 284, 319i, 331i, 341ff, 353ii, 354i, 364iii, 375i, 375ii, 379iv, 380i, 385i, 391ii, 391iii, 392iii, 393ii, 394i, 400ii, 403iii, 404, 408ff, 410i, 410ii, 410iv, 410v, 417iii, 419, 420, 425ii, 426ii.

In common use: 285, 286.

The SPCK Book of Christian Prayer SPCK (1995) 335.

The Spirit of the Sacred Heart (1891) 191, 368v, 401i, 405iii, 421ii, 431ii.

The Poetical Works of St Robert Southwell Stewart (1876) 421iii.

Unknown 194iv, 200i, 213iii, 217all, 218, 372ii.

Altar Servers' Manual Burns & Oates (1907) 195i.

John Donne: *The Complete English Poems.* Penguin (1973) 197iii, 375 iv.

The Crown of Jesus Richardson (1862) 205i,ii, 217v, 337, 367i, 367iii, 368ii, 368iii, 380iiff, 385ii, 385iii, 406i, 406ii, 386i, 392ii, 436iii, 437ii.

Simple Prayer Book Catholic Truth Society(1891) 208.

A Catechism of Christian Doctrine Catholic Truth Society (1889) 301iv 443iv, 444iii, 444vi.

The Way of Perfection, St Teresa of Avila, Stanbrook ed. Baker (1925) 303i.

The Primer, Fr Thurston, Burns, Oates & Washbourne (1923) 305ff, 324ff.

An English Primer of c.1400 Longmans, Green & Co. Ltd. (1891) 331ii.

A Prayer Book O'Connell & Martin, Catholic Press Chicago. 315ii 315iv

316iii, 317i, 317iii, 322i, 322ii, 346i, 347i, 348i, 395ii, 433iii, 436ii.

A Mediæval Anthology ed. Mary Segar Longmans, Green & Co. (1915) 210i.

The Poems of William Dunbar, Faber & Faber Ltd. (1932), 349.

The Golden Manual Burns & Oates Ltd. (1850) 211i,ii, all prayers addressed to our Lord in the *Ad Libitum* devotions for the Rosary section, and the "Let us contemplate..." introductions in the same section. 291 (alt) 345ii, 345iv, 371i.

The Heart of Thomas More Burns & Oates (1966) 213i, 315iii, 368iv, 369.

The Stripping of the Altars, Eamon Duffy, Yale University Press (1992) 213ii.

These are reproduced from *The Sun Dances* by Alexander Carmichael published by Floris Books and the Christian Community Press: 356ii, 410iii, 414i, 440ii.

Manual of Prayers, Burns, Oates & Washbourne (1886/1922): 214i,ii, 215, all prayers by St Alphonsus in the Stations of the Cross, 359ff, 361ff.

Prayers, Verses & Devotions, Cardinal John Henry Newman, Ignatius Press (1989) 399, 375iii 376ii.

The Raccolta, Burns, Oates & Co. 1873 217iv v, 233ii(alt.).

Garden of the Soul, Bishop Challoner, Burns, Oates & Washbourne Ltd. (c.1930) all prayers by Challoner in the Stations of the Cross, all prayers addressed to our Lady in the *Ad Libitum* devotions for the Rosary section.

Devotions for Holy Communion Alban Goodier, Burns & Oates (1909) 241ii, 317ii, 318i.

Manuscripts, 252ii.

The Rule of St Benedict, Burns & Oates, (c.1892) 297ii.

Gerard Manley Hopkins, Poems & Prose, Penguin (1953) 373iv.

INDEX OF SCRIPTURE

used in the Book of Hours

THEMATIC INDEX

GENERAL INDEX

including people, & better known prayers by title or first line